VIETNAM

Strategy for a Stalemate

The Washington Institute for Values in Public Policy
The Washington Institute sponsors research that helps provide the information and fresh insights necessary for formulating policy in a democratic society. Founded in 1982, the Institute is an independent, non-profit educational and research organization which examines current and upcoming issues with particular attention to ethical implications.

ADDITIONAL TITLES

Stability and Strategic Defense
Edited by Alvin M. Weinberg and Jack N. Barkenbus (1988)

The Political Significance of Latin American Liberation Theology:
The Challenge to U.S. Public Policy
Edited by Richard L. Rubenstein and John K. Roth (1988)

Soviet Nomenklatura: A Comprehensive Roster of Soviet Civilian and Military Officials
Compiled by Albert L. Weeks (1988)

Strategic Defenses and Arms Control
Edited by Alvin M. Weinberg and Jack N. Barkenbus (1987)

The Dissolving Alliance: The United States and the Future of Europe
Edited by Richard L. Rubenstein (1987)

Arms Control: The American Dilemma
Edited by William R. Kintner (1987)

The East Wind Subsides: Chinese Foreign Policy and the Origins of the Cultural Revolution
By Andrew Hall Wedeman (1987)

Rebuilding A Nation: Philippine Challenges and American Policy
Edited by Carl H. Landé (1987)

VIETNAM

Strategy for a Stalemate

F. Charles Parker IV

A Washington Institute Book

PARAGON HOUSE
New York

First edition, 1989

Published in the United States by

Paragon House Publishers
90 Fifth Avenue
New York, NY 10011

A Washington Institute Book

Manufactured in the United States of America

Library of Congress Cataloging-in-Publication Data

Parker, F. Charles, 1947—
Vietnam : strategy for a stalemate.

"A Washington Institute book."
Bibliography: p.
Includes index.
1. Vietnamese Conflict, 1961-1975.   I. Washington
Institute for Values in Public Policy.   II. Title.
DS557.7.P35   1989   959.704′3   88-25482
ISBN 0-88702-041-0

For
Harry Hayes
and
David Hann

Contents

Acknowledgments

Usually, an author puts here a long list of names of people to whom he is deeply indebted for assistance in preparation of the book. I thought about that—and to be fair can only list one name that fits into that category. That is Dr. Richard C. Thornton of George Washington University, my mentor for my M.A. thesis and my Ph.D. dissertation—and, more importantly, my friend. We forged our friendship initially on the fields of friendly strife on the intramural football team he coached and quarterbacked to numerous playoffs and one championship, the Red Guards.

During over twelve years of M.A. thesis and Ph.D. dissertation work, I could always count on Dick to take the time to review what I had done thoroughly and make incisive and, often, brilliant comments. He was a good enough friend to tell me honestly when what I had written was bad. As a result, one of my worst chapters on the first attempt is now probably the best because, as always, Dick challenged me to "take a stand on the issues."

I must also thank my long-suffering wife Ely, and my children who have had to put up with most of this work being produced on their time. Ely's support has been wonderful and made completion of the book possible.

Of course, responsibility for errors and opinions is mine.

The views expressed in this book are those of the author and do not reflect the official policy or position of the Department of the Army, the Department of Defense, or the United States government.

Note on Transliterations

Where a quotation or reference in a primary or secondary source uses the older Wade-Giles system for transliterating Chinese into English, I have let stand the original. Otherwise, I have used the Pinyin system throughout.

Preface

A commercial for Time-Life Books shows a man and his son in front of the Vietnam Memorial in Washington. The boy asks a series of heart-wrenching questions. The father says nothing. A bumper sticker in the parking lot at Stanford University says, "No Vietnam War in Central America." The motion picture *Platoon* is a box office smash and *Tour of Duty* survives a full season on prime time television. Countless politicians charge us to remember the "lessons of Vietnam" because these "lessons" should somehow lead us to vote for the politician uttering the charge.

In December 1970, I got on a plane at Dulles Airport, my ultimate destination a tiny jungle outpost in Tay Ninh Province, Vietnam, near the Cambodian border. The plane was full, so the window and center seats next to me were occupied. I did not smoke, but I sat in the smoking section because, given where I was going, I intended to have a few drinks in the air. When you sit with the smokers, you know you are sitting with people who already have one vice and probably will drink as well. They are less likely to cluck under their breath when you order your third bloody mary. My compatriots did indeed drink and smoke and this paved the way for conversation. They were both businessmen. One was outraged at having to take this trip so close to Christmas. The other complained about the difficulty of getting good accommodations close to his business location. When my turn came, it occurred to me that my chief concern was that I might very soon get shot. Without being too self-righteous about the whole thing, it seemed to me that our concerns were on a fundamentally different level.

On the way to the airport I had passed Kerlin's Korner in Annandale, Virginia. People were carefully selecting Christmas trees, obviously unconcerned that I was going to war. In fact, there were no signs of war anywhere. No ads to buy bonds or plant a victory garden. No posters saying that loose lips sink ships. Nothing. Somehow, at the age of twenty-three, I *felt* that something was wrong here. I felt, but I didn't know. Now I know.

I am a soldier. I fought in Vietnam. However, those two facts are not why I know. This book is the product of years of research. Being a soldier who fought in Vietnam may account for my interest in the subject and may have spurred me on to complete the project when it was costing me weekends and evenings from my normal life. But my experience only gave me an expert view of one small part of the war. And when I had my head down trying to move my buttons out of the way so I could get closer to the ground, my perspective was indeed limited. Any attempt to generalize from my own experience would be useless. Instead, this book resulted from research and analysis and puts the war in a global context. It has the side benefit of explaining to people like me, finally, what happened and why. Knowing the answers does not equate to being happy with the answers, but at least they are clear.

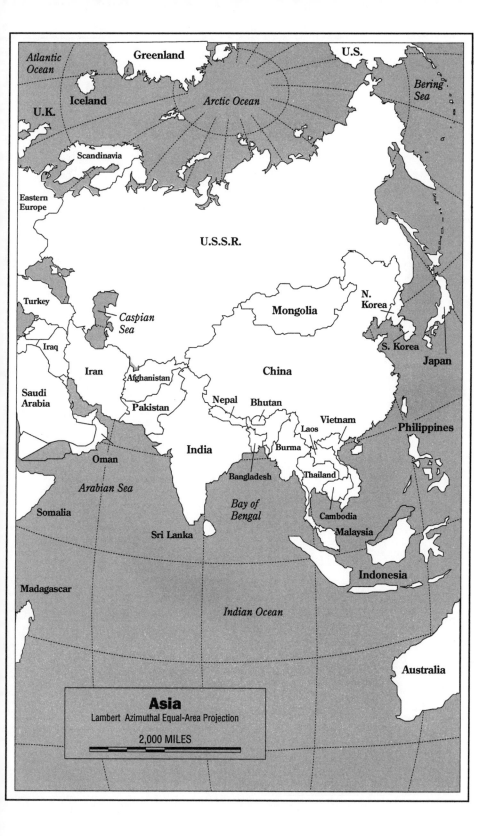

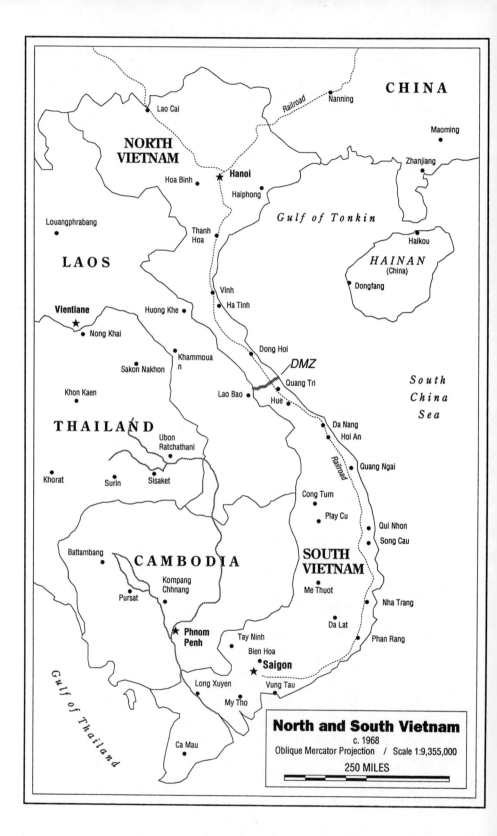

CHINA

Lao Cai

Nanning

Maoming

NORTH VIETNAM

Zhanjiang

Hoa Binh

★ **Hanoi**

Haiphong

Gulf of Tonkin

Louangphrabang

Thanh Hoa

Haikou

HAINAN (China)

LAOS

Dongfang

Vinh

Vientiane ★

Huong Khe

Ha Tinh

Nong Khai

Dong Hoi

South China Sea

Khammouan

DMZ

Sakon Nakhon

Quang Tri

Khon Kaen

Lao Bao

Hue

THAILAND

Da Nang

Hoi An

Ubon Ratchathani

Railroad

Quang Ngai

Khorat

Surin

Sisaket

Cong Tum

Play Cu

Qui Nhon

Song Cau

Battambang

CAMBODIA

SOUTH VIETNAM

Kompang Chhnang

Me Thuot

Nha Trang

Pursat

Da Lat

★ **Phnom Penh**

Tay Ninh

Phan Rang

Bien Hoa

Gulf of Thailand

Long Xuyen

★ **Saigon**

Vung Tau

My Tho

Ca Mau

North and South Vietnam

c. 1968

Oblique Mercator Projection / Scale 1:9,355,000

250 MILES

Introduction

Much has been written about Vietnam. Most of the time the authors set out to explain (a) why the United States lost, (b) why the North Vietnamese won, or (c) both. The principal actors are usually the United States and the Vietnamese, and quite often only the United States really counts. But the war actually was played out against a larger backdrop. The United States wanted to preserve an independent non-communist South Vietnam. But more than the welfare of the people in Vietnam had to have been at stake for the United States to commit an army to combat in Asia. The United States thought it was containing communism in general and Chinese communism in particular when it developed an open-ended commitment to the Republic of Vietnam. The Soviet Union made a fundamental commitment to supply North Vietnam with the military materiel that gave the North Vietnamese the capability to match the American buildup. Without Soviet support, the North Vietnamese could not have escalated the level of conflict. Yet the reason the Soviets bore the costs and took the risks had less to do with Vietnam and more to do with China. And in China there was a violent struggle for power. The issue which ultimately decided which camp a Chinese politician supported was whether the United States military presence in Vietnam threatened China. One group said yes and China should therefore cooperate with the Soviet Union. The other group said no and there was no need to cooperate with the Soviet Union. Forces external to the conflict had a great impact on the conflict. The conflict had great impact beyond Vietnam.

The Soviet Union exploited the conflict by supplying weapons to North Vietnam that resulted in an escalating conflict and an escalating requirement for US troops. The Soviets portrayed the fact of growing American presence in their diplomacy and propaganda as a threat to the entire socialist camp in general and to China specifically. As a result, the Soviets made "unity of action over Vietnam" the centerpiece of their diplomacy within the socialist camp. They hoped to force China to reestablish the Sino-Soviet relationship that Mao Zedong had begun to rupture in 1957. Inside China, Mao favored a continued independent path of development and was against "unity of action" with the Soviet Union, while powerful opponents favored such a course of action.

The United States failed to understand the extent of the Sino-Soviet split, seeing instead a monolithic communist bloc. In fact, the United States viewed the Soviets as the moderate or sane communists while the Chinese were the radical or insane communists. But they were, ultimately, all communists. There can be no doubt that the regime imposed on South Vietnam by North Vietnam is repressive and the desire to prevent this misfortune from befalling those people was a legitimate desire on the part of a United States government that had declared that it would go anywhere and pay any price in the defense of freedom. But this was only a small part of the US decision to fight in Vietnam. The United States perceived strategic interests in Southeast Asia and felt it was containing communism, especially Chinese communism, as part of a larger global strategy. Because the Kennedy and Johnson administrations failed to understand the Sino-Soviet rift, the United States committed its armed forces on the basis of faulty strategic reasoning. Despite accurate intelligence which showed that the military capabilities of the North Vietnamese were primarily supplied by the Soviet Union, the United States failed to assess correctly the Soviet role in the conflict. Increased Soviet military aid meant, in the American view, increased Soviet influence, which should have led to increasing moderation by the North Vietnamese. Instead, increasing North Vietnamese military capability led to a tougher conflict.

Further, long before the United States committed ground forces, Mao Zedong signaled the United States that China wanted to improve relations with the United States and that Vietnam was not an issue that should stand in the way of rapprochement. The United States, still incorrectly seeing the threat in Southeast Asia as a Chinese threat, failed to understand that improving relations with China was a realistic policy option in Asia.

Colonel Harry Summers in *On Strategy* and former President Richard Nixon in *No More Vietnams* have attempted to come to grips with what the United States could have done to use military force properly to achieve political goals. They moved beyond the typical total-war-or-nothing argument and demonstrated that a limited war can be fought by a democracy and still be winnable. This study has a different approach and shows that the United States initially did have defined goals and a plan to achieve them. Military forces were committed with a mission to achieve a military victory by 1968—in time to make the administration look good for the 1968 election campaign. However, the Soviet supply effort so improved North Vietnam's warmaking capability that the victory, in McNamara's view, could not be achieved before the 1968 elections. Moreover, after a year of ground conflict, the United States finally understood that Mao was seeking improved relations. In other words, we were fighting a war to contain Chinese communists, and they did not need to be contained. These two factors coincided with the startling discovery in 1966 by US intelligence that the Soviet Union was rapidly overcoming American nuclear superiority. American forces had been committed to Asia under the assumption that the United States would maintain nuclear superiority through the early '70s. Now, the massive Soviet spending campaign looked like it would achieve near parity in 1967 or 1968. Given these factors, *the Johnson administration consciously chose to abandon military victory as a goal.*

Once set on a path of de-escalation, the administration failed to redefine new national goals in any meaningful sense, and actually concealed from the public the fact that goals had changed. Secretary of Defense Robert McNamara sought and received assurances from the American commander, General William Westmoreland, that, given an upper limit on US troop strength—a troop-strength ceiling—Westmoreland would not lose. Westmoreland warned that the proposed troop ceiling, however, would make victory impossible in any sort of reasonable time frame—Westmoreland's estimate was at least five years. The decision to limit the US commitment was made anyway, and *this left an army in combat whose only goal was to avoid defeat.*

The decision to de-escalate was made in late 1966, appealed by the military in early 1967, and upheld in August 1967—long before the Tet offensive of 1968. Tet did not change US policy, only the public explanation of US policy. For the last two years of the Johnson presidency, that policy was to use military power to maintain a stalemate on the battlefield in Vietnam.

Soviet strategy achieved almost all of its tactical objectives, but failed to reach its initial strategic goal when the United States and China began concrete efforts toward rapprochement in 1969. The United States based its use of military force on incorrect strategic analysis. Having realized the analysis was faulty, the American leadership decided to scale down its military effort and give up its original national goals, but it failed to establish a clear revised mission for the committed forces. Thus, the Kennedy-Johnson era ended with over a half million soldiers in a war in Asia with no strategy, purpose, policy, or goal, and a set of political policies that limited the options for the next administration. The debilitating effect on the nation and the army has been dealt with in numerous other studies. This book explains how and why it happened.

1

Setting the Stage

Major Events

- *1957*—Great Leap Forward in China begins.
- *1960*—National Liberation Front in Vietnam is established.
- *1960–1962*—Soviet military airlift delivers supplies to Laos and Vietnam.
- *1962*—Geneva agreement declares Laos to be neutral. Soviets cease military aid to communists in the region.
- *1961–1963*—United States deploys thousands of military advisors to Vietnam.
- *Early 1962–mid-1963*—Viet Cong military activity declines.
- *May 1963*—Buddhist crisis in South Vietnam begins.
- *July 1963*—Soviet Union again delivers military supplies to Vietnam. Viet Cong military activity increases.
- *September 1963*—President Kennedy sends Robert McNamara and Maxwell Taylor to Vietnam on fact-finding mission. Kennedy indicates he is worried about a crisis that began in May. McNamara reports that the Viet Cong have improved weaponry.
- *October 1963*—Ho Chi Minh makes pro-Soviet diplomatic gestures.
- *November 1, 1963*—President Diem overthrown and killed with US compliance. This Kennedy administration "solution" to the crisis in Vietnam results in political chaos in South Vietnam.
- *November 1963*—Chinese logistic surge to Vietnam occurs as Soviets curtail military aid and counsel restraint in Hanoi.
- *November 22, 1963*—President Kennedy is assassinated. Lyndon Johnson becomes president of the United States.
- *December 1963–January 1964*—South Vietnamese military and political situation deteriorates.

- *February 1964*—President Johnson makes the decision that the United States will remain committed to Vietnam and will do what is necessary to prevent South Vietnam's fall. He communicates a direct threat to North Vietnam.

It was a confident American president that sought to "contain" communism around the world in the wake of the Cuban Missile Crisis of October 1962. Armed with nuclear superiority, John F. Kennedy set out to restrain China as well as the Soviet Union. Southeast Asia was another test case, a demonstration of the national will "to go anywhere and pay any price" in defense of freedom. But as the Kennedy administration became engrossed in Southeast Asia, it failed to understand a developing drama that would become inextricably linked to American fortunes in Vietnam— the Sino-Soviet rift.

The growing hostility between Russia and China in the early 1960s was not as yet accepted as real by American foreign policy experts in government and academia. Since at least 1957, Mao Zedong had attempted to guide China onto an independent path of development, symbolized by the chaotic "Great Leap Forward." This effort by Mao was a fundamental strategic problem for the Soviet Union and its new leader, Nikita Khrushchev. For the Soviets, one critical outcome of World War II and the subsequent triumph of Chinese communism was a secure eastern border for the Soviet Union. The United States had been virtually excluded from the Asian mainland. Now, in the late 1950s, Mao's independence caused great unease among Soviet leaders.

China was a backward state seeking a path to modernization and development. It faced a full spectrum of possibilities. At one end was continued alliance with and dependence upon the Soviet Union. This meant, however, a continued patron-client relationship and Chinese acceptance of Soviet control over the pace and style of modernization. In the center of the spectrum was self-reliance. China could modernize by using its own resources. This would be a long and difficult path and, from a Soviet perspective, seemed extremely unlikely. At the other end of the spectrum was the path most feared by the Soviet Union—technological and economic assistance from the West, including the United States. Mao intended the Great Leap Forward to move China toward an independent path of development and raised the very real possibility that China ultimately would develop a Western orientation in foreign and economic policy.[1] Such a course would destroy Soviet wartime gains in Asia, raise the specter of hostile borders in the east and west, and alter the world balance of power to the disadvantage of the Soviet Union.

Khrushchev came to power as the Chinese began to show their independence. How could he restore the post-1949 Sino-Soviet relationship? One solution in the eyes of the Kremlin was to entangle the United States in a military conflict in Southeast Asia. If the United States committed military power to an anti-communist conflict on China's border, the Soviets could argue that American military involvement was a threat to China that warranted reestablishment of close Sino-Soviet ties.

Internal Chinese politics gave Khrushchev's plan an excellent chance for success. Mao's decision to launch the Great Leap Forward provoked a major split in the Chinese hierarchy and ushered in a continuous struggle for power. Many Chinese leaders favored continued good relations with the Soviet Union. In their view, it was wrong to give up large-scale Soviet economic assistance. These leaders, notably Liu Shaoqi and Deng Xiaoping, attempted to curtail some of the excesses of the Great Leap Forward while increasing their own personal power at Mao's expense. The group headed by Liu and Deng would come to be named by Mao and his followers "the pro-Soviet group."[2]

Soviet strategy was designed to influence this so-called pro-Soviet group. An American threat would provide the group with an issue about which opposition to Mao could unite. Soviet propaganda and diplomacy would stress the threat to China and the entire socialist camp and call for "unity of action" within the socialist camp over Vietnam. Simultaneously the Soviets would punish China for its failure to act in concert with other socialist states by attempting to isolate China on a state-to-state and a party-to-party level. The Soviets hoped the combination of isolation from support of the socialist camp and increasing

[1] See D.M. Pospelov and E.D. Stepanov, *Pekin protiv V'etnama* (Peking Against Vietnam) (Moscow: Thought, 1983), p. 34 for the Soviet view of this problem. The authors argue that from the beginning of the 1960s Chinese policy was driven by the goal of improving relations with the United States.

[2] See "Peking is fighting Pro-Soviet Clique," *New York Times,* January 17, 1965, and Maury Lisann, "Moscow and the Chinese Power Struggle," *Problems of Communism,* November–December 1969, pp. 32–41. For a more comprehensive discussion of the Chinese power struggle, see Richard C. Thornton, *China: A Political History, 1917–1980* (Boulder, Colo.: Westview Press, 1982), pp. 227–277. (Hereafter referred to as *China.*)

perception of threat brought on by increasing US military involvement in Southeast Asia would propel Mao's opponents to victory in China's power struggle.

Southeast Asia Becomes the Field of Play

The idea for entanglement of the United States in Southeast Asia was not a vision that appeared in the night to the new Soviet leadership. It was rather obvious. First, geography. Southeast Asia bordered China. Second, the 1954 accords that ended French involvement in Southeast Asia left the area in turmoil and conflict. Third, the United States already had a military and political presence along with a stated policy of containment of communism. The United States would base its level of commitment on the existing situation in Southeast Asia. But the Soviet Union had the ability to alter that situation by supplying military equipment to communist movements. Khrushchev chose to use arms and munitions as a thermostat governing the level of conflict in the region.

The Soviets employed a continuous airlift of military supplies to communist guerrillas in Laos in 1960 and 1961. The guerrillas used their increasing capabilities to escalate the level of conflict to such a degree that United States leaders feared a communist victory in Laos. Simultaneously, in 1960, the Soviets encouraged the establishment of the National Liberation Front in South Vietnam. Soviet supplies to Laotian communists coupled with smaller but significant support for the North Vietnamese led to rising expectations in the North Vietnamese leadership. Suddenly, in July 1962, the Soviets curtailed all military supplies to the region, agreed to a neutralized Laotian solution, and reduced their presence to negligible levels.[3] The Soviet military disengagement resulted in a decline in Soviet influence in Hanoi as Hanoi's leaders saw their hopes dashed. North Vietnam turned to China for military assistance and by late 1962 the North Vietnamese had moved to a more pro-Peking posture in the Sino-Soviet dispute.[4]

---

[3]Thornton, "Soviet Strategy and the Vietnam War," *Asian Affairs*, No. 4, (March/April 1974), p. 205. (Hereafter referred to as "Soviet Strategy.")

[4]Seymour Topping, "North Vietnamese Economy Reported Faltering," *New York Times*, December 20, 1963, p. 5. The author identifies a "pro-Soviet faction in the North Vietnamese leadership" that reportedly favored a return to a more pro-Soviet or at least a more neutral orientation vis-à-vis the Sino-Soviet rift that "North Vietnam maintained till a year ago,"(till late 1962). See also Donald Zagoria, *Vietnam Triangle* (Pegasus, 1967), p. 43. Zagoria places the pro-Peking shift in early 1963.

The American reaction to developments in Southeast Asia could have been expected. From the US point of view, the "neutral" solution in Laos had narrowly avoided disaster. As the situation worsened in Laos, the Kennedy administration determined to prevent a similar experience in Vietnam where, it was felt, the United States had a much stronger commitment. Thus, the president rapidly increased the number of US military advisors in South Vietnam.[5]

Mao Zedong understood that confrontation between the United States and China would support his opponents' argument that China should reestablish good relations with the Soviet Union. It was in his interests, under these conditions, to keep the level of conflict in Vietnam low. He used his power to influence the level and type of assistance given to North Vietnam to limit the insurgency in the south. As could be expected, during this period of North Vietnam's pro-Chinese policy, there was a clear decline in the level of conflict in South Vietnam.[6] The North Vietnamese, forced to rely on the principles of "People's War" and little else, did not have the ability to support major Viet Cong initiatives in the south.

Ironically, at this stage, less fighting in Vietnam aided the progress of Khrushchev's plans. The United States could not be expected to become deeply involved in a high-risk low-return venture. Khrushchev had to allow the Americans to develop the perception that the advisory effort was achieving success. Indeed, success encouraged the Americans to proceed with their increasing commitment to South Vietnam. And US policy—the "limited-risk gamble"—seemed to be richly rewarded in 1962 and 1963. The decline of Viet Cong activity provided American policymakers with enticing success as the United States came to believe that the war was being won.[7]

[5]*United States-Vietnam Relations, 1945–1967* (Washington: Department of Defense, 1971), Book 3, "The Advisory Build-up, 1961–1967," p. iii. (Hereafter referred to as *Pentagon Papers*). See also Neil Sheehan, et al., *The Pentagon Papers, The Secret History of the Vietnam War*, fifth printing (New York: Bantam Books, Inc., 1971), pp. 79–114. (Hereafter referred to as *Secret History*.) This is a discussion of the transition during the Kennedy years from a "limited risk gamble" to a broad commitment.

[6]*Pentagon Papers*, Book 3, "Strategic Hamlet Program 1961–1963," Table 3, p. 32. This is a graph which depicts "Viet Cong Initiated Incidents" from January 1962 until March 1963. It shows a steady decline in all categories of Viet Cong activity. See also ibid., Book 12, "State Department Memorandum," Oct. 22, 1963, p. 580. This memorandum states "From January 1962 until July 1963, the total number of Viet Cong armed attacks as well as all other incidents (sabotage, terrorism and propaganda), dropped consistently."

[7]Ibid., Book 3, "The Advisory Build-Up, 1961–1967," p. 33. See also Public Broadcasting Service telecast of "Firing Line" January 27, 1974 "The Revisionist Historians." This was an interview of former Secretary of State Dean Rusk by William F. Buckley, Jr. Mr. Rusk stated "There was once in 1964 when—or '63, as a matter of fact—when we got relatively optimistic about the situation out there [Vietnam]."

Intelligence reports through mid-1963 forecast South Vietnamese military victories and a steady reduction in Viet Cong capabilities. The US intelligence community expected this trend to continue "barring greatly increased Viet Cong reinforcement and supply."[8] American optimism was so high that Secretary of Defense McNamara pushed forward a publicized plan for a phased withdrawal of US forces from the area.[9] Unfortunately for the United States, it was precisely the assumption "barring greatly increased Viet Cong reinforcement and supply" that Soviet plans would undermine.

The Soviets Rejoin the Contest

In mid-1963, the Soviet Union began to increase its shipments of military supplies to Southeast Asia. To ensure rapid employment in South Vietnam, many of these were delivered to Viet Cong forces in Cambodia through the port of Sihanoukville, where they could be forwarded to guerrillas near Saigon or in the Mekong Delta. Better equipped Viet Cong units immediately became more aggressive, operating in larger units.[10]

The Soviets evidently expected the US leadership to show mild alarm. The Americans would not be anxious to see their public pronouncements of optimism proved off-the-mark and setbacks in the war could force the United States to take vigorous measures. The Soviet plan had to be executed with finesse. Khrushchev had to escalate the fighting in Vietnam without letting the conflict get out of hand, without allowing the situation to seem hopeless. Such a shock, before the United States was committed fully, could cause the United States to withdraw. And of course, while the Soviets controlled logistics, the North Vietnamese retained command of their own troops in the field and used Russian supplies in battle to maximum advantage. At least initially, the Soviets had to introduce weaponry discreetly to avoid an appearance of Soviet responsibility for escalating the war. Khrushchev,

---

[8] *Pentagon Papers,* Book 3, "Phased Withdrawal of US Forces in Vietnam, 1962–1964," p. a.

[9] Ibid., pp. i-iii. The American advisory force reached 16,732 by October 1963. An ostensible cutback of 1,000 men did take place in December 1963, although these were the most nonessential personnel. By late 1964, troop strength was 23,000.

[10] Hedrick Smith, "Rise in Red Arms to Vietnam Seen," *New York Times,* January 5, 1964, p. 11. A high level US military spokesman said that "communist bloc" supplies had increased over the last six months and three-fourths of the equipment moved through normal commercial channels into Cambodia through Sihanoukville.

after all, wanted to provoke a Sino-American—not a Soviet-American—confrontation over Vietnam.[11]

Although we do not know for certain, a Soviet-North Vietnamese arms agreement was probably concluded during a July 1963 visit to Moscow by a Viet Cong delegation. At that time, a *Pravda* article indicated that the Soviets would supply substantial aid to the Viet Cong. While socialist states could not "devote themselves exclusively to aiding National Liberation Movements through military and political assistance,"said *Pravda*, "such aid may be given on a large scale."[12]

Evidence of renewed Soviet assistance appeared in the fall of 1963 with a North Vietnamese shift from their public pro-Peking pronouncements. Ho Chi Minh, who had sided with Chinese opposition to the 1963 Nuclear Test Ban Treaty when he refused to sign the document in August of that year (the Soviets had been pressing for unanimous support for the treaty within the socialist camp), responded favorably in October 1963 to a French proposal of assistance to Vietnam in throwing off foreign (meaning Soviet, American, and Chinese) influence.[13]

Ho made known his views through Eastern European diplomats who, in interviews with reporters, alluded to a North Vietnamese desire to move away from "suffocating" Chinese influence. The Soviet Union at this time had been courting improved bilateral relations with France. Ho's positive gesture toward his former enemies—combined with his choice of East European diplomats as the means for release of the information—were clear pro-Soviet signals. The nuances of diplomacy followed the flow of military supplies. On the battlefield there was direct evidence of renewed Soviet aid as Soviet and Czech rifles began to be captured by South Vietnamese forces in October 1963.[14]

The level of conflict escalated quickly. In July there was a sudden increase in Viet Cong offensive operations as a result of the new supply effort.[15] The Viet Cong displayed increased aggressiveness, operated in larger

[11]The Soviet need for discretion has limited the availability of evidence. Moreover, relatively small amounts of arms could affect significantly a war in its early stages. There is sufficient evidence, however, to suggest that the increase in external (external from Vietnam) support for the Viet Cong that clearly began in the summer of 1963 was of Soviet origin.

[12]"On Economic vs. Military Aid to Liberated Countries," *Current Digest of the Soviet Press*, Vol. XV, No. 29, (August 14, 1963), p. 13. (Hereafter referred to as *Current Digest*.)

[13]Adam Ulam, *The Rivals* (New York: Viking Press, 1971), p. 356.

[14]United States Department of State, *Aggression from the North*, Department of State Publication 7839, February 1965, Appendix D.

[15]*Pentagon Papers*, Book 3, "Phased Withdrawal," pp. b, 18–20.

units, and used improved weaponry. This led American officials in Saigon to begin efforts to convince the Kennedy administration that the military situation was deteriorating and that official public optimism was misguided.[16] By September, President Kennedy had become alarmed and dispatched Secretary of Defense Robert McNamara and Chairman of the Joint Chiefs of Staff General Maxwell Taylor to Vietnam on a fact-finding mission.[17]

Interestingly, President Kennedy, in his written instructions to McNamara and Taylor, noted that the Vietnamese situation began deteriorating May 1963 when a Vietnamese political confrontation known as the Buddhist crisis began.[18] The crisis was highlighted by the self-immolation of Buddhist monks and attacks on pagodas by government troops. One common criticism of the US performance in Vietnam is that US leaders never understood the importance of politics and overstressed military factors. Here, at least, is an example of the reverse—overstressing politics. While the political turmoil inside South Vietnam undoubtedly provided the Viet Cong with opportunities, the turmoil did not give them their weaponry. The increased prowess of the Viet Cong derived primarily from the newly arrived weapons, ammunition, and other military supplies. The political crisis began in May, but US intelligence reports on the military situation remained generally optimistic. It was late summer before better equipped Viet Cong units, armed with Soviet and Czech rifles, increased offensive action. Preoccupation with political unrest blurred US understanding of the Soviet role in the military escalation.

The report from the McNamara-Taylor trip reflected, in general, continued confidence in the progress of the war, but took note of the improved Viet Cong military capabilities. "Recent days have been characterized by reports of greater VC activity, countrywide," the report noted, "coupled with evidence of improved weaponry."[19] Later in the month the State Department's Intelligence and Research Bureau circulated a classified memorandum that challenged the overall optimistic assessment of the war's progress, declaring that since July 1963 there had been an un-

[16] "Red Made Carbines Seized in Vietnam," *New York Times,* July 23, 1963, p. 3 and David Halberstam, "US Civilian Aides in Vietnam Press for a Decision on Diem," *New York Times,* September 15, 1963, p. 4.

[17] *Pentagon Papers,* Book 12, "Memorandum for the Secretary of Defense from the President, September 21, 1963," p. 551.

[18] Ibid.

[19] Ibid.,"Memorandum for the President, October 2, 1963," p. 559.

favorable shift in the balance of power.[20] "By the final quarter of 1963," said a March 1964 intelligence report, "despite considerable improvement in offensive capabilities of RVN [Republic of Vietnam], the VC likewise had improved."[21] Although preparations for the publicly announced phased withdrawal of US forces continued, the change in military fortunes had made such plans moot. The December withdrawal of 1,000 men in the form of an accounting exercise was the only troop withdrawal on the horizon.[22] The Soviet decision to inject additional military supplies into the combat zone had altered the set of conditions facing US decisionmakers.

Mao Zedong and John F. Kennedy Respond

The rising level of Viet Cong military operations was a serious problem for Mao and Kennedy. From Mao's point of view, a gradually escalating conflict could lead to a gradually escalating US military presence in Vietnam, which supported his opponents' claims that the US presence in Vietnam was a threat to China. This pushed Chinese leaders back into the arms of their Russian patrons, which, for Mao, was a most distasteful marriage of convenience. For if China were compelled to seek Soviet assistance, Mao would lose on the fundamental question of how China should seek to modernize.

From Kennedy's point of view, the presidential election of 1964 could turn on the United States' success in Vietnam, or the lack thereof. Kennedy's administration had staked a great deal of prestige on the formation of Special Forces (Green Berets), who were the key to American advisory efforts in South Vietnam. The Berlin Wall, the Cuban Missile Crisis, and the war in Laos all had combined to create a reasonably strong public consensus that there was a communist threat. Given this perception, the apparent success of US policy in Vietnam from early 1962 through mid-1963 had naturally been well publicized. The president was not anxious to see the war in Southeast Asia take a turn for the worse.

Both Mao and Kennedy faced a challenge. Both responded.

---

[20]Ibid., "State Department Bureau of Intelligence and Research Memorandum, October 22, 1963," pp. 579–582.
[21]Ibid., Book 3, "US Programs in South Vietnam, November 1963–April 1965: NSAM 273–NSAM 288—Honolulu," p. 41.
[22]Ibid., "Phased Withdrawal," p. 30.

The continuing unrest linked to the Buddhist crisis and its poor handling by the government of Ngo Dinh Diem convinced Kennedy and his administration that the war would be lost if Diem remained in power. Because the administration believed the only real political alternative was the Army of the Republic of Vietnam (ARVN), Kennedy and his advisors encouraged a coup by senior military leaders. Discussions between prospective coup leaders and the US embassy in Saigon had broken off in August 1963, but reopened immediately after the McNamara-Taylor trip to Vietnam at the end of September. On November 1, 1963, the generals killed Diem. The desired stability did not materialize, however, as the generals had neither organized political support nor a way to prevent competition among themselves. The result was chaos.[23]

The widespread confusion following the coup gave Mao an opportunity for bold maneuver. Realizing that the United States had no desire to become entangled in a land war in Asia and had demonstrated caution by announcing plans for a phased withdrawal of military advisors, Mao concluded that a rapid deterioration of the situation in Vietnam would cause the United States to cut its losses and withdraw from the area. A sudden Viet Cong surge amid the post-coup turmoil would change America's "limited-risk gamble" to a high-risk, high-cost, low-return venture. So Mao suddenly increased Chinese military support and there was an attendant jump in Viet Cong activity.[24] By December the United States was fully aware of a quantum increase in Viet Cong battlefield activity. The communist forces had seized the initiative in the Mekong Delta and in key provinces near Saigon. American Ambassador Henry Cabot Lodge reported from Saigon in early December that the only progress made in November was by the enemy. Later in the month Secretary McNamara admitted publicly that there had been "a very substantial increase in VC activity, an increase which began shortly after the new government was formed."[25]

Viet Cong forces were told to initiate a general offensive in December 1963. Their orders stated that the war had moved to a new stage and the United States did not want to become "bogged down in a large scale and

---

[23]The Senator Gravel Edition, *The Pentagon Papers, The Defense Department History of United States Decision Making on Vietnam.* Vol. II, (Boston: Beacon Press, 1972), pp. 201–207. (Hereafter referred to as Gravel).

[24]*Pentagon Papers,* Book 3, "The Overthrow of Ngo Dinh Diem, May–November, 1963," p. 63.

[25]David Halberstam, "Saigon's Control in Two Provinces Periled by Reds," *New York Times,* November 21, 1963, p.1. *Pentagon Papers,* Book 3, US Programs," pp. 16–21.

protracted war" which would throw her into "a very passive position in the world." North Vietnamese documents stressed that armed struggle plays the decisive role, that logistic help would be forthcoming, and that the real target of the offensive against the ARVN was US leadership.[26]

Meanwhile, the Soviets shared Mao's analysis of the situation and feared precisely the outcome Mao was trying to achieve—US withdrawal. Consequently, in the immediate aftermath of the coup, the Soviets publicly counseled restraint by Hanoi, letting the North Vietnamese know they could not expect increased aid. When the Viet Cong, now with sudden Chinese support, went on the offensive, the Soviets curtailed the flow of military supplies.[27]

Hanoi shifted again toward a pro-Chinese orientation. Public manifestations of this were visible in January 1964 when an issue of the North Vietnamese theoretical journal *Hoc Tap* attacked Soviet calls for moderation in the war by accusing "the revisionists led by Moscow" of restricting communist advances throughout the world. A second article appeared in the newspaper *Nhan Dan* and ridiculed all suggestions that Vietnam adopt a neutral solution like Laos, reversing, in effect, Ho Chi Minh's stated policy from early November 1963. To signal closer Chinese-Vietnamese ties, the Chinese republished both of these North Vietnamese articles in the Chinese press just before the arrival of a high-ranking North Vietnamese delegation returning from apparently unsuccessful aid negotiations in Moscow.[28] Mao further signaled increased Chinese support by staging mass rallies in support of North Vietnam. At one such event in honor of the third anniversary of the founding of the National Liberation Front, for example, the president of the All China Federation of Trade Unions, Liu Ningyi, announced that the Viet Cong were "carrying their armed struggle in self-defense forward to a new stage" and he pledged all-out backing for the Viet Cong.[29]

Battlefield conditions continued to worsen for the South Vietnamese army and evidence mounted that there had been a substantial surge of

---

[26]"The Viet-Nam Workers' Party's 1963 Decision to Escalate the War in the South," *Viet-Nam Documents and Research Notes,* Document No. 96 (Saigon: 1971).

[27]Theodore Shabad, "*Izvestia* Derides Revolt Leaders," *New York Times,* November 1963, p. 1, and Seymour Topping, "North Vietnamese Economy Reported Faltering," ibid., December 20, 1963, p. 5.

[28]Max Frankel, "Hanoi Says Peking Would Defend It," *New York Times,* February 14, 1964, p. 1.

[29]"Aid to Vietnam Reds is Pledged at Peking," *New York Times,* December 21, 1963, p. 5.

Chinese-supplied weapons. In December, US advisors were particularly disturbed when ARVN units captured Chinese manufactured 57mm and 75mm recoilless rifles. Later in the month, ARVN discovered a huge cache of ammunition manufactured in China in areas near the Cambodian border. The Viet Cong had begun to convert from a hodgepodge of weapons and calibers to a standard family of 7.62 caliber small arms. The most significant new weapon in early 1964 was a Chinese copy of the Soviet assault rifle, the AK-47.[30] American intelligence reported to Secretary McNamara that the situation had deteriorated rapidly and the Viet Cong were operating in larger, more heavily armed units. The growth in Viet Cong power had begun in July 1963 but had accelerated from November 1963 to February 1964.[31]

Mao's strategy had a good chance for success. The *Pentagon Papers* argues that US complicity in the Diem coup resulted in heightened US "responsibilities and commitment in an essentially leaderless Vietnam."[32] This might have been true if conditions were serious but not desperate, but Mao intended to change the military calculus, presenting the United States with virtually a "no win" situation. Kennedy would be faced with an unpalatable choice—far greater US commitment, a commitment that would imply his advisory effort had failed, or defeat. If he chose a larger commitment, he would have to pour men and materiel into Vietnam during an election year, and in no case would the results be decisive by the time Americans went to the polls. Moreover, in the immediate shock of the post-coup chaos, the American administration concluded that it must have been the victim of deceitful war reports by South Vietnamese officials. The *Pentagon Papers* points out this bit of self-delusion as "the impression developed in many quarters, and eventually spread to all, that *before* the coup, the situation had been much more adverse than we had recognized officially at the time."[33]

---

[30]*Pentagon Papers*, Book 3, "US Programs," p. 50 and Admiral Sharp and General William C. Westmoreland, Report on the War in Vietnam (Washington: US Government Printing Office, 1968) Section II, pp. 88–92; and Hedrick Smith, "Rise in Red Arms to Vietnam Seen," *New York Times*, January 5, 1964, p.1.

[31]*Pentagon Papers*, Book 3, "US Programs," p. 34 and ibid., "Phased Withdrawal," p. e.

[32]Gravel, Vol II, p. 207.

[33]Gravel, Vol. III, p. 23. This explanation in the *Pentagon Papers* serves as the basis for much scholarly interpretation. It is a myth. The US had 17,000 advisors contributing to the reporting. There really had a been a decrease in VC activity in 1962 and early 1963. However, as the Viet Cong military capability increased so did Viet Cong military activity and effectiveness. Quite simply the Viet Cong got better because of greatly increased reinforcement and supply. US intelligence had predicted continued positive trends "barring greatly increased Viet Cong reinforcement and supply."

Washington's disenchantment with the South Vietnamese further contributed to an atmosphere that favored Mao's goal—US withdrawal from Vietnam. Mao hoped Kennedy would cut his losses as far ahead of the 1964 elections as possible. But the American president never faced these troublesome political choices. An assassin's bullets cut him down in Dallas on November 22, 1963.

Assassination Delays the US Decision

President Lyndon B. Johnson was far less secure politically than his predecessor. He had been second man on the presidential ticket, not first, and he faced an election in less than a year with a conservative senator from Arizona, Barry Goldwater, his most probable opponent. In the immediate wake of Kennedy's assassination, Johnson needed to demonstrate continuity in US leadership. This restricted his freedom of action. Moreover, the decline in South Vietnamese fortunes—begun in July—had been gradual, and the administration had not as yet conveyed its alarm to the public. In fact, it would be late December before Secretary of Defense McNamara publicly acknowledged the troubles brewing in Southeast Asia. It was Johnson's misfortune to inherit a public position that suggested US Vietnam policy had been successful until he became president. Worse yet, his opponent in the upcoming campaign would express "hard-line" views, leaving Johnson to find a way to fight an increasingly demanding war while appearing more committed to a peaceful solution than his opponent. Understandably, the president had no ready-made solution. His initial directive on the war continued existing policies.[34] The rapidly declining situation, however, meant that he would soon face fundamental decisions.

By February, it was apparent that the United States would have to increase its military involvement in Vietnam or lose. The Soviet Union and China anxiously awaited signs of a US decision. The signal came in blunt

---

This was a valid prediction. Unfortunately, the increases were not barred. For examples of scholarship that uses "the Vietnamese lied to us" interpretation of Viet Cong progress in late 1963, see Leslie H. Gelb and Richard K. Betts, *The Irony of Vietnam: The System Worked* (Washington: The Brookings Institution, 1979) p. 91 and Kathleen J. Turner, *Lyndon Johnson's Dual War* (Chicago: The University of Chicago Press, 1985) p. 5.

[34]Gravel, pp. 17–20.

fashion from the highest level. On February 21, 1964, President Johnson gave a speech in which he warned those supplying the guerrillas.[35] The following day, administration sources suggested to the media that the war might be widened to North Vietnam.[36] Johnson had publicly decided to accept increased US military involvement. This policy was articulated inside the administration on February 20, 1963, at a National Security Council meeting. There the president ordered more rapid development of detailed contingency plans for pressure against North Vietnam.[37] Consistent with his public views, Johnson considered punitive, overt actions against North Vietnam as attractive options.

Mao's gamble had failed. The United States was more deeply entangled.

[35] "Johnson Meets Mexican Leader: Defines US Aims," *New York Times*, February 22, 1964, p.1. Actually, President Johnson approved a plan known as OPLAN 34A which provided for a spectrum of capabilities for the South Vietnamese to execute against the North on January 16, 1964. He authorized the activities, which were initially very minor, to begin on February 1. One consideration with which the president was concerned was "plausibility of denial." The guidance he gave to the NSC on February 20 was to rapidly develop plans for both overt and covert measures and he announced the possibility of action against the North himself the next day.

[36] Max Frankel, "Washington Hints at Saigon Raids on North Vietnam," ibid., February 23, 1964, p.1.

[37] Gravel, Vol III, pp. 118–119.

2

The Path to Tonkin

Major Events

- *February 1964*—Soviets cease calls for restraint in Hanoi and renew pledges of support. They press for Chinese cooperation to meet the common threat in Vietnam.
- *February 1964*—Zhou Enlai states Chinese desire for improved Sino-US relations.
- *February–June 1964*—Chinese press debate appears over the issue of whether the US presence in Vietnam is a threat to China.
- *March 17, 1964*—President approves McNamara recommendations by promulgating National Security Action Memorandum (NSAM) 288 which calls for plans for "graduated overt military pressure against North Vietnam."
- *April–May 1964*—Viet Cong forces conduct new offensive surge.
- *May 1964*—Viet Cong sink American ship.
- *June 1964*—Americans indicate publicly that the US commitment to Vietnam is unlimited. Privately, the president directs his subordinates to find an act of irreversible US commitment. Maxwell Taylor becomes US ambassador to South Vietnam.
- *August 1964*—The Tonkin Gulf incident is followed by the Tonkin Gulf Joint Resolution of Congress. United States conducts one-time retaliatory bombing strike against North Vietnam and increases air and naval presence in the region.

Johnson's decision to back South Vietnam come hell or high water changed the situation facing the Soviet Union and China. Each reacted differently.

For the Soviet Union, US threats to widen the war to North Vietnam meant its strategy was working. The United States was entangled in a military conflict. This presented the Soviets with two tasks. First, they needed to assure the North Vietnamese of staunch Soviet support in the face of increased US involvement. And indeed, Soviet public pronouncements on the Vietnam war changed immediately after Johnson's February 21, 1964, speech. The Soviets abandoned calls for North Vietnamese restraint and their public line became very militant and included new promises of support. Second, they needed to exploit the fear generated by increased US military action in their diplomacy toward China. The Soviets, therefore, conducted an intense propaganda campaign that stressed the seriousness of the American threat to China and China's isolation from the rest of the socialist camp. Further, the Soviet campaign emphasized the value to the Chinese communists of past Soviet aid, claiming such assistance had been key to the communist victory in China in 1949.

For the Chinese—or at least for Mao—stiffening American resolve was hardly good news. In the wake of Johnson's speech, the Chinese press was silent for two full weeks on the subject of Vietnam as Mao assessed the situation. When Johnson's speech was finally reported in the Chinese press, it received only perfunctory treatment. Conversely, in a remarkable bit of diplomacy, shortly after the threat by the United States to take direct military action against a socialist ally on China's border, spokesmen for Mao signaled the United States that China would like to improve relations with the United States and Vietnam was not an issue that would stand in the way. Spokesmen for Mao would repeat this line for the next four months, but the United States would not respond.

Soviets Launch Propaganda Campaign, February–July 1964

Just two days after specific US threats against North Vietnam, the Soviet Union warned the United States against extending the war to the North. Just as importantly, the Soviet Union renewed offers of "whatever assistance" was necessary to North Vietnam, an obvious reference to military supplies.[1] The propaganda campaign to reassure the North Vietnamese continued over the following months.[2] In late March, *Izvestia* challenged US explanations of events in Southeast Asia, affirmed Soviet political support of North Vietnam, and expressed concern over the "ominous" US threats to widen the war.[3] The result, naturally, was a pro-Soviet shift by Vietnamese communists. North Vietnamese Premier Pham Van Dong, in April publicly thanked the Soviets for assistance and praised Soviet specialists working in Vietnam.[4]

Of course, the North Vietnamese were in a precarious position. The Soviets and Chinese quarreled while North Vietnam fought a war. While China bordered North Vietnam and could meet immediate needs and shortfalls more quickly than the Soviet Union, only the Russians had the modern industrial base to support a large war that might include massive US involvement. Thus, while the Vietnamese often had to conduct their policy toward the Sino-Soviet rift as a balancing act, there was always an incentive to tilt toward Moscow.

While reassuring the North Vietnamese, the Soviets launched a propaganda campaign which portrayed US actions as a developing threat to China. They stressed the seriousness of the American threat to China and China's isolation from the rest of the socialist world. And they emphasized the value to China of past Soviet aid and protection and reassured the Chinese that such support would still be available if the Chinese would make concessions.

The opening of the campaign came in mid-February 1964—before Johnson's speech. Although the speech confirmed the American decision for the Soviets, Soviet analysis would have to have concluded by mid-February that the United States would not give up on Vietnam. No US statements or actions gave any indication of withdrawal or a reduction of the US commitment. From the battlefield situation, it was evident that the United States could only maintain its policy of supporting South Vietnam by increasing its military involvement. While the speech was a surprise to

---

[1] Henry Tanner, "Soviet Warns US Not to Carry War to North Vietnam," *New York Times*, February 26, 1964, p. 1.

[2] "US unmoved by USSR Warning," ibid., February 27, 1964, p.3; and "*Pravda* Scores America's advocating War extension," ibid., February 28, 1964, p. 2;" Izvestia continues USSR press campaign against US extending war," ibid., March 1, 1964, p. 45.

[3] "Phantom of Dienbienphu," *Current Digest of the Soviet Press,* April 15, 1964, p. 19. (Hereafter referred to as *Current Digest*)

[4] "Gratitude for Aid," ibid., May 6, 1964, p. 32.

the US public, it was probably less so for the Soviet leadership.

In anticipation of increased US military involvement, the Soviets took advantage of the fourteenth anniversary of the Sino-Soviet treaty to discuss the history of Sino-Soviet relations in *Pravda*. The article claimed that China had made rapid progress toward modernization with Soviet assistance and went on to say that the Sino-Soviet relationship

> plays an important role in the preservation and strengthening of peace in the Far East and the whole world over. The conclusion of the treaty thwarted the intentions of the aggressive imperialist circles to isolate the Chinese People's Republic and foiled attempts to exert on it economic, political and outright military pressure. The Chinese people have in the Soviet Union a granite bulwark in the preservation and strengthening of their homeland. Every time there has been a threat to the security of the CPR, our country has shown complete willingness to carry out its sacred socialist duty to the full.[5]

Pravda went on to note that "unfortunately" Sino-Soviet relations began to deteriorate rapidly in 1960 and suggested China might not currently be able to count on Soviet aid. "Aggressive imperialist circles," of course, refers to the United States and "outright military pressure" alludes to the Chinese-American military conflict during the Korean War. The Soviet author made the argument that China now faced a new military conflict with the United States but had nothing to fear if China relied on the Soviet Union as an ally. The Soviets further suggested that such alliance and aid would not be possible under current circumstances.

In March, the Soviets introduced a thinly veiled threat to expel China from the socialist camp by proposing an international conference of socialist states to discuss consolidation of the world communist movement. Khrushchev asked for a bilateral Sino-Soviet meeting in May and a conference of all socialist states in the fall.[6] There is ample evidence that the Chinese saw this as a rather heavy-handed tactic, and indeed, that the Soviets themselves thought a little more subtlety was in order. Later in 1964, *Pravda,* responding to Chinese accusations, observed defensively that "the conference of Communist Parties is being assembled not to ex-

---

[5] "14th Anniversary of Soviet-Chinese Treaty," *Current Digest,* March 11, 1964, pp. 30–31.
[6] "Fidelity to the Principles of Marxism-Leninism," *Current Digest,* April 22, 1964, p. 3.

communicate this or that party from the Communist movement, not to arbitrarily expel this or that country from the world socialist system and not for mutual scoldings and accusations."[7] Of course, by electing to use the words "excommunicate" and "expel," they called attention to the potential that an international conference might do just that, despite Soviet protestations that this was not their intent.

In April, *Pravda* printed a Central Committee report by Communist Party theoretician M.A. Suslov which attacked the Chinese Communist Party on a broad range of issues. Suslov pointed out that "everytime a threat to the security of the CPR arose, the Soviet Union displayed its readiness to fulfill to the end its duty as an ally." Although China began to undermine the Sino-Soviet relationship in 1958, he continued that the Soviet Union was again ready to consider aid to China. The only barrier was, of course, China's attitude.[8]

Khrushchev continued the propaganda campaign during an April visit to Hungary. The Kremlin leader charged that American aggression in Vietnam demonstrated that imperialism was the chief enemy of the socialist camp, but that Chinese "splitting" benefited the imperialists.[9] At a Soviet-Polish friendship rally later in April, Khrushchev again attacked the Chinese while emphasizing the "imperialist" threat in Asia and the value of Soviet aid to China during the 1950s.[10]

Future KGB head Yuri Andropov also delivered a few body blows in an April Lenin Day speech on "Chinese Hypocrisy," in which he praised the leader of the 1911 Chinese revolution, Sun Yat-sen, implying that Sun had recognized the leading role of Russia in world revolution and the necessity of Soviet aid to China.[11] Andropov reported that Sun was convinced that "the Chinese people could win freedom and independence only with the support of the Soviet Union." Subsequent articles using Sun as their alleged

---

[7] "A Date Named for Preparatory Meeting of Parties," ibid., August 26, 1964, p. 5. For other evidence see "*Pravda* Series on Chinese CP and Communist Unity," ibid., June 3, 1964, pp. 3–9; "The Prospects for Collaboration With Socialist Parties," ibid., pp. 9–13; "Lessons of the Defeat of 'Splitters' at 1924 Congress," ibid., June 17, 1964, pp. 9–10; "*Izvestia* on Relations Among Socialist Countries," ibid., July 1, 1964, pp. 3–7; "A Familiar Role," *Peking Review*, April 17, 1964, p. 15; "Seven Letters Exchanged Between the Central Committees of the CPC and the CPSU," ibid., May 8, 1964, pp. 7–27; "Thwart Manoeuvres to Split International Communist Movement," ibid., May 15, 1964, pp. 20–23.

[8] "The Soviet-Chinese Polemic: Suslov's Speech-II," *Current Digest*, April 29, 1964, pp. 3–17.

[9] "Khrushchev on Goulash and Some Revolutionaries," ibid., May 6, 1964, p. 4.

[10] "Khrushchev Denounces China at Soviet-Polish Rally," ibid., May 13, 1964, pp. 10–14.

[11] "Andropov's Lenin Day Speech: 'Chinese Hypocrisy,'" ibid., May 20, 1964, pp. 15–17.

subject made the point that China needed Soviet assistance. One quoted the early Chinese revolutionary as saying "we must learn from Russia, learn how to fight, how to organize and how to create discipline."[12]

It is evident from these and other numerous examples that the propaganda campaign had the full support of the most powerful figures in the Soviet Union.[13] Soviet media stressed the danger of the threat to China and the entire socialist camp posed by the US presence in Vietnam, the current isolation of China from the socialist camp, the past value of Soviet assistance to China, and the conditions attached to future Soviet assistance. Against the backdrop of a Chinese power struggle in which the debate raged over the issue of Sino-Soviet relations and the nature of the threat posed by the United States in Vietnam, the Soviets hoped their propaganda would be of assistance to those who opposed Mao Zedong's break with the Soviet Union.

The Chinese Debate the Issues

Events in Vietnam and political pressure from the Soviet Union affected the internal Chinese political struggle. Both Liu Shaoqi and his group, who supported rapprochement with the Soviet Union, and Mao and his followers, who advocated a continued independent course with efforts to improve Sino-American relations, took to the press to advance their views. Liu's group favored continuation of the Chinese policy of high-profile support for North Vietnam, recognizing that an increased adversarial relationship with the United States supported the pro-Soviet point of view. Conversely, Mao's group altered its line immediately and signaled the United States that China desired improved Sino-American relations. According to Liu Shaoqi, there was a US threat to China in Vietnam. According to Mao Zedong, there was not.

Four days after President Johnson made the US decision on Vietnam public, Chinese Premier Zhou Enlai granted a private interview to a

[12]"Great Fighters for Friendship Between the Soviet and Chinese Peoples," ibid., July 29, 1964, pp. 10–11. See also "Book-Life and Legacy of Sun Yat-sen," ibid., May 20, 1964, p. 28.

[13]For example, see "The Plenary Session Resolution on the Struggle of the CPSU for the Solidarity of the International Communist Movement," ibid., April 22, 1964, p. 4; "Suslov's Report on the Struggle of the CPSU for the Solidarity of the International Communist Movement," ibid., pp. 5–16; "*Izvestia* Scores Chinese on Proletarian Dictatorship," ibid., June 17, 1964, pp. 3–9; "The Chinese and the Theory of the Party's Future," ibid., May 13, 1964, pp. 15–20; "Who Killed Soviet Aid," ibid., June 17, 1964, p. 12.

reporter during a visit to Pakistan. Zhou stated that China would welcome any peacemaking effort Pakistan might make between the United States and China. "We would welcome the helpful efforts in this direction," he said, "by our friends who are willing to offer their good offices between China and the United States." Zhou established a change in US policy toward Taiwan as the only precondition for improved relations.[14] This is a remarkable diplomatic signal because the president of the United States had just threatened to attack an ally of China located on China's border.

For those who had eyes to see there was ample evidence that Zhou meant what he said—and his views were no aberration. The Chinese press had remained silent on Johnson's threat for two weeks, and when it finally took notice, the response was mild.[15] Less than a week after the American president's threat, however, the premier of China stated that he wanted to improve relations with the United States. There was no mention that the war in Vietnam was an obstacle. Spokesmen for Mao's position continued to signal China's desire for improved relations over the next four months.[16]

On February 29, 1964, Zhou again said the barrier to normal Sino-American relations was the American "ostrich policy alleging that the Chiang Kai-shek clique represents [all of] China."[17] This presaged a continuous barrage of articles and pronouncements that offered improved

---

[14]Jacques Nevard, "Chou Bids US Pullout," *New York Times*, February 26, 1964, p. 3. The pullout referred to is from Taiwan, not Vietnam. See also "Asian-African Countries' Unity Against Imperialism: Premier Chou En-lai Answers Pakistan Correspondent," *Peking Review*, March 6, 1964, pp. 20–21.

[15]Seymour Topping,"Peking Bids Red imitate Viet Cong," *New York Times*, March 5, 1964, p. 1. This article reports that this is the first mention of the Johnson speech in the Chinese press and that there was nothing alarming in the story.

[16]The Chinese power struggle was extremely complex and the outline I have above may oversimplify it. There were two clear groups, one headed by Mao Zedong and one by the Liu Shaoqi-Deng Xiaoping coalition. There were other powerful figures who were uncommitted and others who changed sides. A Chinese politician had to balance his own views on the issues against the impact a decision to go one way or the other might have on his personal political fortunes. At this time it is difficult to put Zhou in Mao's group as he headed a small but powerful group that was uncommitted. Mao was adept at internal maneuvering and often was able to enlist Zhou's support. Over time Mao and Zhou became allies. In the issue discussed above, the problem with the Liu-Deng position was an increased risk of confrontation with the United States. Mao could make the argument to uncommitted politicians that no matter how one felt about the role of Soviet aid in modernization, the last thing China needed was a military confrontation with the most powerful country in the world. For a fascinating and detailed look at the internal workings of the Chinese power struggle see Andrew Hall Wedeman, *The East Wind Subsides* (Washington: Washington Institute Press, 1987).

[17]"US Policy in Asia Going Bankrupt," *Peking Review*, March 6, 1964, pp. 22–23.

relations if the United States delivered Taiwan concessions.[18] In retrospect, it is clear that the Chinese did not understand the importance of Taiwan in American foreign policy and that the Americans might regard their demands as an indication that China lacked any real interest in improving Sino-American relations.

Mao combined his signals to the United States with a strong anti-Soviet polemic. He attacked "revisionism" and challenged the Soviet right to leadership in the Afro-Asian world. The pro-American, anti-Soviet line was clearly expressed in an April 20, 1964, broadcast by the New China News Agency. Liao Zhengzhi, president of the China-Japan Friendship Association, announced that the Chinese were hoping to improve Sino-American relations. But the path to better relations, as usual, required US withdrawal from the Taiwan Straits. And China would "try not to sever its relations with Russia on its own accord," an attitude that did not preclude a split with Moscow.[19]

The pro-Soviet group, for its part, used the press to advocate its holy trinity—increased Chinese involvement in Vietnam, opposition to the United States, and alliance with the Soviet Union. In March, Liu's group published an article mouthing the Moscow party line. It stressed the need for solidarity in the socialist camp in the face of imperialist aggression in Vietnam, the duty of all socialist countries to support the Vietnamese, and the ominous consequences of US nuclear power.[20] The correlation of nuclear forces, in particular, was a powerful argument, for China was not yet a nuclear power and could only stand up to US nuclear blackmail with the backing of the Soviet Union.

Liu's group continued to press its case in April by reprinting an article from the Vietnamese theoretical journal *Hoc Tap* which had first appeared in early February when Mao still endorsed strong material and political

[18] "China's Sovereignty Over Taiwan Brooks No Intervention," ibid., May 15, 1964, pp 6–8; "Washington's Asian Embarrassment," ibid., March 13, 1964, pp. 10–11; "Vice-Premier Chen Yi Answers Questions by Japanese Journalist," ibid., June 26, 1964, pp. 6–7.

[19] Foreign Broadcast Information Service Bulletin, April 20, 1964, p. BBB 23. Liao was a member of Zhou Enlai's uncommitted group, but Zhou sided with Mao in this campaign. See Wedeman, *East Wind*, p. 274. For other evidence of the anti-Soviet polemic see "Chinese Communist Party Vilified in New Soviet Publications," *Peking Review*, March 6, 1964, pp. 27–29; "V.G. Wilcox's Speech at Party School in Canton," ibid., March 20, 1964, pp. 14–21; "Holding High Six Revolutionary Banners to Smash Revisionism," ibid., March 27, 1964, pp. 16–18; "Carry the Revolution Through to the End," ibid., pp.18–20; "The Proletarian Revolution and Khrushchev's Revisionism," ibid., April 3, 1964, pp. 5–21; "New Triumph for National Independence Movement," ibid., pp. 25–26; "Triumph of the Bandung Spirit," ibid., April 24, 1964, pp. 5–6.

[20] "New Anti-US Upsurge in Japan," ibid., March 13, 1964, pp. 11–13.

support for the North Vietnamese. The United States was accused of war preparation and of organizing aggressive military blocs, and, as a result, "the socialist countries should…give vigorous support and aid to the national-liberation movements."[21] By mid-April, of course, these views no longer coincided with Mao's position and did not serve his interests.

The debate intensified and opposing views on almost every issue appeared frequently. Late in April, the Chinese Foreign Ministry articulated Mao's view by charging that the US plan to expand the war merely "aggravated tension in Indo-China and Southeast Asia"—mild rhetoric for the normally incandescent Chinese propaganda.[22] An editorial in the *People's Daily* addressed the same subject but came to a different conclusion. It charged the United States with seeking a base of aggression against "China and all of Southeast Asia."[23] The issue was whether the US involvement in Vietnam was a threat to China. If the answer were yes, it would support reestablishment of good Sino-Soviet relations. The opposite would be the case if the answer were no. The Foreign Ministry took pains to mention aggravated tension only in Southeast Asia. The *People's Daily* article carefully charged the United States with intending to build a base of aggression against China. It is hard not to sympathize with confused American intelligence analysts, who had difficulty in making sense out of the conflicting signals.

On May 13 Foreign Minister Chen Yi mentioned an American plan to use Taiwanese troops in South Vietnam, but expressed no alarm and included it in a list of American actions designed to aggravate tension in "Laos and Indo-China."[24] The pro-Soviet group, of course, took a dramatically different stand on that issue. Taiwanese troops in Vietnam were a "spearhead…directed against China [that] threatens China's security from the south." The whole subject was reminiscent of the US "war of aggression against Korea," when Chinese troops intervened against a threat to China's security.[25] The reference to Korea went hand in glove with Soviet propaganda about Sino-Soviet cooperation against "outright military pressure by aggressive imperialist circles."

---

[21] "The Correct Way to Defend the Peace," ibid., April 10, 1964, pp. 13–16.

[22] "Chinese Foreign Ministry, Statement on Current Laotian Situation," ibid., May 1, 1964, pp. 20–21.

[23] "Stop US Criminal Activities in Laos," ibid., April 24, 1964, pp. 8–9.

[24] "Vice-Premier and Foreign Minister Chen Yi's Reply to Prince Souphanouvong," ibid., May 15, 1964, pp. 8–9.

[25] "A New Plot in the Making," ibid., May 1, 1964, pp. 21–22.

The anniversary of the French defeat at Dien Bien Phu occasioned a number of articles from Mao's group about the significance of the Viet Minh victory. That triumph demonstrated the supremacy of People's War, through which the Vietnamese defeated a technologically superior foe. As with the French, so with the Americans. The Vietnamese had nothing to fear from the United States and could achieve ultimate victory by relying on their own resources.[26] The pro-Soviet group twisted the Dien Bien Phu theme to its own purposes. The United States feared a Dien Bien Phu-type defeat and therefore was plotting to extend the war. "The United States spread the war in Korea, but the result was a crushing defeat. Will there be a different denouement in South Vietnam?"[27] Using historical analogy, victory would come from China's direct involvement in the war, backed by the Soviet Union.

Both sides in the Chinese debate labeled the United States as the aggressor in the Vietnam war. The question on which they differed was "Is US aggression in Vietnam a threat to China?" If so, alliance with the Soviet Union was essential. If not, they could turn to the West for technology that, in addition to being more advanced, came with fewer political strings because it could be obtained through deals with private corporations.

The United States continued its inexorable move toward increased involvement in the war in Vietnam unaware of the connection between US decisions and the struggle for power in China.

The United States Moves Toward Tonkin

Because of the rapid expansion of Viet Cong military power, the Republic of Vietnam would collapse without additional US support. But the United States had decided to provide that backing in February 1964, when President Johnson threatened to widen the war to North Vietnam. In the aftermath of the Johnson speech, numerous administration spokesmen echoed the American president, leaving no doubt that the United States had accepted a higher level of conflict, increased US aid, and an expanded role for the US armed forces.[28] Nevertheless, the

[26]"Dien Bien Phu Victory Anniversary," ibid., May 15, 1964, p. 4; "Historic Significance of the Dien Bien Phu Victory," ibid., pp. 17–19; "The Battle of Dien Bien Phu," ibid., p. 19.

[27]"Stop New US Imperialist Adventure in South Viet Nam," ibid., May 22, 1964, pp. 8–9.

[28]Jack Raymond, "McNamara Bars Vietnam Pullout," *New York Times,* March 27, 1964, p. 1; Jack Raymond "McNamara Tells Johnson of Gain in Vietnam War," ibid., March 15, 1964, p. 1.

administration faced a complex task. Aside from domestic political considerations, the United States feared a direct confrontation with China. While the United States sought to "contain" the "export of revolution" from Mao and his followers, it had no desire to engage Chinese forces on the Asian mainland. This remained a very great worry as the signals from Zhou Enlai and Chen Yi went unnoticed.[29] And so, the battlefield situation continued to deteriorate. At a conference hosted by the Secretary of Defense on March 6, 1964, the participants agreed that the South Vietnamese position was becoming worse.[30] Later in the month, Secretary McNamara submitted his conclusions to the president and emphasized the gravity of the situation. He recommended that the United States supply more economic assistance to South Vietnam and make plans to initiate, on thirty days notice, "graduated overt military pressure against North Vietnam."[31] The president accepted McNamara's proposals in full and incorporated them in National Security Action Memorandum (NSAM) 288 on March 17, 1964. On the same day, a White House statement declared that US policy is "to furnish assistance and support to South Vietnam for as long as it is required."[32]

While reaffirming the US intent to redress the military imbalance, NSAM 288 actually deferred strong action by placing overt military action on a thirty-day "on call" basis. The United States did not understand but was not oblivious to the Sino-Soviet rift. The president explained why NSAM 288 had postponed stronger measures in a cable to Ambassador Lodge on March 20. "There is reason for avoiding immediate overt action,"

---

[29]For articles that reflect a public discussion of the issue of confrontation with China and American concern with it see *New York Times,* February 28, 1964, p. 1; February 29, p. 1; March 5, p. 1; March 21, p. 1; April 21, p. 5; April 29, p. 5. For a reflection of the internal fears in the administration see *Pentagon Papers,* Book 3, "Military Pressures, Feb–June," p. 17. Secretary of State Dean Rusk, discussing possible confrontation with China, says "we are not going to take on the masses of Red China with our limited manpower in a conventional war." In a personal interview in 1976 at the US Army Russian Institute in Garmisch, FRG, the author asked Roger Hilsman, assistant secretary of state for Far Eastern affairs in early 1964, why the United States had not responded to these extraordinary Chinese overtures. He responded that he could not be expected to remember everything Zhou Enlai ever said. I believe that US obsession with the rhetoric of Chinese revolution and the so-called people's war theories of Mao Zedong caused the United States to be slow to understand the depth of the Sino-Soviet rift and slow to understand that China and the United States may have had common interests in containing the power and expansion of the Soviet Union.

[30]*Pentagon Papers,* Book 3, "Phased Withdrawal," p. e.

[31]Ibid.

[32]Ibid., pp. 35–36 and ibid., "US Programs," pp. iii–iv.

he said, "in that we expect a showdown between Chinese and Soviet communist parties soon and action against the North will be more practicable
after than before."[33] The cable demonstrates that the United States was
aware that Soviet support or lack thereof would be an important factor in
China's willingness to confront the United States, that the United States
was firmly committed to stabilizing the military situation in South Vietnam
through direct US involvement, and that the United States did not believe
improved Sino-American relations possible.

The war news continued to worsen as the Viet Cong overran Kien Long,
a district capital in the Mekong delta, in April.[34] Weekly South Vietnamese
casualties reached 1,000 for the first time that month.[35] The Johnson administration began feeling pressure to move beyond NSAM 288 in efforts
to salvage the military situation. Moving cautiously, it leaked stories that
key leaders did not believe that China would intervene in response to an
expanded US involvement. This permitted the United States to study
Chinese and Russian statements about possible intervention and actual
Chinese troop deployments.[36]

On May 1, 1964 an American transport carrying helicopters was
destroyed by sabotage while it was moored in Saigon harbor.[37] Afterwards,
on May 6, a message from the Commander-in-Chief, Pacific (CINCPAC)
to the Military Assistance Command, Vietnam (MACV) raised authorized
US troop strength from 15,500 to 17,000.[38] In mid-May President Johnson
asked Congress to appropriate a $125 million increase in military and
economic aid to Vietnam and Congress gave its approval by the end of the
month.[39] As feared and expected by the US leadership, however, these efforts were insufficient to slow Viet Cong momentum on the battlefield. By
June, influential members of the Johnson administration were convinced
that an irreversible commitment to Vietnam would be necessary to save the
Saigon regime.

[33]*Secret History,* Document 65, "Cable from President Johnson to Ambassador Lodge, 20 March
1964," p. 285.
[34]Sharp and Westmoreland, *Report,* Section II, p. 93.
[35]Peter Grose, "South Vietnamese Forces Suffer Worst Toll Of War," *New York Times,* April 21,
1964, p. 5.
[36]*Pentagon Papers,* Book 3, "Military Pressures Feb–June," p. xvii. and "Rusk Says Saigon May
Ask for Non-US Military Advisors," *New York Times,* April 21, 1964, p. 5. For evidence that US
intelligence followed Chinese troop movements see Wedeman, *East Wind,* pp. 160–162.
[37]"US Ship Is Sunk by Vietnam Reds; Crewmen Escape," *New York Times,* May 2, 1964, p. 1.
[38]*Pentagon Papers,* Book 3, "Phased Withdrawal," p. f.
[39]Hedrick Smith, "President Seeks More Vietnam Aid," *New York Times,* May 19, 1964, p. 1;
Felix Belair, "House Unit Backs Full Foreign Aid Asked by Johnson," ibid., May 27, 1964, p. 1.

Ambassador Lodge and MACV commander General William C. Westmoreland were convinced that some major victory over the Viet Cong soon was absolutely necessary and they conveyed their concerns to Mc-Namara in early June. McNamara convened a meeting in Honolulu of high level administration insiders to consider the problem and at the meeting a memorandum prepared by National Security Affairs Advisor McGeorge Bundy carried considerable weight. The memorandum highlighted the following statement: "It [the breakthrough of mutual US-RVN commitment] could come from the external actions of the US internal leadership in Vietnam," said Bundy, "or from an act of irreversible commitment by the United States."[40] Although the United States still had not decided on specific measures, there was no doubt that the irreversible commitment was coming. A few days later, on June 23, 1964, General Maxwell Taylor moved from chairman of the Joint Chiefs of Staff to ambassador to South Vietnam. With U. Alexis Johnson as deputy ambassador, this was a new and impressive team to offer prestige to the US commitment. Additionally, Taylor was given greater power and authority by the president.[41] Coupled with the new appointments was a White House statement that "the United States commitment against communist aggression in Asia is unlimited."[42]

The Johnson administration signaled its intention to become more deeply involved in the Vietnam conflict consistently from February through July 1964. The public statements were an accurate reflection of the views of key US leaders and both the Chinese and the Soviets concluded by June that a new US commitment was inevitable. Indeed, Soviet spies seem to have obtained key American war plans. In July, *Izvestia* reported that it was aware of "the Rostow plan No. 6...for blockading, bombing and strafing North Vietnam."[43] Chairman of the State Department's Policy Planning Council Walt W. Rostow had, as charged, prepared a classified scenario for "graduated overt military pressure" against North Vietnam.[44] It should have been obvious to friend and foe alike that US forces would soon become involved. The only question was when—and what event would provide the pretext for the actual beginning of US operations. National Security Advisor

---

[40]*Pentagon Papers*, Book 3, "US Programs," p. 83.

[41]Ibid., p. 84.

[42]Jack Raymond, "US Reinforcing Arms Stockpiles at Thailand Base," *New York Times*, June 21, 1964, p. 1.

[43]"Stop Interference," *Current Digest*, July 29, 1964, p. 24.

[44]Gravel, Vol. III, pp. 109,151.

McGeorge Bundy, in a memorandum to the secretaries of state and defense on June 15, 1964, announced a meeting for that evening in the secretary of state's conference room: "The principal question for discussion will be to assess the desirability of recommending to the President that a congressional resolution on Southeast Asia should be sought. The second question is what the optimum recommendation for action should be if in fact a congressional resolution is not recommended."[45] Given the political necessities of an election year and the need to muster public support for direct US involvement in an Asian conflict, the appearance of bi-partisan backing was critical. A congressional resolution was the preferred way to go and some incident was sought in which the enemy were the aggressor.

In a confused set of events in early August 1964 Johnson found what he needed to obtain the political freedom to take the required measures in Vietnam. On August 2, 1964 three North Vietnamese PT boats fired a couple of torpedoes at the US destroyer *Maddox* and missed. The *Maddox* had been on patrol near the coast of Vietnam as part of the ongoing program to escalate pressure on North Vietnam that had begun in February. Aircraft from the US carrier *Ticonderoga* sank two of the three PT boats. On August 4, 1964 the *Maddox* and another destroyer, the *Joy,* reported they believed they were about to be attacked and US aircraft again responded. Although there was no North Vietnamese attack, the whole affair took a number of hours and there was some confused reporting to Washington. The president seized the opportunity and chose to believe the United States had been attacked a second time and ordered US aircraft to destroy oil storage facilities in Vinh, North Vietnam, in retaliation for the second attack.[46] On August 5, 1964, the president requested passage of a joint congressional resolution supporting US policy in Southeast Asia. On the same day, Secretary McNamara announced that US military capabilities, primarily air and naval forces would be increased significantly in Southeast Asia.[47]

---

[45]Gravel, Vol. III, p. 77.

[46]Vice Admiral James Bond Stockdale, "Our Personal and National Resolve," (Stanford: Hoover Institution Press, 1987) pp. 10–11. Admiral Stockdale led the attack that destroyed the two PT boats and responded to the non-attack on August 4. He also led the attack on the Vinh oil storage facilities.

[47]*Pentagon Papers,* Book 4, "Military Pressures Against NVN, July–October 1964," pp. 12–13. McNamara announced "First an attack carrier group has been transferred from the First Fleet on the Pacific coast to the Western Pacific. Secondly, interceptor and fighter bomber aircraft have been moved into South Vietnam. Thirdly, fighter bomber aircraft have been moved into Thailand. Fourthly, interceptor and fighter bomber squadrons have been transferred into advance bases in the Pacific. Fifthly, an anti-submarine task force group has been moved into the South China Sea."

On August 7 the Tonkin Gulf Resolution was passed by near-unanimous vote of both houses of Congress. It granted the president power "to take all necessary measures to repel any armed attack against the forces of the United States and to prevent further aggression."[48] The president's domestic political constraints had delayed the actual transfer of power and direct action by US forces slightly, but the Soviets and Chinese, understanding that such a commitment was inevitable, already had reacted.

[48]Ibid.

3

Vietnam and the Fall of Khrushchev

Major Events

- *June 1964*—Debate in Chinese press over the American threat in Vietnam ends temporarily with Mao forced to admit that a potential threat to China exists.
- *August 1964*—The Soviets increase seaborne military supply effort to Vietnam.
- *August 1964*—Soviet Union refuses to act in its capacity as co-chairman of the Geneva conference.
- *August 1964*—Both Soviet Union and United States call for United Nations to take up Vietnam issue.
- *August 1964*—Chinese deny Soviet Union land access to Vietnam.
- *September 1964*—Khrushchev calls for cuts in spending for conventional weapons and argues that the risks of the seaborne supply effort outweigh the gains.
- *October 1964*—Brezhnev and Kosygin depose Khrushchev and assume power.

Public statements by Johnson administration officials, increased US appropriations for aid to South Vietnam, and limited covert military activities designed to pressure North Vietnam built an ever-growing impression in China and the Soviet Union that the United States was planning something dramatic in Southeast Asia. After a White House spokesman declared in

34

June 1964 that the US commitment was "unlimited," the Soviets responded with a press campaign that warned China bluntly that it could not count on Soviet support under present conditions.[1] These heavy-handed threats were followed immediately by soothing articles which pointed out how valuable Soviet assistance could be against imperialism—if it were available.[2]

So much for subtlety.

The American slide toward direct military involvement and the Soviet diplomatic campaign raised pressure on Mao to a new level and he responded by withdrawing his unacknowledged—and indeed unrecognized—offer to improve relations with the United States. As late as June 20, 1964, Foreign Minister Chen Yi had repeated China's desire to improve Sino-American relations if there could be some accommodation over Taiwan.[3]

However, the June White House announcement and the late June Soviet press campaign ended temporarily the debate in the Chinese press. Mao acknowledged the potential American threat to China and Chen Yi publicized this new outlook on June 24 at a banquet given by the Mali ambassador to China. He said, "The situation in Indo-China has become graver in the last few days.... It must be pointed out that Indo-China lies alongside China and not the United States.... The Chinese people absolutely will not sit idly by while the Geneva agreements are completely torn up and the flames of war spread to their side."[4]

On July 6, Chen Yi sent a letter to North Vietnamese Foreign Minister Xuan Thuy in which he proclaimed brotherly love for his southern ally. "China and the Democratic Republic of Vietnam," he said, "are fraternal neighbors closely related like lips and teeth. The Chinese people cannot be expected to look on with folded arms in the face of any aggression against the Democratic Republic of Vietnam."[5] Three days later an editorial in *People's Daily* restated that sentiment: "Should the US imperialists attack

---

[1] "China Warned: Don't Be Too Sure of Soviet Support," *Current Digest,* July 15, 1964, pp. 3–5.

[2] Ibid. This is another article under the same *Current Digest* heading. This is a June 22 *Pravda* article entitled "You Cannot Blot the Sun with the Palm of Your Hand."

[3] "Vice-Premier Chen Yi Answers Questions By Japanese Journalist," *Peking Review,* June 26, 1964, pp. 6–8.

[4] "Chinese People Will Not Allow The Flames Of War To Spread To Their Side," ibid., July 3, 1964, p. 13. See also Max Frankel, "Peking Reassures Hanoi on Defense," *New York Times,* July 10, 1964, p. 1. The reference to Chen Yi's speech is in the continuation of the article on p. 2, column 6.

[5] "China Backs The Democratic Republic of Viet Nam," *Peking Review,* July 10, 1964, p. 24.

the Democratic Republic of Viet Nam, thus threatening the peace and security of China...the Chinese people will certainly not allow the US imperialists to play with fire right by their side."[6] On July 19 *Hsinhua*, the Chinese press agency, carried a statement with the same warning: "Despite the fact that the United States has introduced tens of thousands of its military personnel into South Viet Nam and Laos, China has not sent a single soldier to Indochina. However, there is a limit to everything.... "[7] Zhou Enlai, too, provided grist for the same mill at a July Peking rally, where a message of support for Hanoi was adopted with explicit warnings for the United States.[8]

Zhou Enlai and Chen Yi up to this point had been the leading spokesmen for the view that US actions aggravated tensions only in Southeast Asia and did not threaten China. The alarm bells should have been ringing in US intelligence. But the Americans simply did not fathom the depths of Chinese factionalism.

In reality, Zhou Enlai at this time was the leader of a small but powerful group that was as yet uncommitted in the power struggle. Most likely, he decided on his own that the official Chinese line toward the United States needed to change. The shift of Mao's group and Zhou's supporters behind the pro-Soviet faction—and their hard-line views on the war in Vietnam—was truly significant.

Mao, however, continued to maneuver against his domestic rivals. He insisted that the anti-Soviet polemic intensify, apparently gaining support from Zhou for the proposition that the US threat did not yet warrant assistance from the Soviet Union. Moreover, from the US public position it was evident that, despite its unshakable military commitment to South Vietnam, the United States was deeply concerned about the prospect of conflict with China. Mao probably concluded that public statements which threatened direct Chinese involvement in Vietnam would help convince the Americans to proceed cautiously. As subsequent events would indicate, Mao felt he could muster enough support in the Politburo and the Politburo Standing Committee to thwart those who actually favored Chinese intervention in Vietnam and cooperation with the Soviet Union, as long as the United States showed some restraint and, most importantly, did not introduce US ground forces into the conflict.

---

[6] "A Stern Warning To US Imperialism," ibid., p. 25.

[7] "Full Support For Vietnamese Government's Just Stand," ibid., July 24, 1964, pp. 5–6. See also "Chinese Warning Stronger," *New York Times,* July 20, 1964, p. 3.

[8] "Saigon Demands Puzzle US Aides," ibid., July 24, 1964, p. 1.

The continuing anti-Soviet polemic became visible to China watchers through Chinese resistance to and criticism of the Soviet pressure for an international conference of communist parties. The Chinese refused to support such a meeting, which they claimed was designed to excommunicate China, and they accused the Soviets of attempting to split the communist movement.[9] Attacks against the Soviet's claim to leadership in the Afro-Asian world were unabated.[10] On July 17, 1964, an editorial blasted Khrushchev personally and escalated the virulence of the polemic by charging that the Soviets were no longer communists.[11] With this campaign Mao dwelled on the disadvantages of rapprochement with the Soviet Union. Soviet assistance only came with Soviet dominance. Further, Mao accused Khrushchev of betraying communism and established him as a personal obstacle to improved Sino-Soviet relations. When the expected infusion of US power came in the aftermath of the Tonkin Gulf incident, Mao must have breathed a sign of relief. The United States only beefed up air and naval forces and did not include any sustained operations against North Vietnamese territory. Triumphantly, Mao continued his tough line on the Soviet Union and helped provoke an internal crisis in the Soviet Union that led to the overthrow of Mao's arch-rival Nikita Khrushchev—although Khrushchev's successor proved no less hostile to China.

The Soviets Try to Exploit Tonkin

Air and naval power! The US decision to deploy its high-tech weaponry in the aftermath of the Gulf of Tonkin affair played into the hands of Mao Zedong and his military theories. Quite simply, Mao had long argued that you couldn't win a war without an army—foot soldiers slogging their way through the mud to seize land, buildings, the civilian population and political control. Without American ground forces in large numbers there was no threat to China sufficient to compel cooperation with the Soviet

[9]"Convene a World CP Conference For Unity, Not a Split," *Peking Review*, July 3, 1964, pp. 28–31.

[10]"For an Independent, Prosperous, New Asia," ibid., pp. 18–20.

[11]"On Khrushchev's Phoney Communism and Its Historical Lessons for the World," ibid., July 17, 1964, pp. 7–27. For other examples of the intensified polemic see "The Khrushchev Clique's Anti-Chinese Statements," ibid., pp. 29–30; "What's Behind Khrushchev Group's Opposition to Personality Cult?" ibid., July 24, 1964, pp. 15–18; "CPC Central Committee's Reply to the CPSU Central Committee's Letter of June 15, 1964," ibid., July 31, 1964, pp. 5–11.

Union. Mao managed to expound upon his military theories and used the great respect in which they were held to deny the Soviet Union access to the Chinese railway system for hauling supplies to North Vietnam.

This left the Soviets in a difficult position. With US air-power in support of South Vietnam, the Russians needed to expand their logistic effort if the North Vietnamese were to intensify the conflict. Sufficient tonnages simply could not be delivered by air. So the Soviets had to rely on ocean transport to resupply North Vietnam. The Cuban Missile crisis in late 1962 had demonstrated absolute US naval superiority, and the Soviets now were forced to confront the fact that their long, unsecured sea lines of communication were at the mercy of the US Navy.

The initial Soviet response was canny. They sought first of all to secure transit rights for Soviet supplies across China through a coordinated propaganda and logistic effort. They combined a series of arguments for socialist unity over Vietnam with suggestions of concessions to China. At the same time the Russians increased the flow of supplies to North Vietnam delivered by sea. This surge of arms and munitions was designed to expand the level of conflict in Vietnam, provoke a still larger US military presence in Southeast Asia, and thereby undercut Mao's argument that there was no US military threat to China. When this plan did not achieve quick success, Khrushchev evidently proposed temporary abandonment of the ongoing naval resupply effort because of the risk. His colleagues disagreed with him and used this crisis to remove him from power.

But to return to the diplomatic arena: During the week following the Tonkin Gulf incident, Soviet propaganda directed three themes at China. First, the US presence in Southeast Asia and the new transfer of air and naval power to the Pacific represented a threat to China. Second, Soviet power was the bulwark of the socialist camp. And third, because of China's current estrangement from the socialist camp, Soviet power would only be available after restoration of Sino-Soviet cooperation. The Soviet Union combined its effort to achieve "unity of action" over Vietnam with a posture toward the United States that would characterize the Soviet public position throughout the war. The Soviets avoided any implication that they would interfere with the deployment of American power to Asia by instigating crises in other parts of the world, thereby restricting the US ability to shift its military to the Pacific. And they answered Chinese criticism on this point by returning to their propaganda theme. The US aggressors were trying to take advantage of the Sino-Soviet rift; without the rift, there would be no imperialist encroachment in Asia; and the only way to stop US aggression in Asia, then, was for China to join in a united front that relied on Soviet power.

As early as August 6, 1964, the Soviet press began to charge that the US response to the Tonkin Gulf incident threatened China. Queried *Pravda,* "Why did the American warships and planes show up in the Gulf of Tonkin...? After all, everyone knows that this gulf washes the shores only of the DRV and the CPR, protruding far into the territory of these countries. The wholly unwarranted presence here...cannot be appraised as other than an overt hostile act toward the states of this region."[12]

The following day, *Pravda* reported a Chinese protest against the United States and emphasized part of a Chinese statement that accused the United States of having "crossed the threshold of war" in Asia. Other articles followed expanding this theme.[13]

In conjunction with this official propaganda exaggerating the extent of China's danger, Khrushchev personally emphasized the importance the Kremlin attached to the whole subject. During a speech on agriculture on August 8, 1964, Khrushchev suddenly changed the topic to Vietnam, noting that the Soviets would "stand up for their homeland and for the other socialist countries.... The USSR has enormous military strength at its disposal and...will continue to do everything necessary to strengthen the unity of the international communist movement."[14]

On August 10 the Soviets proposed a definite date, December 15, 1964, for the convocation of the conference of communist parties that was being used to pressure China. The timing, during a military crisis in Southeast Asia, was intended to place maximum pressure on the Chinese leadership. At the very moment China seemed to be facing possible confrontation with the most powerful nation in the world, the Soviet Union would not tolerate China's independent path of development and would take action to cut China off from support in the socialist camp. The Soviets charged that Chinese "splitting" had provided the United States with an irresistible temptation to exploit the Sino-Soviet dispute. They charged, "More and more facts indicate attempts are being made in the camp of imperialism and reaction to take advantage of the disharmony that has arisen in the ranks of communists on the initiative of the CPC leaders.... The fact that the American imperialists and the South Vietnamese military machine...have stepped up their aggressive activities in Southeast Asia is further testimony

[12] "Aggressive Actions of USA in Gulf of Tonkin," *Current Digest,* September 2, 1964, pp. 25–26.
[13] "CPR Government Statement," ibid., p. 26; "Cease Provocations," ibid., p. 24.
[14] "North Ossetian Anniversary; 'US Aggression' in Vietnam," ibid., August 26, 1964, pp. 3–5.

to our enemies' desire to profit from the differences...."[15] The Soviets placed the blame squarely on the Chinese. The way to restrain the United States was for China to once again cooperate with the Soviet Union so that a solid and unified socialist camp could deter US aggression.

As the campaign developed to frighten Chinese politicians, so also did a campaign to reassure the American political leadership. If there were to be a legitimate threat to China, the United States had to feel free to transfer power to Southeast Asia. Indeed, throughout the war, US leaders discussed the effect of shifting power to Asia and the risk that the Soviets would respond by staging a crisis where geography was in their favor—like Berlin or Turkey. Was the US strategic reserve up to such a challenge?

The Soviets, to encourage the United States to mire itself in rice paddies, adopted a "strikingly mild" response.[16] The most serious Soviet threat was an implication that the Vietnam crisis could impair United States-Soviet relations! The American air and naval buildup, said the Soviet press, "created a situation fraught with dangerous complications" and "the people and government of the Soviet Union resolutely condemn the aggressive acts of the USA."[17] These pro forma protests, impossible to take seriously when compared to the usual Soviet rhetoric, were even further qualified. The reason that the situation was "fraught with dangerous complications" was because—over the long term—there would be a possible deterioration in other regions of the world if the United States did not alter its present course. These subsequent problems would occur "because other imperialists are inspired" by the United States. Moreover, despite American provocations, Khrushchev would continue to implement "peaceful coexistence of states with different social systems."[18]

Khrushchev was not known for his restrained rhetoric. There could be little doubt among American analysts that the Soviet leader was avoiding a direct challenge to the United States. The US military measures in Southeast Asia simply were not going to create a United States-Soviet confrontation. And if there was any doubt about Khrushchev's intention, the Soviet Union refused to act in its capacity as co-chairman of the fourteen-nation Geneva conference. This or-

---

[15]Ibid.

[16]Henry Tanner, "Moscow Assails US 'Rash Steps,'" *New York Times,* August 6, 1964, p. 8.

[17]"Aggressive Actions of USA in Gulf of Tonkin," *Current Digest,* September 2, 1964, pp. 25–26; "Cease Provocations," ibid., p. 24.

[18]"North Ossetian Anniversary; 'US Aggression' in Vietnam," ibid., September 9, 1964, pp. 10–12.

ganization represented the one diplomatic avenue open to the Soviet Union to limit deployment or use of US power. Since the spring of 1964, France had pushed for a convocation of the conference to discuss Laos, urging that the Vietnam war be considered as part of any settlement.[19] On August 5, 1964, United Nations Secretary General U Thant also proposed the fourteen-nation conference as the proper forum in which to decide the issue in Indo-China.[20] North Vietnam and China supported the French proposal.[21]

These initiatives placed diplomatic pressure on the United States to place resolution of the Vietnam war in the hands of this international body. The United States felt such a move would negate the positive psychological impact of its firm stand in the wake of the Tonkin Gulf incident. The United States, therefore, wanted to postpone the conference "to give the political and military situation in South Vietnam time to be improved" by the new demonstration of US power.[22] The American leadership felt that a rush to the conference table would be a sign of weakness to both the communists and the South Vietnamese.[23] Aside from the one-time retaliation bombing of North Vietnam and the transfer of air and naval forces, the United States had not yet done anything to redress the balance of power in the conflict. The threat of air and naval power was intended to intimidate North Vietnam.[24] The Geneva conference would represent a diplomatic constraint on the use of that force.

The Soviet Union refused to back the French/Chinese/North Vietnamese initiative in its capacity as co-chairman of the conference and instead proposed that the question be referred to the United Nations Security Council.[25] But the United Nations offered little hope of effective discussion, let alone sanctions. In fact, the United States also proposed bringing the

---

[19]*Pentagon Papers,* Book 4, "July–October," p. 17.

[20]Ibid., p. 18.

[21]Ibid., and "Chinese Government Replies to Soviet Government's Proposal for Convening 14-Nation Conference," *Peking Review,* August 7, 1964, p. 22.

[22]*Pentagon Papers,* Book 4, "July–October," pp. 16–18.

[23]Ibid., p. 19. For example, Ambassador Maxwell Taylor cabled Washington that a rush to the conference table would confirm the Chinese view that US retaliation was a transient phenomenon. See also ibid., "Rolling Thunder Begins," p. 4, for an example of the American desire to "negotiate from strength."

[24]For an interesting discussion of what happens when a nation tries to convey sophisticated "messages" through the use of military power, see Wallace Theis, *When Governments Collide* (Berkeley: University of California Press, 1980).

[25]"Democratic Republic of Vietnam Ready to Smash Enemy Invasion," *Peking Review,* August 14, 1964, pp. 23–25, and Thornton, *China,* p. 264.

Vietnam War to the United Nations for interminable speeches delivered in almost-empty rooms.[26]

Perhaps the absence of Soviet threats over Vietnam can be explained by a Soviet fear of a US-Soviet confrontation. The Soviet failure to act in its role as co-chairman of the Geneva conference cannot be explained the same way. This diplomatic gambit would have been risk free, a natural and legitimate expression of international law recognized by the West. No, the Soviets did not wish to limit US deployments because such deployments were being exploited as a threat to China by the Soviet propaganda apparatus.

Mao Zedong Responds to the Gulf of Tonkin Affair

The nature of both the Soviet and US responses to the Tonkin Gulf incident supplied Mao with strong arguments against his internal opponents. American concern with the possibility of Chinese intervention caused the United States to stress the limited nature of its military objectives, to rely on a psychological threat to North Vietnam rather than military operations that inflicted significant damage. The US response thus allowed Mao to claim that a potential US threat to China existed—an unwanted admission for Mao, to be sure—but ultimately not very damaging. When the Soviet effort to encourage US transfer of power to Asia was manifested by mild propaganda against the United States and by a refusal to promote the Geneva conference, Mao turned the whole affair to his advantage. He reasserted his familiar charge that the Soviet Union was an unreliable ally that would not be of help even if the United States attacked China directly. Using this argument, Mao intensified his anti-Soviet propaganda campaign and denied the Soviet Union land access to Vietnam.

Although the Americans decided to attack North Vietnamese oil storage facilities in reprisal for the Gulf of Tonkin incident, American planners remained acutely sensitive to the possibility of Chinese intervention. The United States, as a result, devoted considerable effort to convincing China that its goals were limited. The oil storage facilities at Vinh had been carefully selected as "limited and fitting" targets for the reprisal raid. The United States wished to intimidate North Vietnam while reassuring the Chinese, however odd that may sound.[27] Not that odd, evidently, to Chairman Mao.

[26]*Pentagon Papers*, Book 4, "July–October," pp. 18–20.
[27]*Secret History*, p. 264.

Because the United States did not mount a sustained bombing campaign and did not move ground forces to the region, Mao concluded that the United States was responding to specific acts, rather than seriously preparing for war. Mao would continually point out in China's internal debate that "war is won on the ground."[28]

In addition to the restrained US response, the United States took pains to publicize its well-known fear of a land war in Asia. Members of Congress were enlisted in this effort. Representative Melvin Laird stated that the Tonkin Gulf resolution was appropriate, but that a policy still needed to be developed with respect to the possibility of a ground war in Asia.[29] Representative Alger said he supported the resolution but was concerned over "the danger of being dragged into war by other nations seeking help."[30] Several other congressmen declared that the resolution "did not constitute a declaration of war, did not abdicate congressional responsibility for determining national policy commitments and did not give the President *carte blanche* to involve the nation in a major Asian war."[31] Senator Fulbright, who helped push the Tonkin Gulf Resolution through Congress, expressed his view that congressional approval could be withdrawn in the future by concurrent resolution.[32] Further revealing a general reluctance to do anything that might be construed as a threat to China, US Ambassador to the United Nations Adlai Stevenson made a speech at the UN on August 5 affirming that "US policy in Southeast Asia had limited aims."[33]

It should be recalled that Mao had ceased his offer to improve relations and acknowledged the possibility of a US threat to China in June, *before* the Tonkin Gulf incident. Mao conceded the potential of a US threat before the United States took action in order to influence the way the United States went about taking its now inevitable step toward deeper entanglement in the war. His warnings that China would not stand idly by while the flames of war spread to her side were designed to encourage a careful and limited use of US power.

He was successful.

---

[28]For the clearest articulation of this Maoist argument see an article which appeared in February 1965, in which Mao's group clung to this line shortly before US Marines landed in Vietnam, undercutting the argument. "Johnson Administration in a Dilemma," *Peking Review*, February 26, 1965, pp. 11–12.

[29]*Pentagon Papers*, Book 4, "July–October," pp. 13–15.

[30]Ibid.

[31]Ibid.

[32]Ibid.

[33]Ibid.

As a result, there was no change in Chinese propaganda toward the United States after the Gulf of Tonkin affair. Having already charged the United States with moving to the brink of war in June, post-Tonkin Gulf statements repeated the charge with the additional explanation that the United States had only "made the first step in extending the war in Indo-China."[34] In other words, the first step, though important, had not yet brought the war to China. Moreover, Chinese statements explicitly stated that China would not intervene under present conditions. According to China, North Vietnam had now gained the right to strike back in self-defense and "all countries upholding the Geneva agreements have also gained the right of action to *assist* the Democratic Republic of Vietnam" (emphasis added).[35] The North Vietnamese would fight and the Chinese would support their efforts.

American caution permitted Mao to continue to push his view that the Vietnamese would defeat the Americans by relying on People's War. *People's Daily* carried an editorial, for example, stating that the United States would "receive due punishment at the hands of the Vietnamese people."[36] People's War and not reliance on Soviet power was the way to deal with the United States.

Mao argued that socialist countries should help each other on the basis of mutual equality rather than dependence on one country that might be more powerful. The Chinese experience, according to Mao, demonstrated that the only way to make progress toward socialism was for each country to rely on its own strength. True socialist solidarity could be based only on the independent, self-reliant strength of each socialist nation. Rather than supplying aid to Vietnam organized and dominated by the Soviet Union, each country should individually assist Vietnam, offering whatever it could to help the Vietnamese develop the strength to defeat the United States themselves.

In a lengthy article in mid-August, Ai Ching-chu criticized the Soviet Union for attempting to establish hegemony over countries it supported. Socialist powers, argued Ai, should treat each other as equals and exchange "what it has for what it hasn't" so that each country can properly develop

---

[34] "Chinese Government Statement," *Peking Review,* August 7, 1964, pp. ii–iii; "US Imperialism Must Immediately Cease Its Armed Aggression Against Viet Nam Democratic Republic," ibid., pp. iii–iv.

[35] "Chinese Government Statement," ibid., pp. ii–iii.

[36] "US Imperialism Must Immediately Cease Its Armed Aggression Against Viet Nam Democratic Republic," ibid., pp. iii–iv.

self-reliance. The author continued, "Some might ask: Is this not in conflict with the principle of mutual support among the people of different countries? No, not in the least. Only on the basis of self-reliance is it possible to render mutual support."[37] The Chinese would assist Vietnam, but would not yield to Soviet pressure for unity of action over Vietnam because "the form this assistance will take is our own affair."[38]

In coordination with this propaganda campaign, Mao continued to attack the Soviet Union as an unreliable ally. Under the guise of a review of world condemnation of US aggression, the *Peking Review* noted that, apart from Khrushchev's speech on August 5, "the Soviet Government has up till then not made an official statement on the Tonkin Gulf Incident. Neither the Tass statement, nor that of Khrushchev referred to giving support to the just struggle of the DRV against US aggression."[39] Other Chinese statements alleged that the Soviet Union had finally been forced into token protests by the "rising tide of indignation everywhere."[40] According to Mao, the Soviet Union had acted "with kid gloves" because the Soviets were "worried about losing the White House's blessings."[41]

Soviet failure to seize the diplomatic initiative in the Geneva conference gave Mao his best ammunition to attack the Soviet Union. On August 12, 1964, Chen Yi sent a letter to North Vietnamese Foreign Minister Xuan Thuy which focused criticism on the Soviet Union's proposal to have the United Nations consider the Vietnam issue. Chen initially attacked the United States for its call for the United Nations Security Council to consider the Vietnam question as the "tactic of a villain, suing before he himself is prosecuted. Naturally, the DRV cannot possibly agree with this, nor should any socialist country agree with it.... A peaceful settlement can only be found in the way provided by the Geneva agreements.... The co-chairmen of the Geneva Conference, in particular, have an unshirkable responsibility in this regard."[42]

Chen also mentioned the Korean war, but not to recall Chinese intervention. Rather, he alleged that the United Nations could be manipulated by the United States, as had occurred in the Korean war. That manipulation

[37] "China's Economic and Technical Aid to Other Countries," ibid., August 21, 1964, pp. 14–15.

[38] "Chen Yi On US Aggression In Vietnam and Congo," ibid., p. 7; "China Is Well Prepared To Assist DRV Against US Aggression," ibid., February 12, 1965, pp. 6–7; "Warning by Soviet and Chinese Governments," *New York Times,* February 10, 1965.

[39] "US Imperialism Stands Condemned," *Peking Review,* August 14, 1964, pp. 26–27.

[40] "Aggressor Must Not Be Allowed To Act As Prosecutor," ibid., August 28, 1964, pp. 23–25.

[41] Ibid.

[42] "The UN Has No Right To Consider The Indo-China Question," ibid., August 14, 1964, pp. 8–9.

had been made possible because of the Soviet "error" of walking out of the United Nations before the critical Security Council vote. Chen implied that the current Soviet cooperation with the United States over the Geneva Conference was a similar error.[43]

The pro-Soviet group headed by Liu Shaoqi and Deng Xiaoping was caught off guard by Mao's maneuvers. While not banished from the press, they were relegated to writing low-key articles hinting at the seriousness of the threat to China. In one piece, the pro-Soviet group emphasized the common border between China and Vietnam. "Here in Toulung," it said, "13 villages and settlements border on 15 Vietnamese villages. People in Yakow in China and Malishan in Viet Nam actually drink water from the same well."[44] Weak rhetoric, indeed.

Mao had won, at least for a while, on two key points—the United States had not yet deployed a military force that was a legitimate threat to China and the Soviet Union was an unreliable ally.

The Soviets Reassess Their Asian Policy

In the first weeks after the Gulf of Tonkin incident two facts became painfully clear to the Soviet Union. First, the United States had increased its military presence in Asia, demonstrated a willingness to apply that power, and—as a result—put itself in position to restore the military balance in Vietnam. And second, the American military measures had not forced the Chinese to adopt a more cooperative policy toward the Soviet Union. In fact, Khrushchev's transparent effort to focus the crisis in Asia, which included a Soviet policy that encouraged US transfer of air and naval power, hardened Chinese opposition. The Chinese would permit the Soviet Union neither transit rights on the Chinese railway system nor overflight rights for Soviet aircraft.[45]

The Soviet Union now was faced with the fundamental question, Do we continue our strategy or abandon it? Up till now the Soviet Union was able

---

[43]Ibid. See also "US Aggressors Must Not Be Allowed To Take Refuge in UN," ibid., pp. 14–15. Other articles repeated this argument throughout August. See "Aggressor Must Not Be Allowed To Act As Prosecutor," ibid., August 28, 1964, pp. 23–25; "Democratic Republic of Vietnam Ready to Smash Enemy Invasion," ibid., August 14, 1964, p. 23.

[44]"Nationwide Support For Viet Nam Continues," ibid., August 21, 1964, p. 3.

[45]See Henry Tanner, "China Said to Balk Soviet's Hanoi Aid," *New York Times*, March 29, 1965, p. 1.

to pursue its goals at relatively low cost. But costs and risks were rising. To give the North Vietnamese even more supplies could prove extremely expensive. The Soviets weren't in a position to make the outcome a test of industrial production—a test they were sure to lose. And in any case, the United States would be crazy to allow the war to become a logistical contest when a vastly superior US Navy could impose a blockade. The Soviets did not wish to suffer another humiliating defeat by the United States— another Cuba. Moreover, any large conflict involving the superpowers ran the risk of escalating out of control. Still, the Chinese power struggle was far from over. Increased conflict in Vietnam might tip the balance in favor of the pro-Soviet faction.

From mid-August to mid-September 1964, Khrushchev supplied Vietnam by sea, defended his actions against criticism by Mao, and pleaded for land access. By mid-September the intense anti-Soviet and anti-Khrushchev campaign coming from China made it clear that Mao was in control— at least for the near future. Moreover, the extensive personal attacks on Khrushchev made it obvious that Khrushchev himself was a personal impediment to rapprochement. The Soviets faced an extended period of increased risk before the military situation could be expected to force compromise from China. Under those conditions, Khrushchev apparently decided that the strategy should be changed. Instead, the strategy continued and Khrushchev's colleagues removed him from power.

In mid-August Khrushchev already was on the defensive, responding to Chinese charges that the Soviet Union was not a reliable ally. On August 18, 1964, *Pravda* accused China of attempting "to isolate the national-liberation movement from its faithful ally and reliable bulwark.... "[46] The article argued that backward countries need outside aid in the "form of funds, technical cadres and modern machines." A note addressed to all Asian and African countries in August criticized "crude attempts by certain circles" to thwart consolidation against imperialism.[47] Khrushchev went on the road in late August to enlist support from other socialist countries in condemnation of China. In visiting Czechoslovakia, he publicly declared that the war in Vietnam was of "special importance" for the struggle for unity within the socialist camp. The schismatic activity of "the Chinese leaders evokes special alarm.... They act to the advantage of imperialism.... The imperialists understand they can profit from schismatic

[46]"China's Dealings With Developing Nations Deplored," *Current Digest,* September 9, 1964, pp. 17–18.
[47]Ibid.

Chinese acts. They are gambling on this."[48] In early September, *Pravda,* perhaps responding to the personal criticism leveled at Khrushchev, attacked Mao by name. According to the Soviets, Mao "has injured the struggle for peace and national liberation" by falsely portraying Soviet protests against American action in Vietnam.[49]

Soviet propaganda had no apparent effect on China and Khrushchev evidently decided that the strategy to continue escalating the conflict should be abandoned. Hints of this appeared in a September 19, 1964, speech by the Soviet leader. He suggested that the logistic effort to Vietnam and thus the overall strategy should continue only if China granted land access:

> If the countries that are struggling against colonialists need weapons and *if they are able to be delivered from the Soviet Union* we can provide them.... But everything cannot be reduced to weapons. Why? Because the struggle of the peoples unfolds under different conditions and it is necessary that these conditions be ripe.... Viet Nam is divided into two states.... Korea is also divided into two states.... Why is the ground burning under the feet of the Americans in South Vietnam and why do they still stroll about comparatively freely in South Korea? Imperialism is the same everywhere, but apparently conditions in South Korea have not yet become fully ripe.... (emphasis added)[50]

Khrushchev clearly believed that the Soviets should supply weapons to North Vietnam. But his doubts about Russia's ability to continue its efforts in the face of Chinese opposition were beginning to surface in public. Weapons were to be sent if "they are able to be delivered"—but they could not be delivered safely because of Chinese refusal to allow rail transshipment of Soviet supplies. "If they are able to be delivered" could not have been in reference to Korea, since Korea and the Soviet Union share a common border.

Sometime in the next few days, evidently, Khrushchev became convinced that the Chinese would not yield and that the supply effort should be stopped. On October 2, 1964, he called for a cut in defense spending so

[48]"From Khrushchev's Speech to Czechs and Slovaks," ibid., September 30, 1964, pp. 3–6.
[49]"China Is Waging Expansionist 'Cold War'—*Pravda,*" ibid., September 16, 1964, pp. 3–6.
[50]"Khrushchev Address To International Youth Forum," ibid., October 14, 1964, p. 10.

that investment could be shifted to consumer goods.[51] This was coupled with a criticism a few days earlier of spending for conventional weapons.[52] A policy of reducing defense spending, especially for conventional weapons, was inconsistent with an expanded logistic effort to support the war in Vietnam.

Khrushchev's colleagues refused to support him. They had no intention of cutting defense spending. They did not want to lose China to the West, an outcome that loomed as more threatening than the risk entailed in supplying North Vietnam by sea. Since Khrushchev disagreed and had become a personal symbol of Sino-Soviet estrangement, the solution was to dump Khrushchev. The Soviet leader's colleagues understood, as did Khrushchev, that Khrushchev's removal could be viewed as a concession to China. This might give the Liu-Deng group an opportunity to support enthusiastically criticism of Khrushchev but argue that his removal had changed things. In mid-October, Khrushchev was removed from power.

The new Soviet Premier, Alexei Kosygin, later provided strong evidence that Khrushchev's removal was prompted by the need for socialist unity to meet the Vietnam crisis. At the end of his February 1965 visit to Asia, Kosygin, speaking in Korea about the situation in Vietnam, called socialist solidarity and unity "a reliable guarantee of all our victories.... Our fraternal commonwealth of independent states is a great and formidable anti-imperialist force. But it is one thing when each state acts by itself and a completely different thing when we come forth in a united front.... *A plenary session that was a major event in the life of our country was held in October.... [It] created new possibilities for...the growth of the solidarity of the Socialist Commonwealth.*" (emphasis added)[53]

---

[51] Roman Kolkowicz, *The Soviet Military and the Communist Party* (Princeton: Princeton University Press, 1967), pp. 298–299.

[52] "Khrushchev Address to International Youth Forum," *Current Digest,* October 14, 1964, p. 10. Khrushchev said that he spent the day looking at conventional weapons and it made him "ill.... After all, we are spending a lot of money to build tanks."

[53] "Kosygin in Pyongyang: Press Stress Need of Unity," ibid., March 10, 1965, pp. 6–9. See also "Khrushchev Out, Brezhnev and Kosygin Appointed," ibid., October 28, 1964, pp. 3–6. This contains the well known *Pravda* editorial of October 17, 1964, that accused Khrushchev of harebrained schemes and other sins. Undoubtedly there were many reasons for a coalition strong enough to topple Khrushchev to form and the organizers of the overthrow plot may have had to appeal to a variety of constituencies in the party power structure to pull off the coup. But the catalyst was the problem with China and the immediate issue of whether to continue with the ongoing strategy that used the conflict in Vietnam as its focus. Even this editorial mentions the issue of China as equal in importance with harebrained schemes. The editorial says: "The Communist Party of the Soviet Union is fighting with persistence to strengthen the unity and solidarity of the Communist ranks...."

The October plenary session Kosygin referred to is the plenary session that removed Khrushchev and installed Leonid Brezhnev and Alexei Kosygin. According to Kosygin, the removal of Khrushchev should have created new possibilities for the Soviet Union and China to act in concert over Vietnam. In the aftermath of Khrushchev's fall, the competing Chinese factions were faced with the question, Does Khrushchev's fall make any difference? Not surprisingly, they came to different conclusions.

4

The Chinese Debate
Over Khrushchev's Fall

Major Events

- *September 1964*—Viet Cong sabotage and sink US ship. US does not retaliate.
- *September–December 1964*—Soviets maintain logistic surge which equips 9th Viet Cong Division.
- *October–December 1964*—North Vietnamese regular units begin moving toward South Vietnam. US intelligence detects movement.
- *October 1964*—China suspends anti-Soviet polemics.
- *October 16, 1964*—China detonates its first nuclear weapon.
- *November 1, 1964*—Viet Cong mortar attack on US base at Bien Hoa kills four Americans. US does not retaliate.
- *November 1964*—Johnson defeats Goldwater in presidential election.
- *November 1964*—Zhou Enlai travels to Moscow.
- *November 1964*—China resumes open polemics against Soviet Union.
- *December 1964*—Zhou publicly renews subject of improved Sino-US relations.
- *December 1964*—Mao grants interview to American writer Edgar Snow. Mao predicts that the United States and China would eventually be on friendly terms again.
- *December 1964*—Soviets postpone scheduled conference of world communist parties to March 1965.
- *December 1964–January 1965*—9th Viet Cong division destroys two South Vietnamese battalions in battle of Binh Gia. This is first time VC stand and fight.

- *February 1965*—Kosygin travels to Hanoi to discuss increased Soviet military and economic aid.
- *February 1965*—Viet Cong attack US base at Pleiku as Kosygin arrives in Hanoi. United States conducts limited retaliatory bombing.
- *March 1965*—American sustained bombing campaign called Rolling Thunder begins.

Nikita Khrushchev was the world's leading "revisionist." He was the object of great scorn in the Chinese press and a personal impediment to improved Sino-Soviet cooperation. But now he was gone. And the new Soviet leaders were the ones who removed him. They suggested that this event should pave the way for improved relations. The question for Mao, Liu, Deng, and Zhou was, "Does it make any difference?" Mao answered no, Liu and Deng yes, and Zhou wanted to think about it.

In fact, Liu and Deng had attempted to seize the initiative in the power struggle shortly before Khrushchev was deposed. In September, Liu promulgated a set of organizational procedures designed to resist penetration of the provincial communist party apparatus, which he controlled, by personnel loyal to Mao.[1] On October 1, 1964, Liu and his ally Peking Mayor Peng Chen made speeches celebrating National Day in which they alleged that the primary mission of socialist countries was to achieve unity in the socialist camp.[2] The fall of Khrushchev gave Liu's efforts a boost.

Liu argued that Khrushchev had been an obstacle and that his removal paved the way for rapprochement with the Soviet union. Liu apparently won a concession from Mao, probably with Zhou Enlai's support, as the Chinese press ceased anti-Soviet polemics against the Soviet Union for several weeks after Khrushchev's demise. This moratorium was maintained even though there was evidence that the new Soviet leaders intended to adhere to Khrushchev's policies.

In the Chinese message of congratulations to the new Soviet leaders— signed by Mao, Liu, Deng, and Zhou—there was no mention of the Sino-Soviet dispute and indeed there was a call for "unity on the basis of Marxism-Leninism."[3] This pro-Soviet catch-phrase was followed by what appeared to be an official change in position. Peng Chen, at a reception

---

[1] Thornton, *China*, p. 269. These procedures were known as the "Revised Later Ten Points."

[2] "Chairman Liu Shao-chi's Speech," *Peking Review,* October 2, 1964, p. 8, and "Comrade Peng Chen's Speech," ibid., p. 9.

[3] "Chinese Leaders Congratulate LI Brezhnev and AN Kosygin on Their New Posts," ibid., October 23, 1964, p. 4.

celebrating the Soviet October Revolution hosted by the Soviet Ambassador, noted that "we have always regarded the Chinese revolution as a continuation of the October Revolution.... Even before the victory of our revolution, Comrade Mao Tse-tung had pointed out that the Chinese people had to follow the path of the Russians, i.e., the path of the October Revolution.... Peoples...want unity always.... History has proved...[that] those who attempt to create splits...are merely transient figures.... We are convinced we can be united."[4]

Peng Chen conceded the leading role in the communist movement to the Russians. The main obstacle to Sino-Soviet unity, Khrushchev, had proved to be a temporary aberration. His removal, in Chen's view, meant that the Soviet Union and China could again act together.

Mao, of course, wasn't convinced and several factors combined to help him reduce the impact of Khrushchev's removal. On October 16, 1964, the day before Khrushchev's departure, China successfully detonated its first nuclear weapon.[5] The big bang gave Mao an excuse to take to the press and stress self-reliance, a theme easily manipulated to circumvent restrictions on open polemics against the Soviet Union. Mao also seized on indications that the new Soviet leaders would continue Khrushchev's policies. And he continued to point to restraint on the part of the United States in Vietnam—the lack of new deployments or use of US military power in the fall and early winter.

Mao claimed that the Chinese nuclear success demonstrated the correctness of his policy of self-reliance because it had been accomplished without Soviet assistance. The Chinese government announcement of the blast said that the nuclear test was "due to the hard work...of China's workers...who, under the leadership of the Party, displayed a spirit of relying on their own efforts."[6] As a spate of articles extolled China's independent path of development, several twisted the theme to criticize the Soviet Union. On October 22, 1964, in *People's Daily*—and later in other periodicals—articles discussed the nuclear weapons program and ostensibly criticized the United States. In reference to imperialists, "from the very day of the founding of new China they have been sneering at its poverty and backwardness, predicting that it cannot achieve this or that. It seems as though the Chinese people can do nothing unless they do their bidding and rely on their

---

[4] "Comrade Peng Chen's Speech at Soviet Ambassador's Reception," ibid., November 13, 1964, pp. 9–10.

[5] "China Successfully Explodes Its First Atom Bomb," ibid., October 16, 1964, pp. ii–iii.

[6] "Press Communique—*Hsinhia*," ibid., p. iii.

assistance and benevolent grants."[7] This criticism can only have been meant for the Soviet Union. The Sino-American relationship had been adversarial since the "founding of new China," including actual combat in Korea. The only country that wanted China to do its bidding and "rely on their assistance" was the Soviet Union.

The Brezhnev-Kosygin team promptly provided Mao with substantive evidence that Khrushchev's downfall did not solve the problems between China and the Soviet Union. In public statements and private conversations with Zhou Enlai, Brezhnev and Kosygin made it clear that they would continue to push for reestablishment of the Sino-Soviet ties that had existed prior to the rift. This meant a dependent relationship for China. Brezhnev, in a speech at Red Square on October 19, 1964, indicated that there would be continuity in foreign policy:

> The unshakable foundations of the Soviet Union's foreign policy are the Leninist principles of the peaceful coexistence of states with different social systems.... The Soviet Union sees its international duty in supporting the just struggle of the peoples against imperialism, colonialism and neocolonialism for their social and national liberation.... In our times the cause of peace and social progress depends to an increasing degree on strengthening the solidarity of all anti-imperialist forces and first of all on the unity of the socialist countries, of the World Communist movement.... The CPSU will actively conduct a line toward convening a conference of the World's Marxist-Leninist parties.... [8]

With these words, Brezhnev gave a complete summation of what had been Khrushchev's position on foreign policy. The Soviets still intended to convene the world conference of communist parties to isolate China from the rest of socialist camp. In other words, nothing in the fundamental Soviet policy formulation on China had changed. The Soviet Union still demanded restoration of the alliance on Soviet terms.

Brezhnev and Kosygin conveyed this message personally to Zhou Enlai during his visit to Moscow for the celebration of the October Revolution. The impasse reached at these talks is revealed by *Pravda* and *Izvestia,* which listed the participants but did not describe the talks as "useful" or "produc-

---

[7] "Break The Nuclear Monopoly, Eliminate Weapons," ibid., October 30, 1964, pp. 5–7.

[8] "Brezhnev and Kosygin Speeches Hailing Cosmonauts," *Current Digest,* November 4, 1964, pp. 3–7.

tive." There were no joint statements issued and the press reported only that the discussions had been conducted "in a frank, comradely atmosphere."[9] Zhou returned to China with the Soviet message on November 13.[10]

In addition to indications that the Soviet conditions for rapprochement remained unchanged, American inaction helped Mao maintain his position that the United States wasn't a threat to China. The United States concentrated, but did not apply, a great deal of combat power during the final months of 1964. During the presidential campaign Johnson was reluctant to permit open escalation of the conflict, as he wanted to appear more moderate than his opponent, Senator Barry Goldwater. "Some say I ought to go North and drop bombs," said the president, "but we don't want to get involved in a nation with seven hundred million people and get tied down in a land war in Asia."[11] A second political consideration was the instability of the Saigon regime, as evidenced by a series of coups and counter coups. Johnson was hesitant to commit additional forces. How could he claim that the United States was responding to a South Vietnamese request if the government collapsed during deployment?[12] The United States continued to hope that the mere presence of US air and naval forces in Southeast Asia, while providing a psychological lift to the South Vietnamese, would intimidate their northern enemy.

United States Strengthens Mao's Hand

Indeed, the United States failed to respond to two separate provocations, each more serious than the original Gulf of Tonkin incident, in the fall of 1964. On September 18, 1964, North Vietnamese PT boats attacked a US destroyer. The president elected not to retaliate and also suspended naval patrols off the North Vietnamese coast.[13] On November 1, 1964, three days prior to the US elections, the Viet Cong executed a mortar attack on the US airbase at Bien Hoa, killing four American soldiers and destroying several aircraft. Again the president did not retaliate.[14]

[9] "On Meetings of Leaders of Communist Party of Soviet Union and Soviet Government With Chinese People's Republic Party and Government Delegation," ibid., December 9, 1964, p. 18.

[10] "CPR Party and Government Delegation Leaves For Home," ibid.

[11] *Pentagon Papers,* Book 4, "Rolling Thunder Program Begins," p. 8. The *Pentagon Papers* discusses political considerations impacting on Vietnam decisions.

[12] Ibid., "July–October," p. 34 and ibid., "November–December," p. 71.

[13] Ibid., pp. 8–9. See also ibid., pp. 21–22. These pages discuss the "Rostow Thesis" which theorized that "the threat implicit in US action is more important than the military effect of the actions."

[14] Ibid., "November–December," p. viii.

The successful detonation of a Chinese nuclear weapon, the reaffirmation of Soviet policy on China by Brezhnev and Kosygin, and the US reluctance to escalate its actual military involvement in the Vietnam war strengthened Mao's hand. On November 21, 1964, an article in *Red Flag* initiated a new propaganda offensive against the Soviets by accusing the new Soviet leaders of following a policy of "Khrushchevism without Khrushchev."[15] The basic tenet of the campaign was that Khrushchev's fall had been a good thing but that his replacements were no better. Unity with the Soviet Union could not be achieved unless it was on the basis of opposition to "bourgeois nationalism and Great Power Chauvinism."[16] Mao lambasted the Soviet Union for demanding that other socialist states be dependent on Moscow. "Although Khrushchev has fallen," Mao's spokesmen said, referring to the new leadership, "his supporters—the US imperialists, the reactionaries and modern revisionists—will not resign themselves to this failure. The hobgoblins are continuing to pray for Khrushchev, so that 'Khrushchevism without Khrushchev' may prevail."[17]

In late November Mao personally reaffirmed his faith in People's War, which he interpreted to mean that China need not be involved in the Vietnam war. The United States was a "paper tiger," internally weak, and able to be defeated by the Vietnamese people. In a speech which ostensibly supported the Congolese, Mao expressed the view that "US imperialism and the reactionaries of all countries are paper tigers. The struggle of the Chinese people has proved this. The struggle of the Vietnamese people is proving it.... By strengthening national unity and persevering in protracted struggle, the Congolese people will certainly be victorious."[18] If the Vietnamese could win on their own, clearly the US presence in Southeast Asia was of little consequence to China.

It was clear to any country with an intelligence service that the South Vietnamese military situation was deteriorating. And it was also clear that—when the elections were over—Johnson would be free to take new American military action, action that would result in an escalating

---

[15] "Why Khrushchev Fell," *Peking Review,* November 27, 1964, pp. 5–9.

[16] "United Under the Banner of the Great October Revolution," ibid., November 13, 1964, pp. 14–17.

[17] "Why Khrushchev Fell," ibid., November 27, 1964, pp. 5–9. See also "'Problems of Peace and Socialism' Attacks Chinese Communist Party," ibid., pp. 25–26; "US Tycoons in Moscow," ibid., pp. 28–29; "Premier Chou En-lai's Speech," ibid., December 4, 1964, pp. 19–20; "The Militant Unity of China and Vietnam," ibid., pp. 26–29.

[18] "Chairman Mao Tse-tung's Statement," ibid., p. 5.

conflict and an increased US military presence. Mao prepared a theoretical argument to account for this coming development. In December the Chinese honored the anniversary of the founding of the National Liberation Front. "Should US imperialism extend the war..., the Vietnamese people will rise as one" to defeat the aggressors.[19] Other articles developed the same line of reasoning, alleging that "to defeat the US paper tiger, first of all one must not fear it."[20] Even an expanded United States presence was no threat. The conflict was still one that the Vietnamese communists could handle.

Zhou Enlai again sided with Mao in trying to avoid confrontation with the United States and he mentioned the possibility of improved Sino-American relations for the first time since June in a December 1964 speech. He again tied improved relations to the Taiwan issue.[21] A few days later, Mao granted an interview to the American writer, Edgar Snow. Mao reaffirmed his view that the Viet Cong would win the war in South Vietnam by relying on their resources. He then demonstrated that Zhou's mention of better Sino-US relations had Mao's support. A US expansion of the war in Vietnam did not threaten China, he noted, and would not lead to a Sino-American war "as long as China itself is not attacked."[22] Mao concluded by predicting that the United States and China would someday be on friendly terms again.[23]

December also marked the beginning of an intensified attack on Mao's internal opponents. In addition to organizational maneuvers to challenge Liu and Deng's control of the party and state bureaucracies, spokesmen for Mao began to attack those in China "who are taking the capitalist road." Zhou's speech in December to the National People's Congress included criticism of "class enemies at home" who "quite actively advocated the liquidation of the struggle in our relations with imperialism, the reactionaries and modern revisionism." Zhou, referring to the organizational battles in the provinces where Mao and the Liu-Deng machine maneuvered for control of the provincial party apparatus, expressed confidence "that the masses of the people, who constitute more than 95 percent of the population...firmly

[19] "Heroic Struggle Supported," ibid., December 2, 1964, pp. 9–11.

[20] "A Great People, A Glorious Banner," ibid., p. 11; "Solidarity With The Vietnamese People Against US Imperialism," ibid., December 4, 1964, pp. 25–26.

[21] "Premier Chou En-lai Reports on the Work of the Government," ibid., January 1, 1965, pp. 6–20.

[22] "Mao is Said to Bar War Unless China is Attacked by US," New York Times, February 12, 1965, p. 1.

[23] "Mao Said to Assert Viet Cong Will Win," ibid., February 5, 1965, p. 2.

support the lines and policies laid down by our Party...although a part of them may follow our lead somewhat hesitantly."[24]

In mid-January 1965, Mao's faction openly accused a "pro-Soviet clique" of revisionism. These pro-Soviet Chinese "distort and obliterate the thought of Mao Zedong by every conceivable means.... *They act in coordination and sing in chorus with the forces of revisionism in foreign countries."* (Emphasis added.)[25] Mao accused the Liu-Deng machine, which controlled the provincial party apparatus, of using Mao's own directives to counter Mao's policies.[26] And he accused Liu and Deng of advancing arguments consistent with Soviet propaganda on "unity of action."

By January 1965, the Soviet supply effort to North Vietnam had so turned the military situation against South Vietnam that it was obvious that the Americans had to become involved directly in the fighting. Mao's attacks on his opponents had established a good defensive position for the political onslaught that would come once the United States entered the conflict in a sustained manner. The wily communist leader must have known what was coming, for he predicted that the struggle to defeat his internal opponents would take six or seven years.[27]

Brezhnev, Kosygin Stay the Course in Vietnam

There is irony in Khrushchev's fall. He was ousted so that his policies could continue! Thus, instead of a dramatic change, the evidence indicates continuity in Soviet strategy. The Russians continued to increase the flow of seaborne supplies to North Vietnam.[28] This caused greatly expanded North Vietnamese/Viet Cong military capabilities during the last months of 1964 and first months of 1965. By January 1, 1965, in fact, the situation was deteriorating much faster than had been expected by the Americans

---

[24]"Premier Chou En-lai Reports on the Work of the Government," *Peking Review,* January 1, 1965, pp. 6–20.

[25]"Peking is Fighting Pro-Soviet Clique," *New York Times,* January 17, 1965, p. 5.

[26]Thornton, *China.* See this book for a complete and detailed look at the fascinating bureaucratic maneuvering that took place.

[27]Ibid., p. 270.

[28]The discussion in the remainder of this section should serve to confirm this point. For some direct evidence see "Chinese Deny They Block Flow of Soviet Aid to Hanoi," *New York Times,* April 2, 1965, p. 16, and "Report Heard in Hungary," ibid., March 29, 1965, p. 2. The articles discussed Soviet charges that the Soviet Union had been denied land access to Vietnam and were therefore required to supply Vietnam by sea.

even a few months earlier. In coordination with the logistic effort designed to escalate the conflict in Vietnam, Brezhnev and Kosygin used Soviet diplomacy and propaganda to demand united communist action over Vietnam, continuing to threaten China with expulsion from the socialist camp unless it cooperated.

Toward the United States, Brezhnev and Kosygin adhered to Khrushchev's policy line of "peaceful coexistence." Although they intimated that events in Vietnam could not be divorced from US-Soviet relations, the new leaders implied that improved relations were possible.[29] Their public posture perpetuated the mistaken American analysis that the Soviets were the "moderating influence" in the socialist camp.[30] This appearance of moderation, and an overall nonthreatening attitude reduced the chance that the United States would initiate a Soviet-American confrontation on the high seas and it encouraged the Americans to continue deploying military forces to the Far East.

In Vietnam the Soviet supply effort paid dividends. Viet Cong forces increased in size and effectiveness.[31] From September to December 1964, the rate of infiltration from North Vietnam to South Vietnam quadrupled.[32] Even more ominously for the Americans, US intelligence detected North Vietnamese regular army units moving into South Vietnam in late 1964.[33]

---

[29]For example see "Kosygin's Report to the Supreme Soviet," *Current Digest,* December 30, 1964, pp. 3–13. Kosygin expressed a desire for better relations with the United States, reduction of tension, and disarmament. Both Brezhnev and Kosygin advocated coexistence.

[30]See "Reds Charge US Seeks Wider War," *New York Times,* February 15, 1965, p. 1. This article discussed an exchange of notes between the Soviet Union and China. The Soviet note, said the article's author, was "mild by comparison." It was most popular for the press during this period to explain the Sino-Soviet rift as Russia's dispute with her more "militant" Chinese allies.

[31]Sharp and Westmoreland, *Report,* Section II, p. 84.

[32]*Pentagon Papers,* Book 4, "November–December," pp. 1–2. These pages reveal an increase in infiltration that began approximately September 1, 1964. As of September 1 the total number of infiltrees was estimated at 4,700 for the year. Ambassador Taylor feared that, because of the increase, this total might reach 10,000 by year's end. His worst fears were realized. General Westmoreland tells us in *Report,* Section II, p. 95 that the total number actually reached 12,500.

[33]The exact time US intelligence became aware of the presence of North Vietnamese Army (NVA) units in the South is not clear. Individual NVA soldiers were detected as early as October 1964, according to *Secret History,* p. 338. *Secret History,* p. 409 reveals that one regiment of the 325th NVA Division was detected in South Vietnam in February 1965, though not officially added to the enemy order of battle by the CIA until April 21, 1965. George McT. Kahin, *Intervention; How America Became Involved* (New York: Alfred A Knopf, 1986) p. 307 attempts to demonstrate that the North Vietnamese had no aggressive intentions and only responded belatedly to the US escalation of inserting Marines in March of 1965 by saying "In fact the available record indicates that it was not earlier than April 21, 1965, that US intelligence first confirmed that a North Vietnamese combat unit was operating in South Vietnam." While April 21 was the day the intelligence bureaucracy officially added the regiment to the "order of battle," this does not mean the unit instantaneously

Two communist regiments mounted a sustained offensive in South Vietnam's largest province, Binh Dinh, in late November—which, according to General Westmoreland, resulted in loss of control over the countryside and loss of the military initiative.[34]

By the end of December, Viet Cong action convinced many Americans at high levels in the Johnson administration that the war had progressed to the "final phase" of People's War, the mobile offensive. The 9th Viet Cong Division, armed with sea-delivered weapons in the fall of 1964, fought the battle of Binh Gia during the last days of 1964 and the first days of 1965. The communists stood and fought for four days, nearly destroyed two ARVN battalions, and inflicted heavy losses against armored and mechanized forces attempting to relieve the trapped units. This was the first time communist forces remained on the battlefield and met government forces in sustained battle.[35] Binh Gia marked the failure of the US counterinsurgency effort, a failure that was evident to the North Vietnamese as well as the Americans. North Vietnam's military leader Vo Nguyen Giap, looking back at those events, recalled that "the Binh Gia victory...marked the fundamental defeat of the special war strategy of the US imperialists."[36]

The evidence is overwhelming that there was a major communist escalation of the level of conflict in South Vietnam in the last months of 1964. Very simply, communist forces were exceedingly well armed and equipped. Since North Vietnam did not have the industrial capacity to manufacture and support the equipment necessary for this escalation, and it is stupid to suggest such an offensive could have been supported by

---

materialized in South Vietnam on that date. A unit, presumably observing some normal operational security measures to avoid detection, is detected by a series of clues that intelligence analysts analyze. Once an analyst makes his case for a conclusion, the proposal is "staffed" and finally adopted as the "agency position." Then other intelligence agencies (DIA, NSA) are allowed to concur or not to concur. The date a unit is added to the official order of battle in no way approximates the date of first detection. Actually the available record, to include even Gareth Porter's *A Peace Denied,* (Bloomington: Indiana University Press, 1975) p. 27, indicates the United States detected the North Vietnamese moving south in 1964. Porter says the North Vietnamese were forced to send 3 regiments south in late 1964. A recent Soviet work by SA Mkhitaryan and TI Mkhitaryan, *V' etnamskaya Revolutsiya (Vietnam Revolution)* (Moscow: Science Press, 1986) p. 218 states "From 1961 through 1963, more than 40 thousand personnel were sent from North to the South and thousands of tons of supplies including 165 thousand weapons, were delivered." This Soviet source confirms a massive North Vietnamese support effort for the supposed "civil war" in the south long before Kahin would have us believe the North Vietnamese were involved.

[34]Sharp and Westmoreland, *Report,* Section II, p. 95.
[35]Ibid.
[36]Vo Nguyen Giap, *Big Victory, Great Task* (New York: Frederick A. Praeger, Publishers, 1968) p. 5.

people's warriors fighting with captured weapons, the supplies must have been provided by an outside source.

The outside source was the Soviet Union—not China. Escalation supported Soviet propaganda about the need for unity of action and China's return to the Moscow camp. Moreover, Soviet sources discussed the issue directly with Western journalists in the spring of 1965 as the Soviet-Chinese struggle over Soviet transit rights on the Chinese railway system came to a head. "Communist sources" in Moscow told a reporter that the Soviet Union had been forced to supply Vietnam by sea because the railway system had been closed to Soviet use.[37] These reports were intended to place pressure on China to open the railway system, but they also confirmed the existence of an ongoing Soviet seaborne supply effort. In addition, the 9th VC Division had enjoyed considerable success against ARVN armored and mechanized formations by using antitank weapons, specifically the Soviet RPG-2.[38] The US intelligence community supplied analysis to the National Security Council concluding that the Soviet ability to assist Hanoi in a manner that would sustain such dramatic military surge was far greater than that of China—although this analysis fell on the deaf ears of America's political leadership.[39]

As the battlefield situation developed, the Soviets adjusted their line toward China. They continued a self-imposed moratorium on open polemics, despite the resumption of public attacks by the Chinese press. By continued restraint, they hoped that the pro-Soviet group would gain strength. The new Soviet leaders repeatedly advocated that socialist countries "strive to overcome the difficulties in the ranks of the movement."[40] While the differences between the Soviet Union and China could not be resolved quickly, they should be put aside to meet the common enemy in Vietnam.

Later in the Chinese power struggle, Mao's supporters openly accused Liu Shaoqi of having advocated the Moscow party line, quoting Liu arguing "We should unite with [the Soviets], seek common ground while

[37] Henry Tanner, "China Said to Balk Soviets Hanoi Aid," *New York Times,* March 29, 1965, p. 1; "Report Heard in Hungary," ibid., p. 2.

[38] Sharp and Westmoreland, *Report,* Section II, pp. 88, 95.

[39] *Pentagon Papers,* Book 4, "November–December," pp. 11–12. This was the analysis of the US intelligence community in estimates supplied to the National Security Council.

[40] "Soviet-Czechoslovak Communique on Stay in Soviet Union of Party and State Delegation from Czechoslovakia," *Current Digest,* December 30, 1964, pp. 19; "Kosygin's Television Report on Trip to Far East," ibid., March 24, 1965, pp. 3–6. Kosygin argued for united action over Vietnam and for cessation of open polemics.

resolving differences and together oppose imperialism."[41] The new Soviet propaganda, evidently, had some effect.

In December, on the eve of the world conference of communist parties, the Soviet Union postponed the meeting and rescheduled it for March 1, 1965.[42] On the surface this appeared to be a concession to China and supported the view that the Soviet Union was actively seeking better relations with its neighbor. Actually, this maneuver assisted the Kremlin's hard-line strategy in two ways. First, it gave two additional months to apply pressure on other socialist countries— some of whom were not anxious to attend the meeting. And second, and more important, it placed the convocation of the conference at a time likely to coincide with stepped up American reinforcements in Vietnam. The Soviets knew that their supplies had greatly affected the military balance in late 1964 and that President Johnson had more latitude to take action now that the presidential elections were over. An American response could reasonably be expected in the first quarter of 1965. The rescheduled conference thus would likely coincide with a new military crisis in Vietnam. At a time in which the Chinese perception of the extent of the US threat was likely to increase, the Soviets would be increasing the isolation of China in the socialist camp.

Brezhnev and Kosygin, as a prelude to the conference, developed the propaganda line that China need not be alone in her struggle. In Late November, the Soviet Union conveyed this message in a *Pravda* article celebrating Albanian National Day. In the days before open polemics erupted in the Sino-Soviet rift, the two countries used surrogate whipping boys with China attacking Yugoslavia and the Soviet Union railing against Albania. The Soviet treatment of Albanian National Day actually carried a message for China:

> The Soviet Union...extended the hand of fraternal assistance to them.... True to its internationalist duty, the Soviet Union rendered...assistance...on Albanian [Chinese] soil with direct assistance of Soviet workers, engineers and technicians...[and] enabled them to transform their once backward agrarian country to an agrarian-industrial state.... The Soviet people have built their relations...in full conformity

[41] "Along the Socialist or the Capitalist Road?" *Peking Review,* August 18, 1967, pp. 10–18.

[42] Henry Tanner, "Aims of Parley Change," *New York Times,* March 1, 1965, p. 10. The author reports that, on December 12, 1964, the Soviet Union announced the postponement of the conference from December 15, 1964, till March 1, 1965.

with the principles of proletarian internationalism, equality, respect for national independence, sovereignty and territorial integrity and noninterference in internal affairs, and on the basis of close cooperation and mutual aid.... Life has shown that the strengthening of friendship and cooperation between the Soviet Union and Albania [China] answers the vital interests of the Albanian [Chinese] people themselves and the cause of the consolidation of the unity of all countries of the Socialist Commonwealth.[43]

This was a good summation of the Soviet position on China, which emphasized the past value of Soviet aid and the future value of cooperation with the Soviet Union in serving China's vital interests.

As part of the overall campaign to pressure China, Kosygin journeyed to Vietnam only a month before the rescheduled conference of communist parties. He stopped in Peking both coming and going. The composition of his party, which included the Deputy Defense Minister and the Chief of Civil Aviation, indicated that the official purpose of the trip was to consider new Soviet military and economic aid.[44] Although it is not possible to prove that the Viet Cong attack on the American base at Pleiku during Kosygin's visit to North Vietnam was planned with Soviet concurrence, it certainly was well planned and executed and it occurred as Kosygin arrived in Hanoi.[45] Without a doubt an attack of this importance was ordered at the highest levels in Hanoi. The planning and issuance of the necessary orders would have taken some weeks and could have been postponed had the Soviets objected to the timing—as well they might. An attack on US soldiers would undoubtedly provoke an American response. But this is precisely the kind of thing the Kremlin wanted. From Hanoi, Kosygin could call for unity and act as spokesman for the socialist camp in a crisis.

Throughout his visit, Kosygin stressed the special need for unity because of Vietnam and increasingly claimed to speak for China.[46] "Neither the DRV nor the Soviet Union nor the CPR nor any socialist state wants war," said Kosygin, but they must be ready "by strengthening the might and

[43]"National Holiday of the Albanian People," *Current Digest*, December 23, 1964, p. 17.

[44]"Visit to the Democratic Republic of Vietnam by Delegation From Soviet Union," ibid., February 24, 1965, p. 17.

[45]*Pentagon Papers*, Book 4, "Rolling Thunder Program Begins," p. 23.

[46]"Kosygin Warns US on Worsening Ties," *New York Times*, February 13, 1965, p. 1.

defense capacity of the socialist commonwealth."[47] Finally, in a stop in Pyongyang, Kosygin pleaded for land access across China in the name of socialist solidarity.[48] The end of Kosygin's visit to Asia coincided with the anniversary of the Sino-Soviet treaty. The escalating conflict in Vietnam and Kosygin's attempt at personal diplomacy forced Mao to agree to exchange delegations with Moscow in honor of the treaty. To increase pressure for compromise, the Soviets capitalized on the treaty celebrations by reporting that "our alliance...is a barrier on the path of the aggressive imperialist circles.... [The alliance] will continue to serve as an important factor for ensuring peaceful conditions.... It is to the benefit of our common interest to further develop relations ... [and] to eliminate step by step the accretions that have arisen in the past."[49]

For the Soviets, the "elimination of accretions" included the opening of the Chinese railway system. They highlighted their concerns by selecting the Soviet Minister of Transportation, Beshchev, to make a major speech on the significance of the Sino-Soviet treaty. Beshchev pointed out that "the close alliance of the Soviet and Chinese peoples sealed by the treaty, and especially those of its clause directly concerned with the ensuring of peace and security in the Far East, assume special significance in present conditions."[50]

The cumulative effects of Soviet efforts both to escalate the conflict in Vietnam and to pressure China reached a crescendo with the Kosygin trip. As it turned out, even though the United States conducted some retaliatory raids for the Viet Cong attack on Pleiku, Kosygin's presence in Hanoi caused the United States to delay its planned sustained bombing campaign. The delay was brief, however, as the United States in March began this aerial campaign against North Vietnam, code named "Rolling Thunder," and, more importantly, decided that American ground forces would participate directly in combat. The transition to war for the United States had begun.

[47] "Kosygin Visit to Hanoi; The American Bombing," *Current Digest,* March 3, 1965, pp. 3–13.
[48] "Kosygin in Pyongyang: Press Stress Need of Unity," ibid., March 10, 1965, pp. 6–9.
[49] "Anniversary of Soviet-Chinese Mutual Aid Treaty," ibid., March 10, 1965, pp. 9–10.
[50] Ibid.

┌─────┐
│ 5 │
└─────┘

The American Ground War

Major Events

- *November 1964*—President Johnson approves a plan for increased covert aerial harrassment of North Vietnamese supply routes to be followed by a gradually escalating bombing campaign against the North. He holds implementation of the bombing campaign in abeyance.
- *December 1964–January 1965*—Battle of Binh Gia results in major VC victory.
- *January 1965*—2,000 South Korean troops deploy to Vietnam.
- *January 1965*—Johnson approves implementation of bombing campaign. Orders naval patrols off North Vietnamese coast to commence February 4, in the hope of provoking a North Vietnamese attack that would help justify the bombing.
- *February 1965*—Naval patrols postponed because of Kosygin visit to Hanoi.
- *February 7 and 10, 1965*—VC attack US bases in South Vietnam.
- *February 13, 1965*—President makes formal decision to initiate sustained bombing campaign called Rolling Thunder.
- *February 25, 1965*—McNamara orders US Army logistic planning group enroute to Thailand diverted to Vietnam.
- *March 2, 1965*—First Rolling Thunder attacks occur.
- *March 6, 1965*—Logistic planning group arrives in Vietnam and begins survey for port, depot, and support command facilities.
- *March 8, 1965*—First of two Marine battalions land at Danang with the announced mission of airfield security.

- *March 12, 1965*—Army Chief of Staff publicly recommends deployment of a US Army division to Vietnam.
- *March 30–31, 1965*—China opens its railway system to Soviet supplies for North Vietnam.
- *April 1, 1965*—Logistic planning group formally established as 1st Logistical Command with a mission of supporting ground forces. President approves deployment of additional 18–20,000 soldiers primarily to supply needed logistic personnel. President also approves two more Marine battalions and secretly approves the use of the Marines in combat operations.
- *April 7, 1965*—Johns Hopkins speech by Johnson warning of a long war.
- Mid-April 1965—Construction begins on Soviet SAM sites around Hanoi.
- *April 20, 1965*—US troop ceiling raised to 82,000.
- *May 11, 1965*—VC overrun provincial capital of Song Be and hold town for two days.
- *Early June 1965*—Department of Defense develops a 44-battalion "package" for deployment.
- *Mid-June 1965*—Westmoreland recommends deployment of reinforcements. McNaughton sends memorandum to JCS with guidance on the definition of victory and allowable methods to accomplish same.
- *July 20, 1965*—McNamara sends memorandum to the president recommending that US troop strength be increase to 175,000 by the end of 1965, that 100,000 be added in early 1966, and that the United States be prepared to add an unknown number thereafter.
- *July 28, 1965*—President approves increase of US troop strength to 175,000 by the end of 1965.

In the late fall of 1964, evidence of the increasing military imbalance in Vietnam compelled President Johnson to decide that the United States had to exert military pressure against North Vietnam.[1] By February 1965, and probably earlier, the United States leadership had decided to execute a sustained bombing campaign against the North and to deploy US ground forces to bear the brunt of the fighting in the South. The details of the ground commitment were worked out between February and July 1965, when deployment began in earnest. Initially, military actions by the United States appeared cautious—indeed, indecisive—as the Johnson administration gradually attempted to increase pressure against the North. A Special Work-

---

[1]*Pentagon Papers*, Book 4, "November–December," p. i.

ing Group of the National Security Council completed a policy review and submitted a two-part proposal to the president in late November 1964. The president approved both parts, but held implementation of part two in abeyance. Part one called for an intensification of existing "covert" aerial harassment of North Vietnamese supply routes into Laos and Vietnam. This would be followed after thirty days by part two, a sustained and slowly escalating bombing campaign against North Vietnam.[2] Phase one, code named "Barrel Roll," began on December 14, 1964.[3] This program was so ineffective that the North Vietnamese did not notice the "escalation" until January 1965.

As the planning for military action continued, the United States moved to try to "internationalize" the war by pressuring allies for aid and troops.[4] The first tangible result of this effort came on January 8, 1965, when 2,000 South Korean soldiers departed for duty in South Vietnam.[5]

With conceptual approval already obtained from the president for a sustained bombing campaign, a consensus at the highest levels of the administration began to develop that ultimately only US ground forces would save the situation. During a mid-November strategy debate in the Special Working Group, Walt Rostow had urged the deployment of US ground forces.[6] On January 6, 1965, Assistant Secretary of State William Bundy would write a memorandum indicating that introduction of US ground forces "still has a great appeal to many of us."[7]

By mid-January Bundy was pushing forcefully for US action, to include use of American ground troops.[8]

After the battle of Binh Gia at the end of December, the Johnson administration was convinced that the United States had no choice but to proceed with phase two, the plan for a gradually escalating bombing campaign.[9] As a first move, the president ordered naval patrols again to commence off the coast of North Vietnam which, hopefully, would draw fire from North Vietnamese vessels. The United States would then retaliate but

[2]Ibid.

[3]Ibid., p. xiii.

[4]Ibid., p. xvi; "Lodge Passes the Hat," *Current Digest*, September 16, 1964, p. 23.

[5]*Pentagon Papers*, Book 4, "November–December," p. xvi. This is further evidence of an intention to commit ground forces. South Korea would not have committed its own ground forces without some assurance they would be joined by American forces.

[6]*Pentagon Papers*, Book 4, "November–December," p. xvi.

[7]*Secret History*, p. 342.

[8]*Pentagon Papers*, Book 4, "November–December," p. 77.

[9]Ibid., "Rolling Thunder Program Begins," pp. 9–15.

would link reprisals to the larger pattern of aggression in Vietnam. In other words, the United States was searching for a public relations ploy to help justify moving away from a tit-for-tat response to a sustained bombing campaign.[10]

The naval patrols off the North Vietnamese coast were scheduled to begin on February 4, 1965, but the Johnson administration postponed them to avoid an incident during Kosygin's visit to North Vietnam. The need to find a pretext that would justify retaliation to the public was removed, however, when the Viet Cong staged a well-executed mortar attack on the American base at Pleiku, South Vietnam, shortly after Kosygin's arrival in Hanoi. In response, the president ordered bombing strikes against North Vietnam and withdrew US dependents from Vietnam to "clear the decks for action."[11] On February 10, 1965, the Viet Cong again attacked a US base.[12] As a result of the Viet Cong assaults the administration felt sure of public support and the president made the formal decision to initiate the sustained bombing campaign on February 13.[13] After several delays, operation Rolling Thunder began on March 2, 1965.[14]

Crossing the Rubicon — The Ground Forces Are Committed

Although the sustained bombing campaign was important, it could be stopped on a moment's notice—and bombing is somehow not as "personal" as ground combat. The dispatch of troops and the support structure necessary to sustain combat was a more momentous step, a step from which the nation would find it difficult to retreat, for it meant the nation was at war. A dramatic change in American Vietnam policy occurred at nine o'clock on the morning of March 8, 1965, when US Marines landed at Danang.[15] President Johnson, as a result of a decision in February (February 25 at the latest), had crossed the Rubicon. US

---

[10]Ibid., pp. 16, 25.

[11]Ibid., p. 27.

[12]Sharp and Westmoreland, *Report,* Section II, p. 107.

[13]*Pentagon Papers,* Book 4, "Rolling Thunder Program Begins," p. 48.

[14]Ibid., p. 64. See also Wallace Theis, *When Governments Collide* (Berkeley: University of California Press, 1980), pp. 73–103. Theis criticizes the assumptions of US policy upon which the bombing decision was based. The Americans equated governments to single rational actors. (Hereafter referred to as Theis).

[15]Gravel, Vol. III, p. 417.

ground forces would be involved in Vietnam.[16] Although the public explanation of the Marines' purpose was Danang airbase security, the fact remained that the two US infantry battalions were the leading edge of a far larger commitment.[17]

Soviet, Chinese, and North Vietnamese intelligence analysts surely concluded that a substantial ground force commitment was being planned. US force deployments from February through July 1965 grew steadily. Moreover, there was no indication that the United States had placed any limit on the size of its forces. Evidently, deployments would be decided by battlefield necessity. Just as importantly, the United States began to perform concrete tasks necessary to support a large army. On February 25, 1965, for example, the Secretary of Defense approved the introduction into Vietnam of lead elements of an expanded logistic apparatus.[18] Modern combat forces in the field have an exceedingly large "tail" providing weapons, munitions, fuel, repair parts, tools, recovery and repair facilities, and food. As a result of McNamara's February 25 order, a logistical planning group of seventeen officers and twenty-one enlisted men enroute to Thailand was diverted to Saigon, where they arrived on March 6, 1965. Once in Vietnam the American logisticians proceeded to conduct

---

[16]Ibid., p. 401.

[17]This interpretation is in apparent disagreement with existing literature, which places the final decision to commit ground forces on July 28, 1965. Herbert Y. Schandler, for example, in *The Unmaking of a President*, takes the position that the decision for a sustained bombing campaign was taken in February, but that President Johnson's decision to commit US ground forces was in July, after much debate and a formal request in June by General Westmoreland. Larry Berman in *Planning a Tragedy: The Americanization of the War in Vietnam*, using much of the same evidence used in this study, is noncommittal on whether the commitment of Marines was considered to be the first step in a larger commitment. Robert Komer in *Bureaucracy at War: US Performance in the Vietnam Conflict*, concludes that as a result of the US desire to do only what was minimally necessary, ground strategy evolved through three schools of thought, progressing from base "enclave" strategy and finally to the "search and destroy" strategy of July 1965. This book's conclusion that the decision was much earlier is not so much in disagreement as it appears. Richard Betts and Leslie Gelb in *The Irony of Vietnam: The System Worked*, describe the July decision not as a go or a no go decision, but a change in the order of magnitude. The focus of their work is on the US decision-making process. They agree that there was great pessimism at high levels by the end of 1964. If this book is correct and the decision to deploy US units was made early, the details of "how many soldiers" and "when" still needed to worked out by many people with differing views and some with grave reservations. It is this process that Gelb and Betts so ably describe. The point is, the United States had accepted the need for ground forces and was willing to commit them. The fact that some in the administration may have hoped that it would not take very many soldiers to do the job does not alter the fact that the Rubicon had been crossed.

[18]Lieutenant General Joseph M. Heiser, Jr., *Vietnam Studies, Logistic Support* (Washington: Department of the Army, 1974) pp. 9–10.

inspections of places like Qui Nhon, Nha Trang, and Cam Ranh Bay to determine real estate requirements for depot and support command areas.[19] On April 1, 1965, a general order designated these personnel officially as the 1st Logistical Command with a mission of providing logistic support to all of Vietnam, except the air force, navy, and army advisors serving with South Vietnamese troops.[20] If we eliminate these groups, we are left only with US ground forces.

Further indications of the coming buildup came in mid-March with a highly publicized trip to Vietnam by Army Chief of Staff General Harold K. Johnson, after which he publicly recommended that a US Army Division be committed.[21] Following General Johnson's trip, General Westmoreland completed a voluminous "estimate of the situation" in which he echoed the prevailing pessimistic view of the war.[22] Westmoreland's report was presented at a strategy conference in Washington on April 1, 1965, and he asked for commitment of a force that would include seventeen maneuver battalions to be used in combat operations.[23] Secretary McNamara, who was present, distributed a memorandum prepared by Assistant Secretary of Defense McNaughton which asked whether the situation in South Vietnam could be saved "without deployment of large numbers of US (and other) combat troops inside SVN." The answer was "perhaps, but probably no."[24]

Westmoreland's recommendation proved to be too conservative for Johnson and the president instead approved an "18–20,000 man increase in military support forces to fill out existing units and supply needed logistic personnel."[25] In other words, the president chose to build the support structure for a larger commitment rather than provide a small, easily deployable force. Additionally, Johnson approved the deployment of two more marine battalions and a change of mission that permitted their use in combat "under conditions to be established by the Secretary of Defense in

[19]Ibid., p. 15. The fact that McNamara had the authority to order deployment of these logistic forces indicates that the decision to prepare for a ground force commitment had already been made by the president.
   [20]Ibid., pp. 9–10.
   [21]Jack Langguth, "US Army Division is Expected to go to South Vietnam," New York Times, March 13, 1965, p. 1.
   [22]Gravel, Vol. III, pp. 406–407.
   [23]Secret History, p. 398. It should be noted that two Marine battalions were already in Vietnam and two more would soon follow. A US Army division usually would have 11 or 12 maneuver battalions. Thus the 17 battalion proposal and General Johnson's recommendation to deploy a division were mutually supporting.
   [24]Secret History, p. 398.
   [25]Gravel, pp. 702–703.

consultation with the Secretary of State."[26] A decision in February resulted in the initial marine landings on March 8. On April 1, their use in combat was approved.[27]

If the Johnson administration expected the ground force requirement to be large and require a prolonged effort, it soon had reason to believe that the United States was in for an even more difficult task. In early April, the Chinese relented and opened their railway system to Soviet supplies bound for Vietnam, a change that was soon detected by the United States.[28] Construction also began in April on the first Soviet-supplied surface-to-air missile (SAM) site around Hanoi.[29] Additionally, Soviet hints at possible cooperation with Britain at the Geneva conference suddenly stopped and Soviet diplomacy moved to intransigent support of North Vietnam.

The United States, as a result of detecting the opening of the railway system and observing Soviet behavior in early April, girded for a long war. In a speech by the president on April 7, 1965, at Johns Hopkins University, Johnson warned the nation for the first time to be prepared for a long conflict. And he signaled the North Vietnamese that the American commitment was open-ended: "We will not be defeated. We will not withdraw, either openly, or under the cloak of a meaningless agreement. We hope that peace will come swiftly, but that is in the hands of others besides ourselves. And we must be prepared for a long continued conflict. It will require patience, as well as bravery—the will to endure as well as the will to resist."[30]

---

[26]Ibid.

[27]Also supporting the view that the ground force decision was made earlier than July is Ambassador Maxwell Taylor's response to the Marine deployment. He expressed puzzlement that the less entangling bombing decision took a year of debate within the administration, but the decision to put marines ashore was made without discussion. Indeed, Schandler, p. 20, reveals that the decision was made with little discussion and was made at the highest level of the administration. In April, the administration ordered the deployment of the 173rd Airborne Brigade from Okinawa and it caught Taylor by surprise. Taylor had grave reservations about US involvement in a land war in Asia and he expressed the reservations when apprised of the deployment of the 173rd. His objections were overridden the following day in a cable from Assistant Secretary of Defense McNaughton which cited the president's (highest authority) intention to step up actions in South Vietnam. See *Secret History*, p. 404. By June, the use of US forces in combat was so generally accepted within the administration that a State Department spokesman inadvertently revealed the still secret marine change of mission to the press. See "The news-briefly," *Christian Science Monitor*, June 9, 1965, p. 2; *Secret History*, p. 386.

[28]Thornton, "Vietnam War," p. 202.

[29]Sharp and Westmoreland, *Report*, Section I, p. 18.

[30]"President Makes Offer to Start Vietnam Talks Unconditionally; Proposes $1 Billion Aid for Asia," *New York Times*, April 8, p. 1; *Pentagon Papers*, Book 12, "Negotiations, 1965–67: Announced Position Statements," p. 13.

The opening of the Chinese railway system quickly demonstrated that still more forces would be needed. Without even notifying Ambassador Taylor, the president ordered deployment of the 173rd Airborne Brigade from Okinawa on April 14, 1965. At a high-level strategy conference in Honolulu on April 20, American policymakers hastily worked out a semblance of a plan for use of the deploying troops.[31] United States forces would be raised to 82,000 and employed in a so-called "enclave strategy." The forces would form and secure key coastal enclaves from which they would conduct limited offensive operations, generally within a fifty-mile radius. This strategy was intended to reduce the security burden on the South Vietnamese army, freeing them for offensive action.[32] Before the strategy could be implemented, however, battlefield reverses proved that an even larger commitment had to be made quickly.

The Ground War Begins in Earnest

During the American policy transition in March and early April 1965, the Viet Cong had been unusually inactive.[33] Even though the administration realized this was a temporary lull, the decisions of the April 20 Honolulu conference seemed reasonable as a measured step. The dam burst, however, with a new Viet Cong surge in May and June. On May 11, 1965, the Viet Cong attacked a provincial capital, Song Be, with a force larger than a regiment, overrunning the town and its American advisory compound and holding its ground for a day prior to withdrawing.[34] Later in May, two ARVN battalions were decimated in the battle of Ba Gia.[35] By mid-June, the Viet Cong summer offensive was in full stride, causing General Westmoreland to conclude "I see no course of action open to us except to reinforce our efforts in [South Vietnam] with additional US or Third Country forces as rapidly as is practical during the critical weeks ahead."[36] Adding to the crisis,

---

[31]*Secret History,* pp. 405–406. Present at the meeting were McNamara, William Bundy, McNaughton, Taylor, Admiral Sharp, General Wheeler, and General Westmoreland.

[32]Gravel, Vol. III, p. 410 and *Secret History,* pp. 397, 402–405.

[33]Gravel, Vol. III, p. 436.

[34]Ibid., p. 438.

[35]Ibid.

[36]Ibid., p. 440. The Viet Cong offensive was reported in the American press. See Takashi Oka, "Viet Cong accelerates," *Christian Science Monitor,* May 13, 1965, p. 2; Takashi Oka, "Step-up sighted in Viet conflict," ibid., June 7, 1965, p. 1; Takashi Oka, "War thins Saigon reserves," ibid., June 12, 1965. See also Schandler, p. 26.

in mid-June the Quat government fell and the Thieu-Ky regime came to power.[37]

At this point, only the concrete details of who would go and when needed to be worked out. Some writers have argued that the troop decision came after a formal troop request was received from Westmoreland. This is true, but implies the initiative lay with Westmoreland. On the contrary, the entire senior leadership of the administration was pressing ahead to work out the details of a larger troop deployment. Westmoreland's detailed troop recommendation came during a McNamara visit to Saigon in July that was preceded by a cable from McNamara which explained that the purpose of the visit was "to receive from you your recommendations for the number of US combat battalions, artillery battalions, engineering battalions, helicopter companies, tactical aircraft, and total military personnel to be assigned to South Vietnam between now and the end of this year."[38] Given this guidance, Westmoreland would have been insubordinate not to have submitted a detailed troop recommendation.

The July troop request had been preceded by administration discussion of deployment of a fourty-four-battalion "package" to Vietnam. The impetus to develop a specific final recommendation for the president had been provided on June 18, 1965, when McGeorge Bundy passed on to McNamara the desire of the president that "we find more dramatic and effective action in South Vietnam."[39] This nudge from the president spurred the secretary of defense to recommend deployment of an additional fourty-four battalions. On July 1, 1965, in a draft memorandum for the president, McNamara recommended sending fourty-four battalions (thirty-four US) to Vietnam in the next few months.[40] Further, he decided to go to Saigon in mid-July. As part of his preparation for the trip, he asked the chairman of the Joint Chiefs of Staff, General Wheeler, for an assessment of "the assurance the US can have of winning in South Vietnam if we do everything we can."[41] General Wheeler formed a study group under the direction of the assistant to the chairman, General Andrew Goodpaster. McNamara also asked Assistant Secretary of Defense John McNaughton to work with the study group.[42]

[37] "Rift topples Saigon regime," *Christian Science Monitor,* June 14, 1965, p. 2; Takashi Oka, "Saigon turns to military," ibid., June 15, 1965, p. 1.

[38] *Pentagon Papers,* Book 5, "US Ground Strategy and Force Deployments, 1965–1967, pp. 7–8.

[39] Ibid., pp. i and 1.

[40] Ibid.

[41] Ibid., p. 1.

[42] Ibid.

After McNamara directed McNaughton to work with General Goodpaster's study group, McNaughton wrote a memorandum to Goodpaster. In it he wrote that Secretary McNamara "indicated he wanted your group to work with me and that I should send down a memorandum suggesting some of the questions that occurred to us." The tone set by "send *down* a memorandum" and "questions that occurred to *us*," meaning McNaughton and the secretary of defense, clearly shows that the Joint Chiefs were receiving guidance from superiors.[43] McNaughton, responding to his charge, continued "I do not think the question is whether the 44-battalion program (including 3rd country forces) is sufficient to do the job.... Rather, I think we should think in terms of the 44-battalion build-up by the end of 1965, with added forces—as required and as our capabilities permit—in 1966." Here McNamara and McNaughton were trying to get the military to think beyond the immediate deployments—the commitment to a full-scale ground war had been made. Yet, although the military was being challenged to think big and try to win, McNaughton established two fundamental restrictions that characterized the Johnson administration's prosecution of the war. First, McNaughton wrote, "I would assume that the questions of calling up the reserves and extending tours of duty are outside the scope of this study." Second, with regard to increasing strategic bombing or putting a quarantine on North Vietnamese harbors, McNaughton wrote that "the study group probably should not invest time in trying to solve the problem by cutting off the flow of supplies and people by either of these methods."[44]

In addition to these restrictions, McNaughton expressed the view that the ARVN could not improve quickly, thus making the ground war an American battle. This clearly demonstrates an administration commitment

---

[43]See *Vietnam: A Documentary Collection—Westmoreland vs. CBS*, Clearwater Publishing Company, Inc., 1987. This is a microfiche record of the Westmoreland libel suit against CBS in 1984. At this writing, the index for the use of the voluminous transcript is unavailable. McNamara's deposition is on card 331 and his trial testimony is on cards 947 and 948. This will hereafter be cited as *Trial*. McNamara was very evasive in his testimony, claiming that his memory was imprecise. When asked if others shared his views he would argue that he did not know and could not speak for others—except for John McNaughton. He and McNaughton were, according to this testimony, of one mind. He refused to characterize the views of anyone else in the Johnson administration except for McNaughton saying "I say there was one individual in particular who shared my view and I will name him simply because I know precisely what he thought. He's dead. He can't respond. I want it on the record that he did share that view and that was John McNaughton, the Assistant Secretary of Defense for International Security Affairs." This further supports the view that McNaughton was in a position to send down guidance to the JCS.
[44]Ibid., pp. 1–4.

to take over almost total responsibility for the war. Further, McNaughton defined the words "assurance" and "win" for the military. He wrote that "the degree of 'assurance' should be fairly high—better than 75% (whatever that means.)" (Parenthetical remarks were in the memorandum.) Regarding the word "win" McNaughton wrote: "This I think means that we succeed in demonstrating to the VC they cannot win."[45] In brief, the United States would fight a protracted ground conflict without taking the offensive against enemy forces in his own territory or attacking the enemy's strategic lines of communication. In other words, the United States was willing to make an unlimited commitment to fighting a war exclusively on its adversaries terms!

General Goodpaster's study concluded that "within the bounds of reasonable assumption...there appears to be no reason we cannot win if such is our will...." The United States and third country forces "by offensive land and air action, would locate and destroy VC/DRV forces, bases and major war-supporting organizations in [South Vietnam]." The ARVN "would retain control over areas now held, [and] extend pacification operations and area control where permitted by the progress of major offensive operations."[46] The study outlined the concept for the Johnson administration's prosecution of the war.

When McNamara journeyed to Saigon in July to receive Westmoreland's advice, it appears that the general's recommendations relied on calculations that were remarkably similar to those prepared for McNamara by his staff in Washington. Westmoreland and McNamara assumed that a four-to-one superiority would provide a high probability of victory and that the Viet Cong could not mount simultaneous attacks in each corps area exceeding 1) one reinforced regiment (four battalions) and 2) a single battalion attack at any time.[47] At any rate, Westmoreland analyzed the forces available, the enemy's strength, and his guidance from

[45]Ibid. See also Gabriel Kolko, *Anatomy of a War* (New York: Pantheon Books, 1985) p. 177. Kolko argues that part of the US defeat resulted from the United States accepting the strategic defensive and refusing to go over to the strategic offensive.

[46]*Pentagon Papers*, Book 5, "US Ground Strategy and Force Deployments, 1965–1967, pp. 5–6.

[47]Ibid., p. 7. See p. 10 for the *Pentagon Papers* analyst's view that Westmoreland merely ratified McNamara's recommendations rather than the other way around. See Berman, pp. 99–100 for a fascinating discussion of the McNamara trip and subsequent internal debate over the fourty-four-battalion recommendation that turned out not to be much of a debate. See Theis, pp. 100–101 for the view that the fourty-four-battalion recommendation did touch off a debate. Theis says McNamara argued for a change in strategy from denial of victory for North Vietnam to a more aggressive strategy of "search and destroy." Here, Theis has confused a strategic objective with a tactic.

McNamara and developed a three-phase concept for the war:

- Phase I — The commitment of US/third country forces necessary to halt the losing trend by the end of 1965.
- Phase II — The resumption of the offensive by allied forces during the first half of 1966 in high-priority areas, leading to the destruction of enemy forces and the reinstitution of rural construction.
- Phase III — If the enemy persisted, a period of a year and a half (in other words, war until 1968) following Phase II to defeat the remaining enemy forces.[48]

After McNamara's trip to Saigon, he spelled out troop requirements in a July 20, 1965, memorandum for the president. McNamara recommended that forces should be brought up to a strength of 175,000 by the end of 1965 (troop strength in early July had reached 60,000), while "it should be understood that the deployment of more men (perhaps 100,000) may be necessary in early 1966, and that deployment of additional forces thereafter is possible, but will depend on developments."[49]

After troop strength in Vietnam reached "the appropriate stage," according to McNamara, "the concept of tactical operations will be to exploit the offensive, with the objects of putting VC/DRV battalion forces out of operation and destroying their morale.... The operations should combine to compel the VC/DRV to fight at a higher and more sustained intensity with resulting higher logistical consumption."[50] Having said this, McNamara noted "US and South Vietnamese casualties will increase—just how much cannot be predicted with confidence, but US killed in action might be in the vicinity of 500 a month by the end of the year."[51]

While it was clear that several hundred thousand American soldiers would be sent into combat, the issue of political palatability was not tackled head on. The administration let some of its plans become public by leaking stories to the press about an internal "debate" over strategy.[52] McNamara also issued a statement as he departed Saigon hinting at the now

[48]*Pentagon Papers,* Book 5, "US Ground Strategy and Force Deployments," 1965–1967, pp. 8–9.

[49]The report that troop strength hit 60,000 can be found in "The news-briefly," *Christian Science Monitor,* July 8, 1965, p. 2. McNamara's memo can be found in *Pentagon Papers,* Book 5, "US Ground Strategy and Force Deployments 1965–1967, p. 10.

[50]Ibid., p. 11.

[51]Ibid., p. 12.

[52]Robert R. Brunn, "Vietnam strategy choices," *Christian Science Monitor,* July 21, 1965, p. 1.

inexorable military build-up.[53] These stories were followed quickly by others which raised the issue of a possible reserve call up.[54] In the absence of aggressive presidential leadership, however, calling up the reserves and involving the American people in the war directly met with a negative political response. As a result, the president, on July 28, 1965, approved the introduction of 175,000 troops by the end of the year, disapproved a recommendation to call up reserves, and held the decision for additional forces in abeyance.[55] The regular army would fight the war. The American people, unless they happened to be related to a draftee, would not be involved. The war had begun without the public preparation necessary to secure long-term support in a democracy and without a concept of victory that could lead to a swift decision.[56]

In any military operation, a senior commander causes a subordinate commander to move his unit to action by giving an order. In the United

[53]Takashi Oka, "McNamara hints US build-up," ibid., July 22, 1965, p. 1.

[54]Robert R. Brunn, "What would a call-up of US troops mean?" ibid., July 24, 1965, p. 6; Richard L. Strout, "Vietnam impact hits home, ibid., July 24, 1965, p. 1.

[55]*Pentagon Papers,* Book 5, "US Ground Strategy and Force Deployments, 1965–1967," pp. 12–13. See also Gelb and Betts, pp. 131–133. This is an excellent discussion that focuses on the issue of whether the military deceived decisionmakers in order to gain incremental increases in troop strength. The answer, clearly stated here, is no. Herring, p. 140, says that in response to Westmoreland's recommendation for 179,000 troops President Johnson approved the immediate deployment of 50,000 troops and privately agreed to 50,000 more. He cites President Johnson's *Vantage Point,* p. 146. However President Johnson on that page concurs with the 175,000 figure with 100,000 to follow. It may be that Herring took his number from the public announcement which was designed to minimize the impact of the decision and stated that US authorized troop strength would increase immediately from 75,000 to 125,000.

[56]*Trial,* cards 331, 947, and 948. When asked when the decision to commit ground forces was made in the Westmoreland/CBS trial, McNamara responded that he did not know. He called it a gradual process and his memory was imprecise. Given his role outlined in this chapter, his contention is difficult to believe. On the other hand, he may have wanted to conceal that the decision was made earlier than July, as I argue above. The following exchange during McNamara's sworn deposition supports this contention.

> Q: When General Westmoreland assumed command of American troops in Vietnam you were Secretary of Defense at that time?
> A: Yes.
> Q: Approximately how many American troops were in Vietnam at that time? A: I don't recall. Q: Do you recall approximately?
> A: No.
> Q. Was it about 16,000?
> A: I have no idea.
> Q: Do you recall in any event that it was less than 100,000?
> A: I have no recollection. I don't recall when he assumed command and I don't recall the number of troops at any date and time.

States the second paragraph of the operations order is a clear statement of the mission. The mission statement answers the questions who, when, where, what, and why.[57] In the above discussion, it is impossible not to criticize the Johnson administration for its failure to formulate a clear mission. The McNaughton guidance to General Goodpaster did not make clear in easily definable terms what "assurance" and "win" meant. McNaughton's guidance could be restated accurately as, winning means don't lose. The third paragraph of an operations order always contains the commander's concept of the operation. As with the unclear mission, it is impossible not to criticize McNamara's concept of the way the military would go about "winning." McNamara's plan, fundamentally, was to deploy US forces to South Vietnam and there kill as many Viet Cong/North Vietnamese as possible, until, by his calculations, US forces would be killing enemy soldiers and using up their supplies at a faster rate than the enemy could field new soldiers and materiel. Military historians have widely criticized this plan for the complete absence of any plans to take the offensive. Both issues, the clearness of mission and the chances of success, are vital for our understanding of the possibilities and limitations of the use of military power. But that is not the focus of this book.

Q: Do you recall when the decision was made to increase the American military commitment in Vietnam from one of having fifteen or twenty thousand American advisers to a commitment of having several hundred thousand combat troops?
A: No.
Q: Do you recall approximately when that—
A: No.
Q: —was made?
A: No.
Q: Do you recall whether that was made in 1965?
A: I don't know that particular decision was ever made as a decision?"

McNamara thus refused to confirm even the year of 1965. This may be because the decision that American ground forces would have to fight in Vietnam was made *before* 1965. The evidence and argument above suggests that it was at least by February 1965. However, since the evidence is an *order* to set up the Vietnam logistic structure, it is likely that the decision and planning preceded the order which means that the decision was probably in 1964. This may be why McNamara evaded the question.

[57] A good example of a clear order might be "Division attacks at 0600 to seize objective alpha in order to secure the left flank of the Corps attack." Who=Division; What=attack; When=0600; Where=objective alpha; Why=to secure left flank of the Corps attack.

The most important thing to understand here is that the United States did give its military a mission and did develop a concept of the operation. If it is difficult from McNaughton's memorandum to figure out exactly how the United States would know it had achieved victory, that does not alter the fact that the mission was to "win." Westmoreland would not have been permitted to develop a plan for the war that did not satisfy his bosses. His three-phase concept ended with something he said would *defeat* enemy forces by 1968. Thereafter, internal administration discussions about troop deployments linked them to Westmoreland's "phases." The 175,000 by the end of 1965 were "Phase I Deployments" and the 100,000 that would follow were "Phase II Deployments." The point at which US forces began to kill the enemy faster than he could be replaced became known as the "crossover point" and Westmoreland understood this was how he would "win."[58]

Clearly the mission statement from the civilian leadership to the field commander, was "Win by 1968." It is not difficult to surmise what this really meant: "Win before the 1968 elections." Just as clearly, the concept of the operation was, "Within the borders of South Vietnam, kill as many enemy soldiers as possible as fast as possible." The result would be the defeat of the Viet Cong, a stable non-communist South Vietnam, assurance of the free world of America's value as an ally, and containment of communist expansion, especially Chinese communism. This is what the Johnson administration thought it was doing. It would continue to try to "win" for exactly one year, when McNamara would begin the process of choosing not to try to "win."

---

[58]In fact, in a later chapter we will see him report his belief that his forces were approaching the "crossover point" in some provinces. McNamara frequently referred to the "crossover point" in his testimony at the Westmoreland vs. CBS trial.

6

Mao's Struggle During the Soviet Escalation, January–July 1965

Major Events

- *End of March 1965*—China opens railway system to Soviet supplies for Vietnam.
- *First Week of April 1965*—Construction begins on first Soviet SAM site in Hanoi.
- *April 10–17, 1965*—Le Duan and Vo Nguyen Giap negotiate new arms agreement in Moscow for increased Soviet military aid.
- *April–June 1965*—Chinese press debate over issue of American threat to China intensifies. PLA Chief of Staff Luo Ruiqing is the leading spokesman for unity with the Soviet Union. Navy commander Li Zuoping makes People's War argument against the need for unity.
- *May 1965*—Unannounced five-day US bombing halt meets with no response from the Soviets or North Vietnamese.
- *June 1965*—US troop strength in Vietnam reaches 60,000.
- *June 12, 1965*—Soviets and North Vietnamese sign new aid pact calling for increases above the April 17 agreement.
- *May–June 1965*—Soviet diplomatic and propaganda pressure on China intensifies.
- *July 1965*—McNamara travels to Saigon. United States announces new troop deployments.

Mao managed to deflect the effects of the developing military crisis in Vietnam during the last months of 1964 and the first months of 1965. Despite increasing US aerial activity in operation Barrel Roll, he argued that the United States could not be a legitimate military threat to China without ground forces in Vietnam. Additionally, he intensified anti-Soviet polemics. When the marines landed at Danang, the bottom dropped out of Mao's policy—especially as it soon became obvious that the marines were the leading edge of a major ground force commitment. As a result, Mao was forced to compromise on the issue of Soviet transit rights in order to avoid defeat in the struggle for power.

Although Mao could not ignore developments in Vietnam, he attempted to minimize their importance. He condemned the arrival of South Korean soldiers in Vietnam but weakened it by pointing out that the South Korean force was of trivial strength. Foreign Minister Chen Yi also issued a statement condemning the South Koreans, but he too vacillated by noting that if the United States continued to expand the war, "the Chinese government and people will have to give further consideration to the duties incumbent upon them for the defense of peace in this area."[1]

Events progressed rapidly, however, and the combination of Kosygin's Asian trip in February and the American retaliation for the Pleiku incident forced Mao to join with Liu Shaoqi in a temporary display of unity. Mao appeared on the Tien'anmen rostrum in Peking at a huge rally. One of the main slogans for the rally was "any aggression against Vietnam is aggression against China." Liu Shaoqi, Deng Xiaoping, and Zhou Enlai also were present as a member of Liu's group; Peking mayor Peng Chen gave the main address. Peng included Mao's line that the United States was a paper tiger but came down on the side of unity within the socialist camp by predicting that "peoples of the socialist camp" would "persevere in unremitting struggle."[2]

The display of unity was for international viewing and the debate over Vietnam developed sharply. People's Liberation Army (PLA) Chief of Staff Luo Ruiqing spoke for the Liu-Deng faction on February 8, 1965, noting that should US imperialism "dare to force an aggressive war on us, we are prepared, and we know how to deal with their aggression."[3] Liu

---

[1] "US Move to Extend War in South Viet Nam Condemned," *Peking Review*, January 15, 1965, pp. 6–7.

[2] "Solidarity With Fraternal Viet Nam," ibid., February 12, 1965, pp. 8–10.

[3] Ibid.

Ningyi, secretary general of the National People's Congress and a supporter of Mao, countered Luo Ruiqing by using similar terminology but concluding that the Vietnamese would win by relying on their own strength. Liu said that if the United States "dare to go their way and persist in spreading the flames of war to the Democratic Republic of Vietnam, the Vietnamese people who have the glorious militant tradition of Dien Bien Phu will certainly be able to completely and thoroughly wipe out the US aggressor on their soil."[4]

Mao's press spokesmen reported Kosygin's presence in Peking only in passing and mentioned that the Chinese and Soviet leaders "had a conversation." Mao refused to concede that recent events threatened China. On February 9, 1965, a *People's Daily* editorial denigrated the danger of US presence in Vietnam by discussing American weakness. The article took the position that actual US strength in the region was proof that the United States was not prepared to fight a major war in Asia. The editorial warned the Americans, "You are really overestimating yourself if you hope to extend the war on the strength of the meager armed forces you now have in Indo-China, Southeast Asia and the Far East."[5] Other articles sponsored by Mao's faction also emphasized the "meager forces" of the United States.[6]

Events moved rapidly and Mao intensified his anti-Soviet campaign as February drew to a close. The Chinese boycotted the March 1 conference of communist parties in Moscow and the Chinese press accused the Soviets of convening it to cause a permanent split in the socialist camp. On February 28, the Chinese News Agency reported that Khrushchev's fall was "merely a change of signboard" and "what is on sale in the shop remains the old wares of Khrushchev revisionism."[7] The Soviets, unable to force China to attend the conference or to gain unanimous support for the condemnation of China among the world's communist parties, downgraded the significance of the meeting.[8]

Despite the increased polemics, Mao felt his anti-Soviet policy was threatened and he generated a violent anti-Soviet incident. On March 4, 1965, Chinese students in Moscow engaged in a protest at the US Embassy. The riot soon took on an anti-Soviet flavor as the rioters attacked Soviet

[4] "Chinese People Ready to Fight Alongside Their Vietnamese Brothers," ibid., pp. 12–13.
[5] "US Aggressors Must Be Punished," *Peking Review,* February 12, 1965, pp. 17–18.
[6] For example see "The Johnson Administration's Gangster Talk," ibid., pp. 19–20.
[7] Seymour Topping, "China Says Soviet Deepens Division of World's Reds," *New York Times,* March 1, 196, p. 1.
[8] Henry Tanner, "Aims of Parley Change," ibid., p. 10.

police.[9] The Chinese alleged that several students were brutally beaten (probably true), but they went on to charge that Soviet police had sided with US imperialism (manifestly untrue, since the Chinese students received the standard treatment for Soviet protestors).[10] On March 6, in an unprecedented maneuver, Chinese demonstrators protested the Moscow incident outside the Soviet embassy in Peking.[11] The "injured" students returned to Peking to a hero's welcome.[12]

Mao's efforts were finally undercut, however, as the US deployed marines to Danang and as other signs emerged that these were the first elements of a larger force. The announcement of the deployment of 3,500 marines from Japan to Vietnam, for example, was accompanied by the announcement that they would be replaced in Japan by a force of 6,000.[13] Army Chief of Staff Harold K. Johnson's trip to Vietnam soon followed and General Johnson publicly recommended deployment of a US Army division.

Mao was forced to compromise on the land-access issue. At the end of March, 1965, Zhou Enlai—whose own faction held the balance of power between Mao and the Liu-Deng group—warned that "the Chinese and Russian people will close ranks" should the US provoke a wider conflict. He went on to allege that the United States had rebuffed Chinese overtures for better relations based on peaceful coexistence and US withdrawal from Taiwan.[14] In late March 1965, the Soviets revealed publicly that the Chinese had denied permission for the transit of Soviet supplies to North Vietnam. And they intensified the pressure by accusing the Chinese of dragging their feet in negotiations on rail transshipments.[15] Sometime in the last days of March or the first days of April the railway system opened.[16] The Soviets

[9]Henry Tanner, "Russian Soldiers Rout 2000 in Riot at US Embassy," ibid., March 5, 1965, p. 1.

[10]"Brutal Beating Alleged," ibid., March 14, 1965, p. 2.

[11]"Students in Peking Protest Outside Russian Embassy," ibid., March 7, 1965, p. 1.

[12]"Farce At Peking Airport," Current Digest, March 31, 1965, p. 6.

[13]Max Frankel, "President and Top Aides Talk at Camp David on Saigon Issue," New York Times, March 11, 1965, p. 1.

[14]Drew Middleton, "Chou Says Russians Would Be War Ally," ibid., March 26, 1965, p. 1.

[15]Henry Tanner, "China Said to Balk Soviets Hanoi Aid," ibid., March 29, 1965, p. 1.

[16]Thornton, "Vietnam War," p. 202. See also, "Chinese Deny They Block Flow of Soviet Aid to Hanoi," New York Times, April 2, 1965, p. 16; "How Low Can They Sink!" Peking Review, January 1, 1966, p. 16. This is a People's Daily editorial from December 23, 1965. The editorial suggests the railway opened at the end of March. Another article "USSR, US Gang Up to Slander China," ibid., p. 17, says that a protocol between the Soviet Union and China was signed on March 30, 1965 that explicitly stipulated that China would transport Soviet supplies for Vietnam free of charge. The article says that "since then, all shipments of Soviet military supplies to Vietnam, which the Soviet side requested China to transport by Chinese railways, were transmitted free of charge in accordance with the protocol."

publicly announced that the transit rights issue had been resolved on April 7, 1965.[17]

The Soviets Expand Their War Support

Soviet strategy was on the brink of success when Mao was forced to capitulate on the issue of land access across China. The Soviets now needed to proceed with two tasks. First, they had to supply the military materiel and diplomatic support to North Vietnam necessary to allow the North to match the United States in an escalated conflict. And second, the Soviets had to exert maximum diplomatic pressure on China to return to the "socialist"—that is, Moscow's—camp.

The popular image of guerrilla war with peasants using captured government weapons does not conform to reality. Once a people's warrior captures a weapon, he must obtain ammunition, and the ammunition must fit the weapon. If he does not have it, or he has the wrong type, his weapon is useless. In a battle with a well-armed soldier from the "corrupt right wing repressive regime propped up by the US CIA," the "noble" people's warrior with the useless weapon will lose. When guerrillas start operating in larger units, such as battalions and regiments, only a standardized system will support combat. A magazine for a semi-automatic weapon with 20 bullets can be expended in combat in a matter of seconds. Give a company of 100 soldiers 200 bullets each—ten magazines apiece—and you have the minimum requirement for a short fire-fight. To replenish this one company, you need 20,000 of the correct bullets. And 20,000 bullets are very heavy. Add repair parts. Add cleaning material and lubricants. Add mortars with ammunition and spare parts. (Mortar ammunition is further broken down into separate propellent, projectiles, and fuzes.) Add fuel. Add mines and anti-tank weapons. Add machine guns with ammunition, repair parts, cleaning materials, and spare barrels. It is evident that the decision to escalate from terrorist attacks to combat with military units must include a logistic system that can haul and distribute efficiently thousands of tons of supplies.

The decision to move to the level of combat that would involve large units, such as those involved in the battle of Binh Gia, was a major decision for the North Vietnamese. That decision would have been impossible without Soviet support. The North Vietnamese did not manufacture their

---

[17]Henry Tanner, "Hanoi Gets Arms," ibid., April 8, 1965, p. 1.

own logistics. They did not capture the bulk of their supplies from the ARVN. The Soviets gave them the wherewithal to wage a conventional war. The magnitude of the change that was taking place in late 1964 and early 1965 was dramatic—and the Soviets, and only the Soviets, could have been behind it.[18]

The Kremlin had undertaken a costly effort, to be sure, but it also was one that required a significant commitment of Russian manpower to work out the countless practical details. What type of weapons and what quantities were needed? What support requirements were unique to those systems? What were the priorities? Could the Vietnamese transportation system support the necessary tonnages? What would be the fuel requirements? Moreover, the net result of a successful Soviet supply effort would be an increase in conflict in an already volatile situation—for there could be no thought that the North Vietnamese would not put the supplies to use.[19] The Soviets decided to spend the money, commit the manpower, and accept the attendant risks because they believed the expanded conflict to be in their interests.[20]

[18]See Sharp and Westmoreland, *Report,* Section II, p. 84. General Westmoreland observed that the simple decision to outfit the Viet Cong with a standard family of small arms "complicated the overall logistic problem in that the newly introduced automatic weapons (especially the AK-47 assault rifle) required larger tonnages for resupply. Thus Hanoi had taken an important decision." See Porter, pp. 24–26 for Gareth Porter's view of the issue from another angle. He argues that Hanoi's decision to intervene militarily in South Vietnam was forced upon North Vietnam because it was apparent the United States would broaden the war and because holding back when revolutionary conditions seemed so ripe might cost the North Vietnamese the strong support of the Soviets. It appears that even Gareth Porter agrees that Soviet support was critical. The point is that the Soviets decided to provide the means to escalate the conflict and without such a Soviet decision the escalation would not have occurred.

[19]In a sort of convoluted logic that stemmed from the view of the Chinese as "radical" communists and the Soviets as "moderate" or at least "sane" communists, many Western observers viewed the massive Soviet military support for a force at war with America as a good sign. It was all a Soviet plot for peace. Step 1 in this plan was to get the North Vietnamese to rely on the Soviet Union. Step 2 would follow when the Soviets used their increased influence to cause the North Vietnamese to negotiate a peaceful settlement. Interestingly, the Chinese picked up this theme from US publications and cited it as evidence of United States-Soviet Union collusion. See Hanson W. Baldwin, "Viet Cong Forming Bigger Units, Hinting War is Near 3d Phase," *New York Times,* April 2, 1965, p. 6; Zbigniew K. Brezinski, "Peace, Morality, and Vietnam," *The New Leader,* April 12, 1965; "Refutation of the New Leaders of the CPSU on United Action," *Peking Review,* November 12, 196, pp. 10–21; Donald S. Zagoria, *Vietnam Triangle* (New York: Pegasus, 1967) p. 49.

[20]Soviet sources explain Soviet actions as a response to US aggression and as fulfilling Soviet internationalist duty. The Soviets also maintain that Vietnam was an outpost of socialism and that the threat affected the entire socialist camp. See M.P. Isaev and A.S. Chernishev, *Istoriya sovetsko-v'etnamskikh otnoshenii* (History of Soviet-Vietnamese Relations) (Moscow: International Relations, 1986) pp. 90–110.

The point bears restating. The North Vietnamese were not capable of matching US power without Soviet aid. The war would not have expanded without this aid. There was no requirement for the Soviets to support the expansion of the war to protect their ally from extinction. The existence of North Vietnam was not the issue. The issue was the existence of the United States' ally, the Republic of Vietnam.[21] If the Soviet Union had wanted to keep the level of US ground force commitment relatively small, the Soviets could have decided to withhold the level of their logistic support. This would not have placed the existence of North Vietnam in jeopardy. The Russians were nobody's fools. They went ahead with a policy of support for North Vietnam knowing it had to lead to a larger conflict with a larger US military presence in Asia. They then used that large US military force in Vietnam as the basis for a diplomatic/propaganda campaign to pressure China to return to the Moscow fold.

As Soviet supplies began moving across the Chinese railway system the Soviets and North Vietnamese undertook high-level planning to work out the complex requirements for an expanded war. They did so without having to worry about the US Navy—although they continued to use sea transport because the United States elected to leave North Vietnam's ports open. A North Vietnamese delegation, including Le Duan and Vo Nguyen Giap, was in Moscow from April 10 to 17 holding discussions with Brezhnev, Kosygin, and Defense Minister Malinovsky. The meetings produced a joint communique which promised aid to Vietnam and highlighted Soviet influence in Hanoi by stating that the Soviet Union and the DRV were "of one mind" on the crisis.[22] Later, in June, an article in *Pravda* provided insight into the specific nature of the agreement. "We expressed readiness," said the report, "to render additional unrepayable aid in strengthening the defense capabilities of Vietnam and to deliver to the DRV necessary military equipment.... During the visit in the Soviet Union of the delegation of the DRV headed by comrade Le Duan in April of this year, agreement was reached on additional aid to the struggling Vietnamese people."[23]

---

[21]Even Soviet sources differentiate between the nature of the threat in the North and in the South. The bombing in the North was "barbaric" but the real war was in the South. The North helped the warriors in the South. The South was, according to a quote from Le Duan, a great front while the North was a great rear area. See *Isaev*, pp. 90, 97, 103.

[22]"Sovmestnoe sovetsko-v'etnamskoe kommyunike," (Joint Soviet-Vietnamese Communique), *Pravda*, April 18, 1965, p. 1.

[23]"Sovetsko-bolgarskaya druzhba budet zhit' vechno" (Soviet Bulgarian Friendship Will Live Forever), *Pravda*, June 5, 1965, pp. 3–4.

Soviet public statements on the nature of their support increasingly specified the military character of their aid.[24] From the beginning of 1965 the Soviet supply effort would dwarf Chinese assistance.[25] The SAM site that the Soviets began to construct in the first days of April 1965 was the first element of nearly 35 SAM battalions that would be operational by 1968.[26] In addition, as the war developed, the Soviets supplied sophisticated communications and radar, modern aircraft, and large numbers of anti-aircraft weapons. The North Vietnamese air defense system prompted the US Commander in Chief in the Pacific (CINCPAC) to call it "the most sophisticated air defense system ever faced by any force in combat."[27] Moreover, the Soviets supplied ground force weapons such as 122-mm and 140-mm rockets, 120-mm mortars, and 130-mm field guns. They supplied most of the vehicles and fuel that moved men and supplies south. They also supplied the necessary road construction, railroad, bridging, and water transport equipment needed to maintain, improve, and operate the transportation system to support an escalated conflict.[28]

Soviet diplomacy reflected the advantage felt by the Soviets when the railway opened. Previously, without a secure line of communication, they hedged their bets by offering some hope to the West of a peaceful negotiated settlement. They had to. A US naval blockade would have rapidly brought the North Vietnamese Army to a halt. Looking at the specter of the US Navy, the Soviets issued especially positive diplomatic signals in February and March, when they hinted that they would accept a US-supported British proposal that Britain and the Soviet Union work together as Geneva co-chairmen to find a common ground for negotiations. When the railway system opened, the Soviets immediately rejected the proposal and hardened their diplomatic support for the North Vietnamese.[29]

Further evidence of the "hardline" Soviet diplomatic position occurred in May when the United States used a five-day unannounced bombing halt to call upon Hanoi to accept a "political solution" in South Vietnam. Neither Hanoi nor the Soviet Union responded. An article in the *Christian Science Monitor* told the story of a meeting of the "Big Four" foreign ministers in Vienna in the wake of the bombing pause. Secretary of State Dean Rusk

[24] "Rech' tovarishcha A.N. Kosygina" (Speech by Comrade A.N. Kosygin), ibid., May 16, 1965, pp. 1–2; "Ruki proch' ot V'etnama!" (Hands off Vietnam!), ibid., May 23, 1965, p. 1.

[25] Sharp and Westmoreland, *Report*, Section I, p. 4.

[26] Ibid.

[27] Ibid.

[28] Ibid.

[29] *Pentagon Papers*, Book 12, "Negotiation 1965–67: The Public Record," p. 4.

waited for a signal from Soviet Foreign Minister Gromyko, but got nothing, not even an "invitation to breakfast."[30]

At the same time, the Soviets pressed China for a unified effort against the United States. Those in the Chinese leadership who supported Moscow's stand seemed to be winning and the Kremlin tried to exploit this momentary advantage. In early April, Politburo member Anastas Mikoyan traveled to Hungary while Brezhnev and Kosygin traveled to Warsaw, all three making strong public statements on the unity-of-action theme. The travelers also caused their Hungarian and Polish hosts to make similar statements.[31] Simultaneously, the Soviet press published similar comments from other communist parties.[32]

The Soviets initially waged their campaign without mentioning their erstwhile ally. In late April, when *Pravda* referred to China, it was in a positive vein, reporting on a resolution supporting Vietnam by the Chinese National People's Congress.[33] A few days later, *Pravda* reported the return of the Le Duan and Giap delegation to Vietnam, noting they had visited the Soviet Union and China.[34]

The beginning of May and the anniversary of victory in World War II occasioned a series of commemorative speeches by Soviet leaders. Brezhnev pointed to parallels between the Nazis and the United States and called the United States the "new strike force of imperialism." He emphasized Soviet military strength and Soviet support for Vietnam. The important message was for the socialist camp to unite and rely on the Soviet Union.[35]

In response, highlighting growing Soviet influence, the North Vietnamese leadership sent a message of congratulations signed by Ho Chi Minh, Chong Tinh, and Pham Van Dong which echoed the Soviet line. "Being an advance post of the Socialist camp in the east," said the note,

[30]Ibid., and Eric Bourne, "The signal that never came," *Christian Science Monitor,* May 18, 1965, p. 2.

[31]"Vengerskii narod uvernno idet vpered" (Hungarian People Faithfully Go Forward), *Pravda,* April 4, 1965, p. 4; "Nasha obshchaya tsel' sotsializm i mir" (Our Fundamental Goal Socialism and Peace), ibid., April 8, 1965, p. 1; "Rech' tovarishcha Vladislava Gomulki" (Speech by Comrade Vladislav Gomulka) ibid., April 9, 1965, pp. 1–2; "Rech' tovarishcha L.I. Brezhneva" (Speech by Comrade L.I. Brezhnev), ibid., pp. 1–3.

[32]"Vernii put' ukrepleniya yedinstva" (The True Path to Strengthening Unity), ibid., p. 5.

[33]"Rezolyutsiya postoyannogo komiteta USNP" (Resolution of the Standing Committee of the NPC), ibid., April 21, 1965,p. 3.

[34]"Vozrashchenie na rodinu" (Return to the Motherland), ibid., April 24, 1965, p. 3.

[35]"Velikaya pobeda sovetskogo naroda" (Great Victory of the Soviet People), ibid., May 9, 1965, pp. 1–3.

"and following the militant courageous example of the heroic Soviet people and its Army, the Vietnamese people are firmly sure that with the great support and aid of the Soviet people, the peoples of fraternal socialist countries and peace loving people the world over, the just business of the Vietnamese people undoubtedly will triumph."[36]

Soviet pressure built throughout April and May with minor but tangible results. On April 29, 1965, the Soviet Union and China signed a new trade agreement which called for a substantial increase and left the door open for future growth.[37] In late May, the Soviets and Chinese concluded a cultural agreement which included a projected visit to Moscow by a song and dance ensemble of the PLA and a return visit to Peking by an ensemble of the Soviet army.[38]

As the Soviets pressed ahead with diplomatic pressure on China and the material and diplomatic support for North Vietnam, they continued to avoid threatening the United States elsewhere in the world. It was especially important to have a stable environment in Europe because this would permit the United States to draw down its European forces and shift manpower to Asia. Mao recognized this part of Soviet strategy and called them to task for being false friends of Vietnam. According to Mao, if the Soviets were really serious about helping Vietnam they would pressure the United States elsewhere to prevent the ongoing massive transfer of power. The best summation of this argument was given by Chen Yi in December 1965:

The Soviet Union is the largest European Socialist Country. If it really wanted to help Vietnam it could have taken all kinds of measures in many fields to immobilize forces of the United States. [But they] have in fact been giving the United States every facility so that it can concentrate its forces against Vietnam.... [They] reduce the important political question of supporting the Vietnamese people's struggle against US aggression...to a matter of transit of aid material for Vietnam.... Soviet leaders harp on the fact the Soviet Union has no common borders with Vietnam, as if all aid material for Vietnam has of necessity to go through China.... There are sea routes between the Soviet Union and Vietnam.... We

[36]Ibid., May 11, 1965, p. 3.
[37]"Sino-Soviet trade," *Christian Science Monitor,* June 1, 1965, p. 6.
[38]"Kul'turnoe sotrudnichestvo" (Cultural Cooperation), *Pravda,* May 26, 1965, p. 3.

know very well what are the things we have helped to transport.... They are far from commensurate with the strength of the Soviet Union. But the Soviet leaders are boasting about this meager aid and have constantly and everywhere spread the rumor that China is obstructing the transit of Soviet aid material for Vietnam. Naturally this cannot but strengthen people's conviction that their aid to Vietnam is given with ulterior motives. In reality the Soviet leaders have not been sincerely helping...but want to make use of their so called aid to control the Vietnamese situation and bring the Vietnam question into the orbit of US-Soviet collaboration.[39]

The United States did reduce its readiness in Europe to support the war. Most units stationed there in the mid and late 1960s were at partial strength. For example, one typical field artillery battalion in the Nurenburg area that was authorized to have thirty-three officers in the ranks of second lieutenant through lieutenant colonel actually had only twelve officers — eleven lieutenants and a lieutenant colonel. Although a normal tour of duty in Germany was three years, the most a commissioned officer or noncommissioned officer could expect was eighteen months before being "curtailed" and reassigned to Vietnam. Some officers spent as little as four months before being "curtailed," departing for Vietnam before their personal automobiles arrived from the United States.[40] The Soviet attitude in Europe helped convince the United States that it could weaken its European forces to support its Vietnam build-up.

The build-up of US power in Asia placed Mao Zedong at great risk.

The Struggle Deepens in China

The pro-Soviet faction seemed to have the advantage in April 1965. Having achieved their first objective—Soviet land access across China—Liu Shaoqi and Deng Xiaoping began to push for more cooperation with the Kremlin. The internal debate took on a new intensity in the Chinese press.

---

[39] "A New and Great Anti-US Revolutionary Storm is Approaching," *Peking Review*, January 7, 1966, pp. 5–9.

[40] This was the 1st Battalion, 94th Field Artillery at William O. Darby Kaserne in Furth, part of the 4th Armored Division.

Although the introduction of US Marines had undercut Mao's position, Mao was able to take advantage of the Johnson administration's unwillingness to confront the American public about the gravity of the situation or the expected size of the developing conflict. The gradual nature of the buildup between March and August, the restrictions placed on committed forces, and the concealment from the American public of the change in mission for the marines allowed Mao to argue that the small size of the American force and the nature of its use did not yet threaten China. He used these months to develop an alternative argument—that reliance on People's War was the proper way to deal with a US threat, should it develop.

On April 5, 1965, an article sponsored by the Liu-Deng faction in *People's Daily* noted US bombing closer than ever to the border of China and called it a threat to Vietnam and "to the socialist countries and all peace loving peoples and countries the world over.... US imperialism is intensifying its military provocations against China."[41] An April 13 editorial by Mao's group, however, called the bombing an act of desperation which reflected US failure and "frailty." The editorial not only scoffed at the notion of a US threat to China, it dismissed the notion of a US threat to Vietnam. The Vietnamese, without assistance, could defeat the United States by relying on protracted struggle.[42]

On April 11, the pro-Soviet group published an editorial by an anonymous columnist in *People's Daily.* Responding to President Johnson's Johns Hopkins speech, the author highlighted Johnson's threat to use military power and took note of his warning to be prepared for a long conflict. More importantly, the article interpreted Johnson's references to China as a direct threat. "By taking so much trouble in repeatedly mentioning China by name," said the editorial, "Johnson evidently intended to make war threats against China and stop the Chinese people from supporting the revolutionary struggles of the Vietnamese and other peoples."[43]

Later in the month, Liu Shaoqi and Deng Xiaoping met with the North Vietnamese delegation returning from Moscow. The announcement of the visit not only discussed the meeting in Peking but noted "the delegation arrived in Peking on April 18 on its way home after visiting the Soviet Union."[44] This was followed by a resolution supporting Vietnam by the Standing Committee of the National People's Congress, which reveals the growing

---

[41] "A Great Victory and the Determination to Win," *Peking Review,* April 9, 1965, pp. 6–7.

[42] "A Short Lived Fraud," ibid., April 16, 1965, p. 12.

[43] Observer, "Johnson's Big Swindle," ibid., pp. 10–11.

[44] "Chinese Leaders Meet Vietnamese Comrades," ibid., April 23, 1965, p. 3.

momentum of those favoring greater Sino-Soviet cooperation. Vietnam is referred to as a socialist outpost "entitled to every assistance from the people of all countries in the Socialist Camp."[45] Moreover, Chinese intervention is hinted at. "The people of the countries in the socialist camp," ended the resolution, "will give the Vietnamese people all out support, oppose the US aggressor, and defend the southeastern outpost of the socialist camp."[46] This exactly replicated the Soviet position on Vietnam.

The Liu-Deng group was especially active in April as it attempted to exploit the aftermath of the US ground force commitment. Key members of the faction gave speeches publicly associating themselves with "unity over Vietnam." Deng Xiaoping, speaking on the anniversary of the Bandung conference, called the United States the "common enemy of Asian-African peoples," referred to the American presence in Vietnam as an international problem and reaffirmed China's "internationalist" duty.[47] Peking Mayor Peng Chen followed with a similar argument.[48] These speeches left some room for maneuver, although probably unintentionally. Mao's group responded by claiming that "internationalist duty" was for *each* country to help Vietnam in its own way rather than *all* countries uniting behind the Soviet Union. But Deng's and Peng's remarks closely approximated the Moscow party line. On April 16, 1965, a *People's Daily* editorial stated flatly that socialist countries needed to distinguish between friend and foe and unite against "the most vicious enemy...US imperialism." The "most pressing task" was to unite over Vietnam. Differences between socialist countries had to take second place.[49]

Liu and Deng's offensive intensified in May as the anniversary of victory in World War II gave the pro-Soviet group a chance for a broadside. PLA Chief of Staff Luo Ruiqing gave a speech on May 7, 1965, which argued that the United States was a clear threat to China and socialism and should be met by the unified might of the socialist camp. Lo, in calling for unity of action with the Soviet Union, noted that "preparation must be made not only against any small scale warfare, but also against any medium or large scale warfare that imperialism

[45]"Resolute and Unreserved Support for Vietnam," ibid., April 23, 1965, pp. 6–7.
[46]Ibid.
[47]"Expel US Imperialism From Vietnam," ibid., pp. 10–11.
[48]"Direct Spearhead of Struggle Against US Imperialism," ibid., pp. 11–14.
[49]"People of the World, Act and Force US Aggressors Out of Vietnam!" ibid., April 23, 1965, pp. 14–17.

may launch."[50] Numerous other articles sponsored by the Liu-Deng group fired away in the same direction.[51]

In response, since at this point Mao's faction had lost the initiative, Mao and his supporters began developing three themes in the press which, over the long run, could undermine Sino-Soviet cooperation. First, Mao's followers pointed out that the post-Khrushchev Soviet leadership continued to adhere to conditions for Sino-Soviet rapprochement that were unacceptable to China. Second, US military action in Vietnam had not yet reached levels that threatened China. And third, if the Chinese did have a confrontation with the United States, the best way to deal with that threat was to rely on the principles of People's War—not the Soviet Union.

Early in April, Mao's group announced that public polemics against the Soviet Union were right and necessary.[52] Shortly thereafter, they repeated charges that "Khrushchev's successors are really following in his footsteps."[53] A *Red Flag* editorial in April also argued that, after Khrushchev's downfall, "The new leadership of the CPSU declared again and again that they would faithfully continue to implement Khrushchev's fully developed revisionist line and practice Khrushchevism without Khrushchev."[54] In addition, other articles denounced all Soviet pronouncements and efforts toward Vietnam as an effort to gain control of the situation in order to betray Vietnam by a negotiated settlement with the United States.[55]

As anti-Soviet polemics continued, Mao's group sought to minimize the threat posed by US ground forces by stressing their weaknesses and vulnerabilities. An April 15 *People's Daily* article said "The US is outwardly strong, but really fragile.... *Militarily their fighting manpower is inadequate, their war front too long, and rear too far away, while morale is low and the terrain unfavorable.*"[56] (Emphasis added.) In other words, if the

---

[50]"Commemorate the Victory Over German Fascism! Carry the Struggle Against US Imperialism Through to the End!" ibid., May 14, 1965, pp. 7–15.

[51]"Escalation Means Getting Closer and Closer to the Grave," ibid., April 30, 1965, pp. 10–12; Observer, "Johnson Administration's Act of Piracy," ibid., May 7, 1965, pp. 23–24 (discusses the "menace to China's security"); "Johnson's Doctrine is Neo Hitlerism," ibid., May 21, 1965, pp. 9–11.

[52]"March 1 Meeting Condemned as a Major Conspiracy," ibid., April 9, 1965, pp. 18–21.

[53]"CPSU 20th Congress—Root of All Evils of Khrushchev Revisionists," ibid., April 30, 1965, pp. 15–17.

[54]"A Great Victory for Leninism," ibid., May 7, 1965, pp. 7–10.

[55]Ibid., and "Soviet-US Plot to Establish an International Gendarmerie," ibid., April 23, 1965, pp. 27–28.

[56]"The People of Vietnam Will Win," ibid., April 23, 1965, pp. 17–18.

military manpower was inadequate and the lines of communication too long even to deal with the situation in South Vietnam, the US military commitment certainly was too small to be a threat to China.

April also was the beginning of Mao's attempt to establish People's War as the proper way for both North Vietnam and China to deal with the United States. In a major theoretical piece early in the month, Li Zuoping, a strong supporter of Mao and Defense Minister Lin Biao (Li, as commander of the Navy, was destined to be purged with Lin Biao in 1971), developed a lengthy treatise on People's War. Li criticized those who had failed to follow Mao's military line in the 1930s and then discussed the war with Japan as an analogy to the present situation. That is, according to Mao, a powerful modern force attacked a relatively weak and backward nation and was defeated by People's War. Finally, Li discussed the Chinese civil war in which, according to the communists, guerrilla forces finally gained victory over the US-supported forces of Chiang Kai-shek. The main source of supply, allegedly, was captured equipment and Li pointed out that "our Army's main sources of manpower and material were at the front."[57]

Maoist articles, which argued that Vietnam could defeat the enemy on its own, could hardly have been popular in Hanoi. Maoists, in essence, were not just telling the North Vietnamese to "bite the bullet," they were telling them to steal it first. In April, one Maoist piece made it sound as if all the people in both North and South Vietnam had risen to strike a United States tottering on the brink of defeat. "For more than a decade...," it said, "the people of South Vietnam have, with their bare hands expanded their own strength in the struggle, built up a powerful people's armed force, destroyed over four-fifths of the 'strategic hamlets' and liberated three-fourths of South Vietnam which holds two-thirds of the population.... Everywhere people hate the US and fight."[58]

In a battle of anniversaries, the Liu-Deng group's celebration of Soviet victory in World War II was matched by a simultaneous Maoist tribute on the anniversary of Dien Bien Phu. A *People's Daily* article on May 7, commemorating the final assault on the French stronghold, explained why the North Vietnamese would win without help.

---

[57] "Strategically Pitting One Against Ten, Tactically Pitting Ten Against One," ibid., April 9, 1965, pp. 12–17. Of course this overlooks the arms and supplies that the Soviets took from the million-man Japanese Army that surrendered in Manchuria. The Soviets turned these supplies over to the Chinese communists.

[58] "The People of Vietnam Will Win," ibid., April 23, 1965, pp. 17–18.

The basic reason for this is that they are fighting a revolutionary war against aggressors, a war waged by the whole people. It is a cause of the people themselves.... This people's war, in which everyone is a soldier, every household a bulwark and every village a battlefield, is like a vast sea that overwhelms and drowns the enemy. Taking the situation as a whole, the United States, because it is engaged in aggression everywhere in the world, has its armed forces dispersed, a long battlefront and is very much limited in its military power. In Vietnam, even if the United States does throw a large amount of armed forces and military equipment into South Vietnam, it will have to confront 14 million South Vietnamese people who are full of hatred for the common enemy.[59]

When taken in context of the ongoing debate, this quote means that (1) the threat has not yet materialized even against North Vietnam and (2) if it does, the Vietnamese can defeat the threat by relying on People's War. The phrase "even if the United States does throw a large amount of armed forces and military equipment into South Vietnam," means "because they haven't yet." In other words, the United States, according to this line of reasoning, had a long way to go before it can deploy sufficient force to threaten China. The serious nature of the debate is highlighted by the fact that Luo Ruiqing delivered his speech arguing precisely the opposite position on the same day the editorial quoted above appeared in *People's Daily.*

The Maoist position, however, was soon undermined by changes on the battlefield and the buildup of US military strength—bringing China one step closer to the Great Proletarian Cultural Revolution.

The Soviets Support a Major War

With the Americans moving toward a major ground war in Vietnam, the Soviets, who had an open-ended commitment of their own, sought to keep up with changing battlefield requirements. It was soon clear that the April 17, 1965 arms agreement negotiated by the Le Duan-Vo Nguyen Giap delegation would be insufficient. As a result, Hanoi's chief aid negotiator, Le Than Nghi, flew to Moscow in June for detailed and lengthy talks about

---

[59] "Unrivaled Power of the People's Revolutionary War," ibid., May 14, 1965, pp. 23–24.

a new and more extensive program of support. A joint communique was soon issued which hinted at the magnitude of Soviet supplies destined for Asia. "These agreements envisage additional assistance," said the two nations, "over and above the assistance being rendered to the Democratic Republic of Vietnam by the Soviet Union on the basis of agreements signed earlier."[60]

The new Kremlin commitment was formalized on July 12, 1965, sixteen days before President Johnson approved an increase in US troop strength to 175,000 by the end of the year—while the war was still going well for the Viet Cong. Still, this agreement was in response to the American build-up. Ironically, even though the US public was not fully aware of US intentions, the North Vietnamese and Soviet intelligence services almost certainly knew that a major escalation in US strength was coming soon. They could see 60,000 American soldiers already deployed, restrictions lifted on the use of the troops in combat, and a large developing logistic infrastructure. Much of this information was available from the open press. And the communists had plenty of spies to fill in the gaps and watch American logisticians as they inspected Qui Nhon, Nha Trang, and Cam Rahn Bay to determine real estate requirements for depot and support command areas.

Soviet propaganda pressure on China built to a crescendo as evidence of the forthcoming US deployment became stronger. An editorial in *Pravda,* highlighting the US ground forces already present in Vietnam, warned that "war like a fire can spread further and can create a threat for other people"—a clear reference to China. This was followed by another obvious jab at the Chinese: "In the hour of danger there cannot be even one [socialist country] that does not participate."[61] At the same time, the Soviets elicited statements from numerous communist parties around the world calling for unity despite differences. A lengthy article on the "most pressing requirement of the antiimperialist struggle" in late June argued that the socialist camp must "consider disagreement in the context of the most important mission.... Even when there is serious disagreement it is necessary to achieve unity." Imperialists exploited the divisions within the communist world, said the Russian author, pointing out that the Soviet Union had

[60]L. V. Kotov and R.S. Yegorov, eds., *Militant Solidarity, Fraternal Assistance* (Moscow: 1970), pp. 77–78. (Hereafter referred to as Kotov); "Priem A.N. Kosyginym" (Reception by A.N. Kosygin), *Pravda,* July 9, 1965, p. 1.

[61]"Solidarnost' s geroicheskim V'etnamom" (Solidarity With Heroic Vietnam), ibid., June 11, 1965, p. 1.

refrained from open polemics against China since Khrushchev's fall.[62] The impact of Moscow's campaign can be seen in China from the almost slavish repetition of Soviet propaganda by the Liu-Deng group (which argued that socialist countries should distinguish between friend and foe and unite against "the most vicious enemy...US imperialism," and that the "most pressing task," like the Soviet "most pressing requirement," was to unite over Vietnam).[63]

A major Soviet media blitz followed in July with lengthy speeches by Brezhnev, Kosygin, and other top leaders. Brezhnev spoke in Leningrad emphasizing that the national liberation movement depended on cohesion in the socialist camp. He acknowledged that differences "do, unfortunately exist," and that the United States exploited those differences. He called for an end to mutual recriminations and encouraged joint practical action over Vietnam.[64] Clearly, the Kremlin was looking for victory by the Liu-Deng faction in China.[65]

Liu Shaoqi and Deng Xiaoping Near Victory

Mounting evidence of the coming American troop deployments steadily eroded Mao's position. In consequence, the Communist party chairman and his supporters talked less and less about American weakness and increasingly shifted their attention to the doctrine of People's War.

Given the mounting evidence of a forthcoming large American ground force, perhaps the question at this point in the chain of events is Why did the pro-Soviet group fail to achieve victory?

The answer, most likely, is that the Kremlin was too heavy handed. Soviet conditions for the reestablishment of a Sino-Soviet alliance included Soviet dominance, a dominance that was, it seems, absolutely unacceptable

---

[62] "Yedinstvo deistvii—povelitel'noe trebovanie antiimperialistiche-skoy borby," (Unity of Action—The Most Pressing Requirement of the Antiimperialist Struggle), ibid., June 20, 1965, pp. 3–5.

[63] "People of the World, Act and Force US Aggressors Out of Vietnam!" *Peking Review,* April 23, 1965, pp. 14–17.

[64] "Hero City Celebrations: I—Brezhnev in Leningrad," *Current Digest,* August 4, 1965, pp. 12–16.

[65] "Hero City Celebrations: II—Kosygin in Volgograd," ibid., pp. 17–21; "Suslov, Kosygin and Mikoyan at Baltic Celebrations," ibid., August 11, 1965, pp. 4–13; "Rech' Tovarishcha L.I. Brezhneva na devyatom kongresse kommunisticheskoy partii Romanii" (Speech by Comrade L.I. Brezhnev at the Ninth Congress of the Rumanian Communist Party), *Pravda,* July 21, 1965, p. 11.

to those uncommitted Chinese politicians who held the balance of power in the internal struggle. Evidently, Khrushchev's replacements felt they had China in such a squeeze that no compromise was necessary. This simply did not give the pro-Soviet group an acceptable position with which to overcome Mao's tenacious opposition.

As US strength hit the 60,000 mark in early June 1965, Mao's group still attempted to denigrate the threat, noting that "the tens of thousands of US troops who are not an impressive number in any case... will drown in the vast ocean of the South Vietnamese people's war."[66] The implications of the McNamara trip to Saigon in July undercut this position, however, and the Liu-Deng group began raising the specter of a Korean type war—an appeal that generated considerable emotion among the Chinese.[67] *People's Daily,* on July 22, 1965, responded to McNamara's trip to Saigon and press reports about the forthcoming decision to raise troop strength by noting that the US press talked about a "willingness to fight a Korean type war in Vietnam." In preparation, said the article, wartime measures "like calling up the reserves are being considered.... The US constructs bases...may call up the reserves...[and] will increase [its troop strength in Vietnam] to 200,000 by year's end."[68] After noting US violations of China's airspace, the article alleged that "when Johnson talked about increased response in the air he meant extending raids north even to China.... Now when he talks about increasing response on the ground, does he not mean to say that the 'ground war' will be expanded without limit? People can still remember clearly how the US war of aggression in Korea was expanded."[69]

Forced to respond, Mao retorted that China hoped the United States would commit large forces, for that would make the American defeat more decisive. Foreign Minister Chen Yi articulated this position in an interview in Algeria, saying "I hope the US sends in two million troops" because a "bigger intervention" means "bigger defeat" in a Chinese People's War.[70] Luo Ruiqing, responding in turn, perverted this argument for the Liu-Deng faction. "We invite them to come on in large numbers," he said in seeming agreement. But then he added that the United States would be defeated

---

[66]"On the War Situation in South Vietnam," *Peking Review,* June 11, 1965, pp. 21–22.

[67]Observer, "A Dramatic Change," ibid., June 4, 1965, pp. 16–17; "China Will Support Vietnamese People Till Final Victory," ibid., June 25, 1965, p. 13.

[68]Observer, "Accelerated Escalation Means Accelerated Defeat," ibid., July 30, 1965, pp. 10–11.

[69]Ibid.

[70]Earl W. Foell, "Peking line stiffens," *Christian Science Monitor,* June 29, 1965, p. 1.

then, not by People's War, but because of the unity of the socialist camp. Lo looked forward to a large war, "for we would then have more opportunities to fight in unity with the revolutionary forces of the world."[71]

Although losing the debate on the character of the American threat, Mao continued to hammer away on the unacceptable Soviet conditions for rapprochement. In addition to denouncing Khrushchev revisionism, Mao's forces raised a fundamental issue broader than foreign policy orientation.[72] What path should China take to modernization? Mao answered "self-reliance," economic and political development independent of the Soviet Union. In an article in mid-June, the Mao faction presented the Great Leap Forward in 1958 as "self-reliance in socialist construction." This resulted in "greater, quicker, better, more economical results" that made "full use of available resources." China was able to gain funds through "internal accumulation...[without] *enslaving foreign loans.*" (Emphasis added.) According to Maoists, foreign aid might be welcomed under some circumstances, but it was necessary to "discern its true nature before accepting it."[73] In other articles that quickly followed, Mao's supporters attributed the obvious economic failures of the Great Leap Forward to a combination of natural calamities, "certain shortcomings and errors [which] cropped up in our own work" and "revisionism" during the period 1959–1961.[74] The accusation of "shortcomings" in the period 1959–1961 refers to the efforts of Liu Shaoqi and Deng Xiaoping to curtail the excesses of the Great Leap Forward while simultaneously extending their control of the party and state organizations.[75] "Revisionism" refers to the Soviet withdrawal of aid that included Soviet factory managers in China removing or destroying vital blueprints as they departed.

Faced with the prospect of open personal attacks by Mao, Liu and Deng

---

[71] "China Stands Ready to Smash US War Schemes," *Peking Review,* August 6, 1965, p. 5.

[72] "Carry the Struggle Against Khrushchev Revisionism Through to the End," ibid., June 18, 1965, pp. 5–10; "New CPSU Leadership Intensifies Sabotaging of Japanese CP and Democratic Forces," ibid., July 16, 1965, pp. 12–15; "US-USSR Get Together," ibid., July 30, 1965, p. 19.

[73] Tseng Yun, "How China Carries Out the Policy of Self-Reliance," ibid., June 18, 1965, pp. 12–15.

[74] Yang Pei-hsin, "China's Stable Monetary System," ibid., June 25, 1965, pp. 15–19; Chin Yu-kun, "Self-Reliance in Making Precision Machine Tools," ibid., July 30, 1965, pp. 15–17.

[75] Thornton, *China,* pp. 253–255. This discussion is a good picture of how the Liu-Deng group came to be called "pro-Soviet" and highlights also why we cannot take the title too literally. Pro-Soviet does not mean Liu and Deng had a congenital predilection to support the Soviet Union. Rather, it simply means that Liu and Deng did not favor giving up Soviet assistance that was already in place. It does not mean that they would not turn on the Soviets down the road, given the opportunity.

responded by signaling Moscow that they needed some sort of compromise on the conditions for rapprochement. Now the pro-Soviet group attacked the Soviet Union for its refusal to compromise.

In late May, Peng Chen made a major speech in Indonesia, presenting a strong argument on the need for united action. He concluded, however, by attacking Brezhnev and Kosygin for adhering to Khrushchev's conditions for unity against the United States. "We are convinced," said Peng, that "dark clouds will ultimately be dispersed...[and] we still place some hope in the leadership of the Soviet Union." But, said Peng, referring to Zhou's conversations with Kosygin in Moscow, despite the victory signaled by Khrushchev's ouster, Khrushchev's successors "to our delegation's face...told us their attitude was the same." As a result, Peng rejected Soviet terms for "unity with the CPSU."[76] While Peng supported unity, the obstacle to that unity was Soviet insistence on having the leading role in the Sino-Soviet relationship. In practical terms, Zhou Enlai was the power broker in the struggle between Mao and the Liu-Deng group. As long as Soviet terms remained unacceptable to Zhou, there could be no rapprochement.

Deng Xiaoping reiterated this position in July with a speech greeting the Ninth Congress of the Rumanian Communist Party. He called for a broad united front based on the principles of Marxism, Leninism, and equality.[77] Some months later, Liu Shaoqi would make the argument clearly himself. Pointing out that China was still a backward country and that "several decades of hard work are still required to make our country really strong.... We must ally ourselves on an equal footing with those among the peoples who treat us on the basis of equality and unite with all countries that can be united in the common struggle."[78] Liu, Deng, and Peng Chen were now adding a qualification to their calls for socialist unity—bilateral equality. The Soviet demand for a patron-client relationship was unacceptable. These public statements were a clear signal to the Soviet leadership that some sort of Soviet compromise was necessary for improved Sino-Soviet relations, no matter who in China had the upper hand in the ongoing factional strife.

It is only possible to speculate on the reasons for continued Soviet in-

---

[76] "Speech at the Aliarcham Academy of Social Sciences in Indonesia," ibid., June 11, 1965, pp. 10–20.

[77] "Teng Hsiao-ping Greets Ninth Congress of Rumanian CP," ibid., July 30, 1965, pp. 8–10.

[78] "Chairman Liu on Dr. Sun Yat-sen," ibid., November 5, 1965, pp. 4–5.

transigence. Perhaps the Kremlin thought the coming US escalation would lead to Mao's banishment from the Chinese political scene—as Khrushchev himself had been. Certainly President Johnson's decision to fight the war without calling up reserves caused disappointment in Moscow, for this took a bit of the edge off the American threat. Even so, the Russians undoubtedly still hoped to "sucker" the Americans into a major ground war in Asia, to force Mao out of the Chinese political scene, and to reestablish Sino-Soviet relations on the Kremlin's terms—perhaps a step up (but a small one, at that) from the puppet regimes in eastern Europe. Mao's position clearly was weakened. Reportedly, he was briefly placed under house arrest in 1965 by Liu and Deng.[79] In 1965, Soviet analysts had every reason to believe that Mao's demise was only a matter of time. Unfortunately for the Soviets, Mao came to the same conclusion. And he preferred to plunge China into a virtual civil war rather than lose. A careful look at some seemingly innocuous articles written in mid and late 1965 reveals the first steps toward the Great Proletarian Cultural Revolution.

---

[79]See Wedeman, p. 172, note 86.

7

Acceleration
of US Buildup

Major Events

- *August 1965*—3rd Marine Division defeats Viet Cong regiment in first major American ground combat of Vietnam War.
- *Early November 1965*—McNamara recommends that United States proceed with Phase II deployment of an additional 112,430 soldiers in early 1966. President approves recommendation.
- *November 1965*—US Army's 1st Cavalry Division wins bloody victory in Ia Drang valley.
- *November 20, 1965*—US intelligence reports that enemy strength in South Vietnam rose from 48,550 in July to 63,550 in November. North Vietnamese regiments increased from one to eight.
- *November 23, 1965*—McNamara cables Westmoreland and asks, "Will it not be necessary to add one or two divisions.... Will even more forces be required in 1966...?"
- *November 23, 1966*—Westmoreland cables CINCPAC and says that more forces would be needed to counter the enemy increase and that ultimately even more forces would be needed to attain Phase II objectives.
- *November 28–30, 1966*—McNamara visits Saigon. Returns to Washington with a Westmoreland request for an additional 41,500 US soldiers to be added to Phase II forces.
- *1971*—*New York Times* publishes its version of *Pentagon Papers* and describes the November 28–30 request for an additonal 41,500 soldiers as a sudden Westmoreland request for an additional 154,000 more men.

- *December 1965*—Administration publicly states it is considering Vietnam force levels of 350,000–400,000.
- *December 10, 1965*—McNamara memorandum for the president says approximately 400,000 soldiers would be required by the end of 1966 and perhaps 200,000 more later.
- *December 13, 1965*—McNamara draft presidential memorandum circulated for staff. Projects troop strength for the end of 1966 to be 367,800.
- *December 16, 1965*—CINCPAC recommends additional helicopter and engineer units plus four tank battalions making the figure 443,000 soldiers.
- *January 1966*—JCS agrees with 443,000 goal, but says it can be achieved by the end of 1966 only if there is a reserve callup.
- February 9, 1966—At Pentagon planning conference, McNamara tells JCS that the 443,000-man goal would be attained without a reserve callup.
- *Late February 1966*—JCS submits deployment schedule to McNamara which does not attain the 443,000-man level until the end of 1967.
- *March 1966*—United States decides to permit American scholars to visit China.
- *March 1966*—Congressional hearings on Chinese-US relations.
- *March 10, 1966*—McNamara rejects JCS proposal and orders more study and review. Says that the JCS should make all possible efforts to meet the 443,000 goal without a reserve callup.
- *April 4, 1966*—JCS submits new proposal projecting troop strength by the end of 1966 as 376,350 and 438,207 by the end of 1967.
- *April 11, 1966*—McNamara demands explanation from JCS for failure to achieve 443,000-man goal but approves the JCS plan, which subsequently is adjusted to a 384,000-man target for the end of 1966.
- *April 12,1966*—McNamara demands that the JCS continue to work to find ways to accelerate the deployments and achieve a troop strength in Vietnam greater than 384,000 by the end of 1966.
- *June 1966*—Vice-president Humphrey in graduation address at West Point suggests that the US attitude toward China is changing.

American ground forces arrived in strength in Vietnam during the second half of 1965. Even as these 175,000 soldiers entered combat, however, the July 12 Soviet-North Vietnamese arms agreement was improving the overall military capability of the North Vietnamese. This meant to US planners that the American military commitment was insufficient to achieve victory according to the original timetable. The

United States was faced with a paradox. It was enjoying tactical success beyond original expectations while the strategic situation was worsening. Since the deployments had gone well and initial battlefield victories were enjoying some fanfare in the press, the administration did not seriously consider responding to the new circumstances in any other way than increasing the troop strength above the level already projected for deployment by mid-1966. From November 1965 through August 1966, the United States continued to send as many soldiers as fast as possible to Vietnam. The only limitations were logistical. In truth, the military establishment could not deploy forces as quickly as the administration desired and McNamara put constant pressure on the Joint Chiefs of Staff to speed up the process.

America Goes to War

As US forces arrived in Vietnam, the JCS worked out guidelines for the conduct of the war. The plan would be

> to intensify military pressure on the DRV by air or naval power; to destroy significant DRV military targets, including the base of supplies; to interdict supporting LOCs in the DRV; to interdict the infiltration and supply routes into the RVN; to improve the combat capabilities of the RVNAF; to build and protect bases; to reduce enemy reinforcements; to defeat the Viet Cong...; and to maintain adequate forces in the Western Pacific and elsewhere in readiness to deter and to deal with CHICOM [Chinese Communist] aggression. By aggressive and sustained exploitation of superior military force, the United States/Government of Vietnam would seize and hold the initiative in both the DRV and RVN.... [1]

American ground forces were to fight inside the boundaries of South Vietnam while the US government remained alert to the possibility of confrontation with China (indeed they were preoccupied by it). US forces were

[1] *Pentagon Papers,* Book 5, "US Ground Strategy and Force Deployments, 1965–1967, Phase II," p. 12. The meaning of the various acronyms is as follows: DRV=Democratic Republic of Vietnam, LOC=Lines of Communication, RVN=Republic of Vietnam, RVNAF=Republic of Vietnam Armed Forces, and CHICOM=Chinese Communist.

committed initially at points of maximum peril.[2] In August the 3d Marine Division engaged a Viet Cong regiment in the first major American combat of the war. In November, the army's First Cavalry Division defeated a large VC/North Vietnamese Army force in the bloody battle of the Ia Drang Valley.[3] America was at war.

The early deployments and battles achieved the primary goal of Phase I, which was to stop losing, and in early November Secretary McNamara recommended to the president that the United States proceed with Phase II. Although the initial recommendation in July had been for an additional 100,000 soldiers, this had been an approximate number only. Given time for detailed calculations, the actual number recommended by McNamara in November was 112,430.[4] Even this recommendation was overtaken by events, however, as US intelligence began to detect the results of the massive Soviet logistic effort. More soldiers than already approved for Phase II would be required to achieve Phase II's goal, "start winning."[5]

Until this point, the Johnson administration had been proceeding under the assumption that it would introduce a total force of about 300,000 by the end of 1966, and that this could be done by activating new units and expanding the draft. The administration was hoping to avoid other alternatives that were politically unpopular (reserve callup) or strategically unwise (draw-down of US forces elsewhere in the world). Now the problem of how to provide a larger force loomed and, partly because of the US force structure, there was no easy solution.

The Administration Wrestles with the Problem

United States national intelligence agencies concluded in November 1965 that North Vietnam's military capabilities were increasing at an alarming rate, provoking a prolonged discussion within the administration.[6] The United States had the luxury of discussing the issue at length since forces scheduled to move to Vietnam through the early part of 1966 already overtaxed existing logistic facilities. Quite simply, General Westmoreland

---

[2]Ibid., p. 14.

[3]Sharp and Westmoreland, *Report*, Section II, pp. 98–99.

[4]*Pentagon Papers*, Book 5, "Phase II," pp. 15–18.

[5]Ibid., p. 16; Sharp and Westmoreland, *Report*, Section II, p. 100. This is Westmoreland's explanation of the situation in late 1965.

[6]*Pentagon Papers*, Book 5, "Phase II," P. 18. See also *Secret History*, p. 465.

could not receive troops at a more rapid rate.[7] Although it was clear from the outset that the administration's response to the rapidly developing North Vietnamese power would be to add US ground forces, the size of the increase needed to be worked out. It would be spring 1966 before a specific decision on the number of soldiers had to be made.

There was no "gradual escalation." There was no civilian-military split within the administration over what to do about improved North Vietnamese strength.[8] These popular myths come from the mistaken belief that the political leadership wanted to win with as a small a commitment as possible while the military, knowing that a much larger force ultimately would be required, attempted to build the force through incremental, ever-increasing troop requests. The administration, according to this commonly held belief, reluctantly granted the initial requests. McNamara at every stage "carefully pruned the military's requests," says one author, in order to fight a cost-effective war and leave resources for the Great Society.[9] Similarly, others termed US strategy "incrementalism," a "strategy of progressive pressure and the progressive failure of the strategy."[10] Still another view is that this was the result of a lack of clear guidance for the military, leaving military leaders to work out military plans for themselves and press for approval through a series of troop requests.[11]

The origin of these interpretations can be traced to the editors of the *New York Times* version of the *Pentagon Papers*. The editors, having discussed the Phase I troop deployments, wrote that General Westmoreland "suddenly found it necessary to request a vast increase in troops for the Phase II part of his plan. The General said he would need 154,000 more men."[12] This explanation badly distorts the actual record. In addition, the *Pentagon Papers* analyst responsible for this discussion in the actual Pentagon study, in commenting on administration discussions over the increase of Phase II forces, said that "from the outset of the American buildup some military

[7]*Pentagon Papers,* Book 5, "Phase II," p. 22.

[8]The term "military" is fairly vague, since it could include everyone in the service from the rifleman in first squad to the chairman of the Joint Chiefs of Staff. In this work the "military" means the collective group that includes General Westmoreland, Admiral Sharp and the Joint Chiefs of Staff. These officers did not always agree with each other, but when talking about US leadership during this period, it is useful to group them as distinct from the political appointees in the Departments of State and Defense, the National Security Council and, of course, the president.

[9]Komer, p. 14.

[10]Gelb and Betts, p. 132.

[11]Schandler, p. 35.

[12]*Secret History,* pp. 465–466.

men felt that winning a meaningful victory in Vietnam would require something on the order of one million men. Knowing this would be unacceptable politically, it may have seemed a better bargaining strategy to ask for increased deployments incrementally."[13] This was the analyst's supposition and is not supported by the evidence in his own section.

There was no "sudden" troop request. There was never any question that there would be an increase in the size of the Phase II force once the intelligence on the increase in enemy strength became available to the Johnson administration. In fact, McNamara prodded Westmoreland to ask for more troops because US policy remained an open-ended commitment to achieve military victory in South Vietnam before the 1968 elections. The ultimate increase in the size of the Phase II force requested by Westmoreland was 41,500. This was the only "request" from the military for a troop increase while US policy remained an open-ended commitment.

There was, however, a civilian-military split that began to develop during the discussions over how the United States should respond to the enemy escalation, although it was not over the size of the response. It was given that the United States would respond. This left two issues. First, what would be the size of the increase of Phase II forces? This issue did not generate significant civilian-military disagreement, except as it related to the second issue. Second, how would the buildup be achieved? This issue did cause a significant civilian-military split, as the military favored a partial mobilization while the civilians in the administration did not. The civilian position on the size of the force, as represented by McNamara, was that the administration desired to have 443,000 soldiers in Vietnam by the end of 1966. The military did not disagree with the desirability of this size force, but believed that it could not be achieved until mid-1967 without mobilization. Thus, the military's projection for end-of-1966 troop strength was 384,000.

The Evidence

The external manifestation of the Soviet/North Vietnamese arms agreement, concluded in July 1965, was a significant increase in enemy

---

[13]*Pentagon Papers*, Book 5, "Phase II," pp. 40–41. The analyst also offered the explanation that maybe nobody really foresaw what the troop requirements would be. A third explanation was a combination of the two.

infiltration from North to South Vietnam with a concurrent improvement in the quality of enemy weapons. United States leaders, having seen American forces enjoy tactical success, were faced with the paradox that enemy combat troop strength in the south had, nevertheless, risen from 48,550 in July to 63,550 in November. The number of North Vietnamese regiments had increased from one to eight.[14] This put the early American victories in the field in an entirely different light, although it did not affect American resolve. There was no question in the mind of either McNamara or Westmoreland that the United States would counter the North Vietnamese buildup.

US intelligence agencies informed high-level officials of the increased North Vietnamese troop strength about November 20, 1965.[15] On November 23, McNamara reacted by postponing his return from a NATO meeting in Paris in order to visit Saigon November 28–30. His November 23 cable to Saigon reveals that the purpose of his trip was to discuss an increase in Phase II troop requirements. "Will it not be necessary to add one or two divisions to the 28 battalions proposed in order to provide forces in the Delta?" asked the defense secretary. "Will even more forces be required in 1966 if the number of PAVN [People's Army of Vietnam] regiments continues to increase?"[16] Earlier in the month McNamara already had recommended, and the president had approved, going ahead with the 112,430-man Phase II deployment in early 1966. Weeks later, the "one or two divisions" and "even more forces" in the cable were intended to be tacked on to the 112,430-man decision.

General Westmoreland analyzed the implications of the North Vietnamese buildup in a cable to CINCPAC on November 23. He noted that US/enemy force ratios would become progressively less favorable over time.[17] Westmoreland estimated the number of units required to offset the enemy's current forces but cautioned that additional units would be required to match further North Vietnamese deployments in the South. Accomplishment of Phase II objectives "will ultimately require much larger deployments."[18] Moreover, he outlined a logistic problem that would play a role in the military-civilian split over mobilization.

[14]*Secret History,* p. 465.

[15]*Pentagon Papers,* Book 5, "Phase II," p. 16. The old Phase II figures were still being used as of November 20.

[16]Ibid., p. 24.

[17]Ibid., p. 21.

[18]Ibid., p. 22.

One of the most pressing needs is to improve the logistic situation in RVN. Phase I logistic units are stretched out through CY (Calendar Year) 66 and into CY 67. It was determined at the Honolulu Conference in September that the preferred schedule for deployment of major Phase II combat units could not be met because the essential logistics units would not be available in the timeframe required. Nevertheless, we accepted marginal logistic support in order to deploy combat units as rapidly as possible. Therefore, the logistics system in SVN cannot accept the even greater burden represented by the required additional combat forces without significant augmentation early in CY 66. We appreciate the fact that this may require extraordinary measures. It has been determined that the ports can accommodate the force buildup if the critical through-put capability can be provided in the form of added logistic units and related facilities. MACV (Military Assistance Command, Vietnam) is prepared to specify the quantity, type and time of phasing of logistics units required to support the buildup.[19]

While General Westmoreland believed that additional Phase II forces would be necessary, he was acutely aware of the American inability to support larger numbers of troops in the field. For a while, at least, without improved logistics, America could only add soldiers to its troop-strength levels—not to the battle in the jungles.

Nevertheless, addressing the problem of increased North Vietnamese strength, Westmoreland concluded that he needed a minimum of 48,000 soldiers above Phase II forces that were already programed. Moreover, his "preferred" increase was for 64,500 troops, a figure that included a total of 23,000 South Korean soldiers. This meant that his "preferred request" was for an additional 41,500 US soldiers.[20]

But the *New York Times* version of the *Pentagon Papers* says that there were incremental military requests from 175,000 to 275,000 to 443,000. "Suddenly," meaning, apparently, out of the blue and totally unexpected, Westmoreland asked for "a *vast increase...* [of] 154,000 more men." But Westmoreland's "preferred request" was 41,500 and he made it knowing

[19]Ibid., pp. 40–41.
[20]Ibid., p. 23.

that the secretary of defense's response to the North Vietnamese buildup had been to cable Westmoreland and ask "Will it not be necessary to add one or two divisions...?" It is obvious that 41,500 does not equal 154,000. Did the editors from the *New York Times* make it up? The answer is no, but almost.

Recall that we are discussing the end of 1965 when Phase I deployment of 175,000 soldiers was supposed to be complete. In fact, as it turned out, end-of-year strength was approximately 180,000. At that time, based on McNamara's early November recommendation to the president, an additional 112,430 soldiers were to begin Phase II deployments. But they were not already in Vietnam, just already committed to go. If we add 41,500 to 112,430 we get 153,930, or approximately 154,000, which is what the editors did. But there was nothing sudden about 112,430 of the 154,000. Moreover, 154,000 may be considered a *vast increase* when compared to 175,000 already in country, but 41,500 is hardly vast when compared to the nearly 300,000 that the administration had already committed before pressuring Westmoreland to recommend "one or two more divisions." Moreover, there were no "incremental" military requests from 175,000 to 275,000 to 443,000. There was *one* initial recommendation from Mc-Namara to the president that the United States deploy 175,000 by the end of 1965 and an additional 100,000 in early 1966; 175,000 plus 100,000 equals 275,000. Furthermore, McNamara's cable to Westmoreland of November 23 talked not only about the immediate need to increase Phase II forces, which resulted in Westmoreland's 41,500-man request, but of even more forces after that. After considering the issue of more forces, McNamara ultimately would conclude that he wanted 443,000 soldiers in Vietnam by the end of 1966. (About which, more later.) The military would argue that, given logistic constraints as described above by Westmoreland, the force could only reach 384,000 by the end of 1966.

The progress of the internal administration discussions further confirms that all major actors, military and civilian, knew from the outset that a much larger force would be required. There was no incremental strategy and no misunderstanding. The point is important to this discussion because it establishes that the United States policy was to increase the size of its force in Vietnam as fast as possible. It was not an accident provoked by military leaders trying to trick the administration into a larger force and it was not an attempt by the administration to up the ante gradually. It was a fundamental US decision to build up a large Army in Vietnam rapidly. When the Soviets, Chinese, and North Vietnamese interpreted American actions to mean precisely that, they were correct.

When McNamara arrived in Saigon on November 28, 1965, it already had been decided that the United States would raise troop levels as high as required. In retrospect, it is clear that what the administration needed from the military was a professional estimate of what the increase should be. Indeed, the secretary attempted to push the military into a more rapid buildup than the military had recommended. The fact that the decision had been made before McNamara journeyed to Saigon is reflected in the public position established by the administration. In contrast to much of the optimistic reporting accompanying the initial deployments and battles of Phase I forces, the administration on November 27, 1965, made information available to the press that resulted in the question being asked, "Will the North Vietnamese try to match us?"[21] The answer to the question, of course, was yes, as the administration already knew. And it soon became public knowledge.

Secretary McNamara, as he departed Saigon on November 30, announced publicly that the United States would supply as many troops as necessary.[22] This was the Johnson administration's way of telling the American public that more troops than originally planned were needed because of changed circumstances. The following day an article appeared detailing increased North Vietnamese strength and cited McNamara's conclusion that there was a "clear decision by Hanoi to escalate the level of conflict." In consequence, said the article, McNamara felt the United States had no choice but "to do something."[23] By December 10, 1965, the administration had admitted publicly that force levels of 350,000 to 400,000 US soldiers were being considered—preparing the public for decisions already made.[24]

Truly, the Johnson administration had a kind of double-mindedness on the subject of Vietnam—absolutely decisive behind closed doors, but eager, in public, to appear to be reacting to events outside their control. Perhaps the closest the administration came to having second thoughts about war, at least early on, was in a memorandum for the president that McNamara prepared upon his November 30 departure from Saigon, in which he noted in passing the option of seeking some sort of compromise solution. But McNamara recommended an intensification of the bombing campaign and a massive buildup beyond that already planned—400,000

[21]Robert R. Brunn, "Viet build-up watched," *Christian Science Monitor,* November 27, 1965, p. 1.

[22]Takashi Oka, "US may stiffen Viet position," ibid., December 1, 1965, p. 13.

[23]"The news briefly," ibid., November 30, 1965, p. 2.

[24]Godfrey Sperling, "Johnson may seek new Viet mandate," ibid., December 10, 1965, p. 1.

soldiers in Vietnam by the end of 1966. He did so while admitting that these deployments "will not guarantee success: US killed-in-action can be expected to reach 1,000 a month, and the odds are even that we will be faced in early 1967 with a no-decision at an even higher level." [25]

The military problem had been outlined by General Westmoreland in his discussion of logistics. Military support units would have to be added before new combat forces could be sent into the field. As a result, the payoff for an increase in troop strength would not be an immediate increase in the size of the force fighting in the jungle. This fact provoked impatience from an administration which was seeking indications of success and trying to minimize the impact of the war at home. [26] Furthermore, the JCS faced a problem in supplying the needed support troops. The US Army is structured with many key logistic forces in its reserves. If the administration would not call up the reserves, the needed support forces would have to come from activation of new units primarily staffed by the draft. Many of the needed skills required extensive training and the units took some time to develop cohesion and teamwork. Some relief could be achieved by drawing down forces elsewhere, but this was strategically risky. The administration proved willing to take the risk but still could not provide the numbers and types of units available in the reserves. [27]

After McNamara departed Saigon, the troop strength requirements that Westmoreland and McNamara had worked out were sent to CINCPAC for review. [28] McNamara wrote a December 10 memorandum advising the president that something on the order of 400,000 soldiers would be required by the end of 1966 and perhaps an additional 200,000 later. On December 13, the defense secretary sent out a draft memorandum for the president for staffing in which he projected troop strength reaching 367,800 by the end of the following year. [29] However, CINCPAC's review was forwarded to Assistant Secretary of Defense Alain Enthoven on December 16 and CINCPAC recommended an even higher figure—443,000 by the end of 1966. This number did not increase the number of maneuver battalions that resulted from the Westmoreland-McNamara talks in November, but did in-

[25] *Secret History,* pp. 488–489; *Pentagon Papers,* Book 5, "Phase II," p. 25.

[26] Ibid., p. 41. This is the analyst's opinion that the president had an interest in keeping the domestic effects of the war as small as possible.

[27] Ibid., p. 27. This points out the administration's preference for drawdown over reserve callup. See Heiser, *Logistic Support,* pp. 8–16 for an excellent exposition on the logistic problem.

[28] Gravel, Vol. IV, p. 309.

[29] Ibid.

crease combat support forces like helicopter and engineer units.[30]

McNamara then passed on the CINCPAC recommendations to the JCS so that the services could develop estimates of their ability to satisfy the requirements.[31] However, the JCS took the position that the only way to deploy the 443,000 troops to Vietnam by the end of 1966 was by calling up the reserves. The JCS worked out deployment schedules based on three different sets of assumptions and submitted them to McNamara as a request for planning guidance. The 443,000 figure for the end of 1966 was based on (1) the draft, (2) new unit activations, (3) draw down from other areas and (4) a reserve callup (case 1). A lower figure for the end of 1966 was based on (1) the draft, (2) new unit activations and (3) draw down from other areas (case 2). The third and lowest figure was based only on achieving the buildup through (1) the draft and (2) new unit activations (case 3). At a February 9, 1966, meeting McNamara responded that the planning should proceed under the assumption that US combat forces in Vietnam would reach 443,000 by the end of 1966 and that reserves would *not* be called up.[32]

In response, the Joint Chiefs submitted a recommended deployment schedule that would reach the levels required by the secretary, but not until the end of 1967.[33] McNamara rejected this proposal on March 10 and directed "more study and review." In the meantime, "you should plan to deploy forces to SVN in accordance with...Case 1.... All necessary actions are to be taken to meet these deployment dates without callup of reserves or extension of terms of service. Troop movements from Europe will be made only by written approval of Mr. Vance or myself."[34]

[30]Ibid., pp. 309–310.

[31]Ibid., p. 310. Numbers in the *Pentagon Papers* are sometimes difficult to follow and someone who already believes that the military lured the civilians along can find support often in the way the analyst has discussed them. What happened here is that Westmoreland and McNamara worked out a requirement for 75 combat battalions. CINCPAC accepted this requirement, but added requirements for combat support units, which Westmoreland and McNamara accepted as legitimate. By the time of a planning conference at the end of January, CINCPAC and Westmoreland had decided they needed some tanks and added 4 tank battalions to make the total 79 combat battalions. But there were also 23 battalions from allied countries. Thus the 4 battalions made the total climb from 98 to 102. Unfortunately, much of the discussion in this section had been about the 75-battalion proposal. The way the analyst wrote up the 4-battalion increase was to write, at the start of a new sub-heading: "However, by 28 January, the CINCPAC/MACV requirements had risen to 102 Free World battalions (79 US including 4 tank battalions...)." This is factual but leads the uncareful reader to believe another massive jump had been injected from 75 to 102 instead of 98 to 102. In essence, there were no surprises in order of magnitude at the January 28 conference.

[32]*Pentagon Papers*, Book 5, "Phase II," pp. 26–27.

[33]Ibid., p. 30.

[34]Ibid., p. 38.

Here we see clearly the dispute between the military and civilian leadership. The issue was not the desired size of the Phase II force, or even when it should be achieved. The issue was how to attain the agreed-upon buildup. The military believed that it was beyond the ability of the United States to field a 443,000-man combat force in Vietnam by the end of 1966 without a reserve callup. McNamara insisted that the reserves not be called up and that the military achieve the 443,000 level anyway.[35]

The Joint Chiefs responded to McNamara with a reworked proposal on April 4, 1966, that would raise troop strength by the end of 1966 to 376,350, rising to 438,207 by the end of 1967.[36] McNamara was infuriated. He immediately demanded an explanation of the failure from the Joint Chiefs. The JCS stood firm. The United States simply did not have it in its power to do what McNamara wanted. McNamara, believing it necessary to make *some* decision to ensure that the flow of troops would be uninterrupted, accepted the JCS proposal on April 11.[37] He remained dissatisfied, however, and directed Assistant Secretary Alain Enthoven to work with the military to try to find ways to accelerate deployments.[38]

Meanwhile, the administration continued to treat American public opinion with a great deal more caution than their enemy in the field. They released information in dribs and drabs, seeking to prepare the public for a larger commitment and a longer war than previously announced. Soviet shipping from the Black Sea to Vietnam, for example, received considerable press attention as the administration released intelligence data on

---

[35]*Trial*, card 608. Further evidence of the administration's, and especially McNamara's, enthusiasm for as rapid a buildup as possible during this period is found in exhibits 215, 215A and 215D of the Westmoreland/CBS trial. This document was drafted by William Bundy and John McNaughton on February 8, 1966 and was titled "1966 Program To Increase The Effectiveness Of Military Operations And Anticipated Results Thereof." Recall that McNaughton was the only person with whom McNamara allegedly shared the same views on the war. The program called for almost doubling the number of battalion-months of offensive operations and expected end-of-1966 strength for US forces to be 429,000 and 79 maneuver battalions. One of the expected outcomes was that the enemy forces would be attrited by the end of 1966 "at a rate as high as their capability to put men into the field." In other words, the crossover point would be reached. This indicates that the administration's thinking still included military victory as the ultimate goal.

[36]Ibid., pp. 38–39.

[37]Ibid., p. 40. There was some modification to the final approved proposal, now having changed from Phase II to Phase IIA to Phase IIA(R)—R meaning revisited. The number would be 383,500 by the end of 1966 and 425,000 by mid-1967; 383,500 later was rounded up to 384,000 in some documents, and this is where my figure of 384,000 as the military position originates.

[38]Ibid.

the expanded Soviet efforts.[39] In February 1966, the administration revealed that 300,000 soldiers would be in Vietnam by late spring and that facilities would be built to support 500,000.[40] Another report suggested that 600,000 troops might not be enough.[41] President Johnson could have committed almost any size force and still have claimed "consistency." But his domestic political opponents could look back—and they did—and wonder whether the administration ever had a clear idea of what it was attempting to accomplish.

The United States Seeks to Prevent Chinese Intervention

As the American buildup proceeded apace, so too did the Johnson administration's concern that hordes of "Red" Chinese soldiers might march south into the battle. McNamara, for example, wrote a memorandum for the president in early December 1965 in which he discussed the impact of the proposed increase of US troop levels in Vietnam to a possible 600,000. "The question of Chinese intervention," said the obviously worried defense secretary, "would become critical.... Any prospect of military success [would be] marred by the chances of an active Chinese intervention."[42] This fear was echoed in a January 1966 memorandum by Assistant Secretary McNaughton and in numerous other administration documents in January and February.[43] Concerned about China, the United States attempted to improve relations with its former adversary, hoping to divorce the status of bilateral relations from the situation in Vietnam and, ultimately, discourage the Chinese from intervening.

Initial gestures included an early March 1966 decision to permit American scholars to visit China and Senate Foreign Relations Committee hearings, obviously prompted by the administration, on Sino-American relations.[44] The hearings, in particular, accomplished a dual objective, sending signals to China and the American public of a possible shift in US policy toward conciliation with "Red China."[45] Well known China scholars

[39]Paul Wohl, "How the Soviets ship arms aid to North Vietnam," *Christian Science Monitor,* January 14, 1966, p. 12.

[40]Robert R. Brunn, "Pentagon eyes Hanoi," ibid., February 10, 1966, p. 11.

[41]"Focus on Washington," ibid., February 11, 1966, p. 1.

[42]*Secret History,* p. 490.

[43]Ibid., pp. 491–492.

[44]"The news briefly," *Christian Science Monitor,* March 11, 1966, p. 2.

[45]Richard L. Strout, "Isolation of Peking opposed," ibid., March 11, 1966, p. 3.

testified before the committee that US policy should end its attempted isolation of the Asian giant.[46] In a rare appearance before Congress that drew attention, Vice-president Hubert Humphrey lent his weight to their testimony by supporting much of the scholars' arguments and advocating "containment without isolation."[47] Moreover, while not officially changing its policy of opposition to a United Nations seat for China, the administration leaked stories that suggested a strong faction existed within the government that would support such a move.[48] The vice-president would make another overture to China in June in his graduation address to the class of 1966 at West Point.[49] Other articles reflected continued suggestions of a developing new attitude toward China.[50]

McNamara's Response—Some Thoughts

Having discovered the impact of the Soviet-North Vietnamese arms agreement, no one in the US leadership, civilian or military, seriously considered any action other than increasing troop strength. What is astonishing is the lack of discord not only on the principle, but on the specific details. Westmoreland's analysis of the situation on November 23 and McNamara's independent review were identical. Westmoreland's cable to CINCPAC talked in terms of an immediate increase in the size of the Phase II force, but treated this as a stopgap measure only, because more troops would be needed later. McNamara's cable to Westmoreland indicated he believed something like two divisions would be necessary to add to Phase II immediately and that more forces would be needed later. Westmoreland's request for 41,500 is of the same order of magnitude as two divisions. McNamara and Westmoreland's talks ultimately resulted in a request for 75 combat battalions, which worked out to be a little less than 400,000 soldiers. CINCPAC accepted the 75-battalion level, but added other types of units that made the total number of American troops a little more than 400,000, but still within the order of magnitude suggested by McNamara

[46]Saville R. Davis, "How US policy shifts on communist China," ibid., March 16, 1966, p. 1.
[47]Ibid.
[48]"The news-briefly," ibid., March 16, 1966, p. 2.
[49]"Vietnam policy explained to West Point graduates," ibid., June 21, 1966, p. 11. Of course, most of the class of 1966 would go to Vietnam, as would the rest of us in the stands from the classes of 1967, 1968, and 1969.
[50]For example, see Roscoe Drummond, "Peking self-isolation," ibid., March 28, 1966, p. 1; Earl W. Foell, "UN sees jujitsu tactic in US-China talks," ibid., March 30, 1966, p. 1.

to the president. How could this process have developed with all major actors in such agreement?

The answer lies in the Johnson administration's pseudo-scientific concept for fighting the war. The McNamara Defense Department approached war as a mathematical equation, one more political science problem to solved—like poverty—through the precise application of resources. A certain-size enemy required a specific-size friendly force. The calculations were reasonably complicated because rates of infiltration, friendly and enemy death, and other factors were considered. But give the Johnson administration a specific number of enemy combat troops and it would calculate the number of friendly combat battalions required to defeat it. Add combat support and combat service support, multiply a few numbers, and it had its answer. And everyone at high levels knew how to do it. When intelligence said that enemy strength had risen from 48,550 in July to 63,550 in November, the administration believed it had a solvable problem. Both Westmoreland and McNamara, using the same intelligence estimates and the same formulas, arrived at the same conclusion. What disturbed them both was that this increase took place during the initial deployment and tactical success of US forces, which exceeded the predictions of their equations. During a period in which the rate at which friendly forces were killing enemy soldiers greatly increased, enemy strength rose by more than 30 percent. The additional forces beyond the 41,500-man increase they both said was needed were the result of calculations using the same formulas, with data based on the trends established during the July–November period. What did the administration expect to happen when it increased the size of US forces?

Secretary McNamara addressed this in his rather pessimistic memorandum to the president of November 30, in which he spelled out the requirement for about 400,000 soldiers by the end of 1966 and perhaps 200,000 more later. He said that this would not guarantee success, that the United States probably would be faced with a stalemate at higher levels at the beginning of 1967, and that the United States might be losing 1,000 men per month. Still, he recommended going ahead with the troop increase, and the president approved it. Why?

The answer, most likely, lies in the administration's rigid approach to both military strategy and political leadership. The Johnson administration's original concept was mathematical—to fight a "meatgrinder" war in which, at a certain point, the level of destruction was such that the United States killed more soldiers than North Vietnam could replace. McNamara's November 30 memorandum reflected this when he said that "the enemy can be expected to enlarge his present strength of 110 battalion equivalents by the end of calendar 1966, when hopefully his losses can be made to equal his input."[51] A very precise concept for prosecution of the war, however misguided.

But Westmoreland's original Phase II was to be accomplished by mid-1966, with the Phase III final victory, assuming enemy persistence, taking until early 1968. The main message of McNamara's memorandum to the president, seen in context, is that the crossover point that was supposed to have been reached in mid-1966 now would not be achieved until, "hopefully," the end of calendar year 1966. All things being equal, this would slide the entire process forward to mid-1968, just before the elections. For the Johnson administration this was still acceptable politically—but just barely.

One can therefore understand McNamara's exasperation with the Joint Chiefs for not being able to deploy the required force by the end of 1966. Everyone agreed on the requirement. The problem was time. If the necessary level of killing required 443,000 soldiers to achieve the Phase II objective, enemy losses equaling replacements—then they had to be in place by the end of 1966. Every month of slippage made it more likely that victory would be postponed until after the election, which, administration officials were convinced, their successors would have the privilege of celebrating.

Having set a 443,000-man target by the end of 1966, the military's subsequent caveat that it would be impossible without a reserve callup gave McNamara apoplexy. The reserve callup in the view of the administration guaranteed defeat at the polls. McNamara, explaining his position to the Joint Chiefs, noted that

> the political aspects of a Reserve callup are extremely delicate. Look, for example, at the Fulbright Committee hearings. One school of thought...is that this country cannot afford to do what we are doing. Another school of thought feels that we plain should not be there at all, whether or not we can afford it. A third school of thought is that although we are rightly there, the war is being mismanaged, so that we are heading straight toward war with China. Furthermore, there is no ques-

[51]*Secret History,* p. 488.

tion but that the economy of this country is beginning to run near or at its capacity with the resulting probability of a shortage of certain skills and material. If this continues we may be facing wage and price controls, excess profit taxes, etc., all of which adds fuel to the fire of those who say we cannot afford this. With all these conflicting pressures, it is a very difficult and delicate task for the administration to mobilize and maintain the required support in this country to carry on the war properly. The point of all this presents extremely serious problems in many areas and a decision cannot be made today.[52]

The Johnson administration, which had no end of courage for fighting communist aggression, had no stomach for domestic political disputes. Foreign communists don't vote. And it had a perverse notion of the patriotism of the American public. Thousands of dead and wounded were more acceptable than a reduction in domestic consumption and living standards. General Johnson, not surprisingly, responded to McNamara with thinly veiled exasperation of his own. "A reserve callup," said the tough veteran of the Bataan Death March, "might be an important factor in the reading of the North Vietnamese and the Chinese with respect to our determination to see this war through...," a factor the defense secretary had ignored. "Reserve callups," he noted with polite disgust, "are traditionally a unifying factor."[53]

The general's arguments were futile and there would be no mobilization. Although the civilian and military leadership were split on how to achieve the buildup, they were, in April 1966, determined to press on with one. Pressure to accelerate deployments would continue from McNamara until August 1966, when he would completely and absolutely reverse his position and argue to abandon military victory as a goal.

[52]Ibid., p. 32
[53]Ibid., pp. 32–33.

8

The Great Proletarian Cultural Revolution

Major Events

- *May 1965*—Pro-Mao forces publish article "Militant Role of China's Trade Unions." Open criticism of "reactionary elements who refuse to be remolded" begins.
- *June 1965*—Pro-Mao forces follow with direct criticism of Liu Shaoqi's and Deng Xiaoping's leadership during 1959–1961.
- *July 28, 1965*—United States announces troop strength would reach 175,000 in Vietnam by the end of 1965.
- *August 1965*—Army Marshall He Long, speaking for Mao's group, criticizes those "infected with bourgeois thinking" regarding the Army.
- *September 1965*—US troop strength in Vietnam reaches 119,000. Chinese Army Chief of Staff Luo Ruiqing, speaking for Liu and Deng, warns that the American threat to China is serious and makes analogy to Korean War.
- *September 1965*—Chinese Defense Minister Lin Biao gives "Long Live People's War" speech, attacks Luo Ruiqing, and dismisses possibilty of Chinese-American conflict.
- *September–October 1965*—Mao creates five-man "Cultural Revolution Group" at a Central Work Conference and Politburo Standing Committee session.
- *October 1965*—Press attacks begin on "capitalist roaders"—meaning Liu and Deng. Pro-Liu articles attempt to deflect Cultural Revolution by "intrepreting" Cultural Revolution instructions for lower echelons. Li

Zongren, former Nationalist Vice President, returns to China, welcomed by Mao.

- *December 1965*—Luo Ruiqing is attacked at Central Committee Conference in Shanghai and accused of "anti-Party" activities by Lin Biao.
- *March 1966*—Luo Ruiqing is arrested. Mao attacks Peking Mayor Peng Zhen. United States offers to exchange scholars and journalists with China.
- *April 1966*—Luo and Peng are removed from their posts. Resistance to Cultural Revolution increases in the Provinces.
- *June 1966*—Central Chinese media under Mao's complete control. Zhou Enlai equates the struggle against Soviet revisionism with the struggle against US imperialism.

Mao Zedong held the line against Liu, Deng, and their many allies in mid-1965, but a major ground role for US forces in Vietnam could tip the balance of power in favor of his enemies—and that was precisely what was happening. Mao knew he had a few months, but only a few months, before he would be faced with a large American army fighting a ground war against a socialist country on China's border. Rather than wait, he took the offensive, seeking to remove the Liu-Deng faction from its positions in the government and party.

As early as mid-May, articles in the Chinese press developed the charges Mao would use to remove the pro-Soviet group from power. For example, "Militant Role of China's Trade Unions," which was published in the *Peking Review,* discussed the primacy of politics in union work and referred to unnamed "reactionary elements that refuse to be remolded."[1] In June, an editorial on China's policy of self-reliance (self-reliance meaning independence from Moscow) mentioned "errors and shortcomings in our work in the 1959–1961 period."[2] From 1959 to 1961, Liu and Deng had gained ascendancy in the party and state apparatus and dominated policy as they attempted to limit economic damage caused by the Great Leap Forward. These "errors," therefore, belonged to Liu and Deng. Later in June, yet another *Peking Review* article, allegedly on China's monetary system, made further reference to the same errors.[3]

[1] "Militant Role of China's Trade Unions," *Peking Review,* May 14, 196, pp. 26–29.

[2] T'seng Yun, "How China Carries out the Policy of Self-Reliance," ibid., June 18, 1965, pp. 12–15. See also Chin Yu-kun, "Self-Reliance in Making Precision Machine Tools," ibid., July 30, 1965, pp. 15–17.

[3] Yang Pei-hsin, "China's Stable Monetary System," ibid., June 25, 1965, pp. 15–19.

The intensity of Mao's campaign increased after President Johnson announced on July 28, 1965, that US troop strength would reach 175,000 by the end of the year. In early August, as part of Army Day celebrations, Politburo member and Army Marshal Ho Lung criticized unnamed people "infected with the habits of the old type Army and those with bourgeois thinking who have stubbornly opposed Comrade Mao Zedong's line on Army building. While opposing the strengthening of absolute Party leadership over the Army, they have used one reason or another, one pretext or another, for opposing the movement for democracy and resisting the mass line."[4]

By September, US troop strength reached 119,000 and included the new airmobile 1st Cavalry Division.[5] PLA Chief of Staff Luo Ruiqing pressed the issue of the growing American threat to China by referring to "Korean War-type" threats by the United States, specifically, American statements that the "idea of sanctuary [for the Viet Cong] is dead." Lo hoped the United States would continue to pour men and material into Vietnam because it would give China "more opportunities to fight in unity" with the Soviet Union.[6] Defense Minister Lin Biao countered on September 2 with a major address—"Long Live the Victory of People's War!"—which has been considered by many to be the opening salvo of the Cultural Revolution. Lin progressed from the familiar, commonplace general argument that revolutionaries everywhere must win victory on their own through People's War to specific and unprecedented attacks on the Liu-Deng group and on Luo Ruiqing personally. Lin Biao dismissed the possibility of a Chinese-American conflict, which he thought very unlikely. Further, even if war came, Lin believed that China would defeat the United States with People's War. He criticized those in the Party who opposed Mao's efforts to combat "revisionism" and especially attacked Luo Ruiqing's position on the American threat. There was no reason to unite with the Soviet Union, no matter what the United States did.[7]

---

[4]Ho Lung, "Democratic Tradition of the Chinese People's Liberation Army," ibid., August 6, 1965, pp. 6–16. This article also appeared in the Party theoretical journal Red Flag, People's Daily, and in Liberation Army Daily. He Long at this point was moving to assert his independence from Liu and Deng and spoke for Mao's camp. In January 1967, when Mao committed a large portion of the PLA to the struggle that had reached civil war proportions, many military leaders including He Long balked. He was attacked and disgraced. See Thornton, China, p. 298, Wedeman, p. 89, and Stanley Karnow, Mao and China, (New York: 1972), pp. 280–281.

[5]Sharp and Westmoreland, Report, Section II, p. 109.

[6]Lo Jui-ching, "China Stands Ready to Smash US War Schemes," Peking Review, August 6, 1965, p. 5.

[7]Lin Piao, "Long Live the Victory of People's War!" ibid., October 15, 1965, pp. 5–7. See Thornton, China, p. 276 and Wedeman, pp. 155–157.

The Onslaught Begins and Luo Ruiqing and Peng Zhen Fall

Behind the scenes, Mao began putting together an organization personally loyal to him that would remove opponents in the party and state apparatus. At a Central Work Conference and Politburo Standing Committee session in September and October, Mao managed to create a five-man "Cultural Revolution Group," ostensibly to study class struggle in cultural and ideological affairs.[8] In October, Mao's supporters in the press began referring to the socialist revolution on the cultural front and the continuing struggle between the "capitalist and socialist roads."[9] It soon became clear that Liu, Deng, and their many followers were the "capitalist roaders."

Mao's initial targets were Army Chief of Staff Luo Ruiqing and Peng Zhen, mayor of Peking and a powerful member of the Party's Secretariat. Removal of these two would pave the way for Mao's control of the capital city and the military. Mao convened a Central Committee Conference in Shanghai in December 1965 to hear charges against Luo Ruiqing. Lin Biao already had managed, as minister of defense, to reshuffle a number of district commanders so that many key leadership positions below the general staff were filled with officers loyal to Mao.[10] At the Central Committee Conference, Lin expanded his criticism of Luo Ruiqing, accusing Luo of a variety of crimes—including an attempt to accumulate personal power and organizing an anti-party faction in the PLA. Luo denied the charges but was arrested in March 1966. Simultaneously, Mao convened an unofficial conference at which he attacked Peng Zhen for permitting the rise of bourgeois intellectuals in Peking. Liu and Deng were indecisive in the face of Mao's attacks and Peng Zhen was removed from his posts by April.[11]

---

[8]Thornton, *China*, pp. 279f. For a more detailed discussion of the Cultural Revolution, please refer to the appendix at the end of the book.

[9]Tien Chu, "Fruits of the Cultural Revolution," *Peking Review*, October 15, 1965, pp. 5–7.

[10]Wedeman, pp. 214–215.

[11]Thornton, *China*, pp. 282–283 and Wedeman, pp. 229–248. This is a very brief summary of the attacks on Lo and Peng. The point is Mao and Lin Biao went after the chief of staff and the municipal leadership of Peking and were successful. See Thornton and Wedeman for detailed and entertaining discussions of maneuvering among the Chinese leaders. While there are many explanations for why the Cultural Revolution began, most scholars agree that late 1965 marked the beginning and that Peng and Luo were early victims. See Karnow, *Vietnam, A History*, A. Doak Barnett, *China After Mao*, and J.K. Fairbank, *The United States and China* for other readings on the subject. For evidence of Mao's initial maneuvers to gain control of the military, see "PLA Conference on Political Work," *Peking Review*, January 21, 1966, pp. 5–6. This discusses the results of a 20-day conference saying "Whatever seems counter to his (Mao's) instructions must be rejected and firmly opposed." This is incumbent "even on more senior cadres."

Mao's opponents soon recognized the threat. Mao had devised an ingenious technique for bypassing the Party and State apparatus. By using Cultural Revolution groups, he was able to mobilize popular support among rank-and-file party members, officials of all ranks and students who venerated Mao for his wartime leadership. Liu-Deng loyalists countered with a clever tactic for resistance. As they would throughout the Cultural Revolution, Liu-Deng supporters pretended to support the Cultural Revolution while manipulating the new verbiage to their advantage. They did this in order to confuse Mao's activists about who the activists were supposed to attack, limit popular participation, encourage public order, and maintain popular obedience to the apparatus which they controlled. For example, in October 1965 a *People's Daily* editorial apparently supported the work of the Cultural Revolution Group and the necessity for struggle between the capitalist and socialist roads. However, much in the manner of the press secretary who says "What the President really meant to say was…" the article went on to explain what all this really meant. In addition to the struggle,

we must also thoroughly transform China's face of poverty and blankness and wage revolution against poverty and backwardness.… [We must] build our country into a powerful socialist state with a modern industry, modern agriculture, modern science and technology and modern national defense.… Taking up an occupation under the leadership of a revolutionary regime is also working for the revolution. Many people lack a clear understanding of what is working for revolution. Some people…think that farming, working in factories, feeding cattle or pigs, hair cutting, cooking meals, standing behind the counter, street cleaning, collecting night soil, making clothes, taking part in sports, treating patients, delivering babies cannot be revolutionary—Is this correct?— certainly not. They only regard class struggle as revolution but not the struggle for production and scientific experiment. They are wrong. The struggle to transform nature is carried out under the leadership of the Party and state and constitutes an integral part in the socialist cause.[12]

[12]"All Our Work Is For The Revolution," *Peking Review,* October 22, 1965, pp. 27–29.

The meaning of this is clear. If people worked under the direction of the existing Party and state structures and went about their normal lives, they would be supporting the Cultural Revolution. In other words, "don't take to the streets." "Continue to follow existing lines of authority." As Mao's opponents controlled the provincial party apparatus and held many positions in the state organization, this would leave Liu and Deng in control.[13]

The Cultural Revolution Deepens

Mao Zedong's assault on Luo Ruiqing and Peng Zhen placed the pro-Soviet faction on the defensive. Open calls for unity over Vietnam began to decline. Liu Shaoqi and Deng Xiaoping ceased to make foreign policy the primary battleground of the domestic power struggle. Instead they adopted the terminology of the Cultural Revolution and used bureaucratic infighting to counter Mao's offensive. There is a kind of grand irony in the rhetorical contest between Mao and the Liu-Deng faction at this point in the struggle. Mao, who recommended against direct military intervention in Vietnam, chose direct political attacks upon his opponents, and Liu and Deng, who preferred direct military action to People's War, chose to counter Mao indirectly by using the weight of the Chinese bureaucracy against him. At any rate, Maoist leaders were soon cautioning their supporters to be alert against those "who wave the red flag to oppose the red flag."

With the formal dismissals of Luo Ruiqing and Peng Zhen in May 1966, Mao solidified control over the Army and the Peking party and government, in essence seizing most elements of the national media. Mao's triumph was near-total when the editorial departments were purged at the end of May. After June 1, 1966, the national press no longer reflected both sides in the debate, although a close reading of the criticism Mao leveled at his opponents provides clues about the continuing struggle.

Mao's position on Vietnam, his view that "unity" was a Soviet trap, increasingly dominated the press in the spring of 1966. The Chinese accused the Soviets of trying once again to become "China's patriarchial father."[14] The Soviet Union had not delivered aid to Vietnam

---

[13]The modernizations referred to later achieved fame in the West as the "pragmatic" program of Four Modernizations of Deng Xiaoping.

[14]"The Leaders of the CPSU are Betrayers of the Declaration and the Statement," ibid., January 1, 1966, pp. 9–12.

commensurate with its ability and was following a policy of appeasement in Europe.[15] At the same time, spokesmen for Mao, acknowledging the escalating conflict in Vietnam, dismissed the US threat in contemptuous terms. If the United States were foolish enough to spread the war to China, the 650 million Chinese people would rise up and defeat them. The possibility of a large and dangerous war did exist, said Mao, but he defined a "large war" as 10 million US troops directly deployed against China. Clearly, the 200,000 soldiers were about as troublesome as a mosquito on an elephant's back. The new party line was simple: 14 million Vietnamese could deal with 200,000 Americans and 650 million Chinese could handle 10 million.[16]

In an effort to keep a low profile, Liu and Deng issued pro forma public statements attacking revisionism and were silent or ambiguous on other issues dividing the two groups.[17] But the situation continued to deteriorate. Mao promptly took advantage of Liu Shaoqi's absence on a diplomatic mission to change the organizational structure of the Cultural Revolution Group. It was placed directly under the Standing Committee of the Politburo, which meant that no party bureaucratic structure stood between it and Mao. Moreover, the Cultural Revolution group which originally had included representation from the Liu-Deng faction now was composed of Jiang Jing (Mao's wife), Kang Sheng, Chen Boda, Yao Wenyuan, and Zhang Chunqiao—all ardent supporters of Mao. (Jiang Jing, Yao Wenyuan, and Zhang Chunqiao would achieve fame in the 1970s when Deng Xiaoping had them purged as members of the "Gang of Four.") In essence, the group became Mao's personal instrument.[18]

The effect of Luo Ruiqing's fall from grace, meanwhile, was reflected in the pages of the *Liberation Army Daily*. On April 18, in a lengthy editorial extolling the thought of Mao Zedong, it was clear that the army was now

---

[15]"A New and Great Anti-US Revolutionary Storm is Approaching," ibid., January 7, 1966, pp. 6; "USSR Refuses to Clear Up Anti-China Rumors," ibid., January 21, 1966, pp. 26–27; "Whom is the Soviet Leadership Taking United Action With?" ibid., February 4, 1966, pp. 10–13; "Malinovsky is a Liar," ibid., May 6, 1966, pp. 25–26.

[16]"Premier Chou's Four Point Statement on China's Policy Toward US," ibid., May 13, 1966, p. 5; "The War Threat of US Imperialism Must Be Taken Seriously," ibid., April 8, 1966, pp. 6–8. Propaganda is usually directed at a target audience. Later we will see that beginning in late 1965, Mao directed another campaign at the US leadership. The message was that China wished to improve relations with the United States.

[17]"Comrade Liu Shao-chi's Speech," ibid., May 6, 1966, pp. 8–10; "Comrade Teng Hsiao-ping's Speech," ibid., may 13, 1966, pp. 16–19.

[18]Thornton, *China*, p. 282.

"the most loyal tool of the Party and the People" in the bitter class struggle with "bourgeois intellectuals."[19]

For a time, evidently, Liu and Deng were able to use their political strength in the provinces to form party "work groups" to "assist" the new Cultural Revolution groups that Maoists were forming. But by May, although some Liu-Deng officials had been criticized and there were a few purges, Mao was out to banish Liu and Deng. Using the forum of the *Liberation Army Daily,* now firmly under his control, Mao attacked "those who...wave the red flag to oppose the red flag.... Taking advantage of the functions and powers given them by the Party and Government, they have put under their absolute control some departments and units, refusing the leadership of the Party and carrying out anti-Party, anti-Socialist criminal activities through instruments in their hands. The people are mostly so-called 'authorities' and they are well-known in society [i.e., Liu and Deng].... Their anti-Party, anti-socialist activities are not isolated, accidental phenomena. They are in tune with the international anti-China chorus raised by...modern revisionists [i.e., Soviets]."[20] Perhaps early on, Mao's goal was to gain control of the bureaucracies, not destroy them. But by the summer of 1966, Mao intended to seize control in the provinces by using the rapidly expanding Cultural Revolution organization—no matter what the consequences.

Mao Tries Again to Improve Relations with the United States

Ordinarily, consistency is a trifling matter in a communist society, because the Party answers to no one. A Stalin can praise Hitler one day and rewrite the history books the next. But Mao, before he had won the internal power struggle, did not want to give his opponents the advantage by appearing to contradict himself. So, as he had accused the Soviet Union of collusion with the United States over Vietnam, he could not overtly offer to improve Sino-US relation without exposing himself to the same criticism. (In fact, the Soviets would later make just this charge.)

Improved relations with the United States were, however, in Mao's interests. This would eliminate the issue of an American threat to China, the argument that the Vietnam conflict necessitated unity with the Soviet

---

[19] "Hold High the Great Red Banner of Mao Tse-tung's Thinking; Actively Participate in the Great Socialist Cultural Revolution," ibid., April 29, 1966, pp. 5–10.

[20] "Never Forget Class Struggle," ibid., May 13, 1966, pp. 40–42.

Union. Moreover, in the longer term, the United States could balance Soviet military pressure and western trade and technology could offset the loss of Soviet economic assistance. Pro-American signals from Mao had disappeared shortly before the Tonkin Gulf Incident but surfaced briefly again in late 1964 and early 1965 with Mao's interview with Edgar Snow. The introduction of US ground forces and Mao's subsequent compromises forced him to cease efforts toward improving relations with the United States until he began his first forceful moves in the Cultural Revolution in the fall of 1965. Given Mao's struggle for power, however, he had to proceed carefully. His problem was to send positive signal to the United States without opening himself to charges of collusion. His solution, once again, was to use criticism of US Taiwan policy to convey the message.

In October 1965, Li Zongren—who had been Chiang Kai-shek's vice-president, had assumed duties as president of Nationalist China when Chiang moved to Taiwan in 1949, and had resided in the United States there-after—returned to the Chinese mainland. Li had been a bitter enemy of Chinese communism for years and the Chinese communists had considered him a leading US "puppet." Now he was welcomed with open arms in Peking. He appeared with Mao Zedong on the Tien'anmen rostrum at a rally and gave a press conference at which it was made clear that his return had been orchestrated by Mao's followers. Moreover, it was also clear that the episode was an overture to the United States. At the carefully staged event, Li, in answering questions, said that he had hoped for good Sino-American relations and peace in the Pacific region while living in the United States. The responsibility for the two countries not being on friendly terms, he added, was entirely that of the US leadership—meaning Chinese leaders were prepared for friendly relations. He further stated that no one could real-ly consider China a threat to US security and downplayed the possibility of a US-Chinese conflict.[21] Li's statements, delivered with the blessing of Mao Zedong as US ground forces were beginning to enter combat in Vietnam in a big way, were meant to be a signal to the United States that Mao favored a broad strategic rapprochement with America. (In fact, this is exactly the message the Soviets took from the Li Zongren affair.)

There is no evidence that the United States believed or even understood that Mao desired better Sino-US relations. A series of overtures from the United States in early 1966, which suggested a more flexible US attitude toward the People's Republic of China, was motivated entirely by US fears

[21] "Li Tsung-jen's Press Conference," ibid., October 1, 1965, pp. 22–27.

over possible Chinese intervention in Vietnam. Whether Mao believed that the United States had finally responded to Chinese diplomatic signals, or he understood that the Americans were merely trying to head off Chinese intervention, the US overtures were an opportunity to begin the process of rapprochement. But Mao—no doubt still constrained by the internal power struggle—continued to use hostile rhetoric, especially over US Taiwan policy, to send his signals for improved relations. Indeed, Mao rejected and even ridiculed US overtures, perhaps hoping to spur caution among American leaders on Vietnam and to encourage the United States to change positions on Taiwan and China's seat in the United Nations. But Mao consistently, despite the surrounding rhetoric, maintained that it was America's fault—not China's—that the two countries did not enjoy good relations. Moreover, he never linked the Vietnam war and rapprochement as issues that had any bearing on the other. But US policymakers, seeing all Chinese acts through an ideological prism, continued to be blinded by the rhetoric.

Mao's response to the US overtures appeared in a March 27, 1966, *People's Daily* editorial, in which the American signal about improved relations was acknowledged. The article listed the alleged US desire to be flexible with regard to China, its claim that it no longer sought to isolate China from the rest of the international community, the American call for peaceful relations, and, specifically, the US request for scholarly exchanges. The editorial rejected US offers and talked about the sixteen-year "hostile occupation" of Taiwan. Further, the United States had shifted the focus of its strategy to Asia and threatened to carry war in Vietnam to China. But in rejecting the specific US proposal of an exchange of correspondents and scholars, the article hammered away on the subject of Taiwan. "Everyone knows the continued cause of strained relations has nothing to do with journalists and scholars—it is the hostile policy of the United States...primarily because the United States is forcefully occupying China's province of Taiwan."[22] It is astounding that American China watchers failed to see the potential room for negotiation in Chinese statements.

Zhou Enlai in April 1966 removed any doubt about the nature of Mao's reply to US overtures with a "Four-Point" statement during a visit to Pakistan. Amid news of the increase in Phase II troop strength in Vietnam, Zhou said that "China will not take the initiative to provoke war with the United

---

[22]Observer, "Old Tune, New Plot," ibid., April 1, 1966, pp. 13–15. Some analysts in the United States detected the focus on Taiwan and not on Vietnam. See Earl W. Foell, "UN sees jujitsu tactic in US-China talks," *Christian Science Monitor,* March 30, 1966, p. 1.

States." Then, according to Zhou's first point, the United States should not send more troops to Hawaii and should withdraw all its armed forces from Taiwan—clearly setting the top price before offering hedges that showed room for negotiation. Second, the Chinese would resist any aggression. Third, China would be ready for any test of strength with the United States—and 650 million Chinese would be able to defeat 10 million US troops. And, fourth, if the United States invaded China, the war would know no boundaries. In other words, when the international situation should have dictated strong Chinese statements on Vietnam, Zhou said his real beef with the United States was Taiwan and the only thing that would cause a Chinese-US conflict was a US invasion of China—not very comforting words for Hanoi.

At the end of June 1966, after complete seizure of the national media by Mao's forces, Zhou began spelling out Mao's position on Sino-US relations with greater clarity—reflecting Mao's growing power as the Cultural Revolution progressed. At a mass rally, Zhou equated the struggle against Soviet revisionism with the struggle against US imperialism.[23] US "imperialism" always had been the chief enemy of the socialist camp. Zhou now had elevated the struggle against Soviet "revisionism" to a new level, on an equal par with US "imperialism." But while the Chinese were unwilling to discuss "unity of action" with the Soviets, they were, it seems, willing to conduct a dialogue with the United States.

Thus, as the Cultural Revolution developed rapidly, to the astonishment of the world, Mao Zedong began signaling the United States with increasing urgency that "radical" communist China wanted to improve relations with the American giant. This time it appears the United States began to understand.

---

[23] "Comrade Chou En-lai's Speech at Tirana Mass Rally," *Peking Review*, July 1, 1966, pp. 25–30.

9

Soviet Adjustments

Major Events

- *October 1965*—Cultural Revolution Group in China formed. Li Zongren returns to China. Soviet press reacts sharply.
- *December 1965*—Soviets and North Vietnamese sign three new agreements which supplement the July 1965 arms agreement. Averell Harriman sent to Moscow to ask Russians to intercede with the North Vietnamese.
- *January 1965*—Shelepin-Ustinov delegation travels to Hanoi. Soviets announce increase in defense budget and attribute it to Vietnam War. Soviets host Indian-Pakistani talks in Tashkent. Soviet-Mongolian Friedship Treaty signed.
- *February 1966*—North Vietnamese announce they will attend 23d Congress of the Communist Party of the Soviet Union despite Chinese boycott.
- *March–April 1966*—23d Party Congress in Moscow. Unity over Vietnam is major theme.

Two events in October 1965 startled the Soviets, giving them their first premonition that Mao was taking the offensive in China's internal power struggle. First, the formation of the Cultural Revolution Group and the subsequent press criticism of those taking the "capitalist road" implied that Mao was ready to attack directly those Chinese leaders in whom Moscow placed its hopes. Second, the return of former Nationalist Vice-president Li Zongren demonstrated clearly—at least to the Kremlin—Mao's intention to move toward rapprochement with the United States as a strategic counterweight to the Soviet Union. These events would combine to end the self-imposed reduction in Soviet polemics against China, ushering in a sharp anti-Mao press campaign.

To the Soviets, who knew how dissent is displayed in a communist regime, the formation of the Cultural Revolution Group and articles attacking those in power taking the "capitalist road" immediately set off alarm bells.[1] Direct attacks on opponents were unusual. Typically, if a Chinese communist wished to find fault with a rival, he would use historical lessons in which the moral of the story was analogous to current conditions, criticizing earlier errors by unnamed people when the origins of the policy errors were clear—or criticizing the work and opinions of lower-ranking officials known to be associated with an opponent's camp. By referring to "those in power taking the capitalist road," Mao clearly was going after Liu and Deng and their pro-Soviet policies with a directness never seen before. (Unfortunately, most of this remained impenetrable and obscure to American analysts.) Moreover, for the Chinese reader, Soviet "revisionism" was an accusation that Soviet economic policies, especially material incentives for workers, amounted to nothing less than capitalism. As Liu Shaoqi and Deng Xiaoping were known to advocate similar economic measures, the attack on "capitalist roaders" was instantly recognizable as an attack on Liu and Deng and their pro-Moscow slant.

The Soviets knew right away that Mao was escalating his attacks to include the senior leadership of the group Moscow hoped would win the struggle for power.

The Li Zongren episode confirmed the Kremlin's worst fears. Li's background as an anti-communist who had resided for years in the United States, and Mao's welcome of him gave credibility to Li's remarks that China would welcome improved relations with the United States. The Soviets viewed this as an obvious diplomatic overture from Mao to his former American adversary—and Sino-American rapprochement was exactly what Soviet strategy was working to prevent.

The Soviet public response was sharp. Two days after Li Zongren's press conference, a signed editorial in *Pravda* scored the Chinese for inviting the return of a "top expert when it comes to fighting against communists." This "war criminal," the article continued, had suddenly done an about-face and was now welcomed by the Chinese Communist party. Significantly, Li "let

---

[1]Thornton, *China*, p. 282–283; Tien Chu, "Fruits of the Cultural Revolution," *Peking Review*, October 15, 1965, pp. 5–7.

it be understood that there were essentially no issues between China and the USA save the problem of Taiwan, which, if they wanted to, they could solve through negotiations with the Chiang Kai-shek camp."[2] The Soviets instantly realized that this was a step toward improved Sino-US relations. Of course, by publicly painting the gesture for what it was, Moscow hoped to expose Mao to the same criticism he had heaped on the Soviet Union—collusion with the United States.

While Liu Shaoqi and Deng Xiaoping attempted to absorb and dissipate the brunt of Mao's attacks, Mao let it be known in unmistakable terms that he would never consider reestablishing close ties with the Soviet Union. Employing as a vehicle an editorial in *People's Daily* and *Red Flag*, Mao's forces put forth the argument that there was no basis for unity with the Soviets under any circumstance. "United action is impossible with those who transpose enemies and friends...," it said. "The new leaders of the CPSU are taking united action with the United States on the question of Viet Nam.... It means splittism.... The new Soviet leaders are more cunning and hypocritical than Khrushchev."[3]

Deteriorating conditions in the internal power struggle with China prompted the Soviets to reinitiate strong open polemics against their neighbor. Articles in the Soviet press accused the Chinese of following a schismatic course that inflicted "especially heavy blows on Vietnam."[4] The polemics continued throughout December as the Soviets began to recalculate, once again, what would be required to keep the war in Vietnam on an ever-escalating spiral. Given the open-ended US commitment, new North Vietnamese military strength surely would provoke the United States to deploy more troops in Southeast Asia. Perhaps this "threat to China" would yet help the Liu-Deng group seize power.

The Soviet Union and North Vietnam Sign New Agreements

From the open press, the Soviets and North Vietnamese discerned that the United States intended to put approximately 400,000 soldiers into

---

[2] I. Ivanov, "Vozvrashenie Li Tsung Dzhena," (Li Tsung-jen Returns), *Pravda,* October 3, 1965, p. 3.

[3] "Refutation of the New Leaders of the CPSU on 'United Action,' " *Peking Review,* November 12, 1965, pp. 10–21.

[4] "International'nii dolg kommunistov vcekh stran," (The International Duty of Communists of All Countries), *Pravda,* November 28, 1965, p. 1.

Vietnam by the end of 1966 with a possible addition of 200,000 in 1967.[5] In response, a North Vietnamese delegation led by chief aid negotiator Le Than Nghi flew to Moscow in mid-December to begin the process of recalculating logistic requirements. The result was the signing of three new agreements on technical and economic aid which were supplements to the July 12, 1965 military aid pact.[6] Despite the fact that weapons were not mentioned, other statements implied the military purpose of the agreements.[7]

The now-predominant Soviet aid was reflected in a more solid pro-Soviet stance by the North Vietnamese—especially on the Sino-Soviet split. Le Duan, the emerging power in the North Vietnamese communist party—who had been trained in China—and Pham Van Dong and Vo Nguyen Giap, made it quite clear that they understood who their benefactor was. The North Vietnamese announced they would send a high ranking delegation to Moscow for the Soviet Union's 23d Party Congress, a Congress boycotted by China.[8]

Following the signing of the December accords, the Soviets decided to send a high-level delegation to Hanoi for further discussions. While the delegation was headed by Politburo member Aleksandr Shelepin, the key man on the team was Politburo candidate-member D.F. Ustinov.[9] Ustinov had been Stalin's wartime minister of armaments and was known as a key figure in the Soviet equivalent of the "military-industrial complex." He later achieved full membership on the Politburo and became minister of defense. Assisting Ustinov, among a large delegation of political and economic experts, was a team of military experts headed by Colonel-General V.F. Tolubko.[10] Ustinov was high enough in the hierarchy to understand Soviet strategic goals and was technically qualified to ensure that the quantities and types of supplies promised to the North Vietnamese would support Soviet strategy. Ustinov was destined to appear at many of

[5] "*Pravda* Scores Chinese Attitude on Help to Vietnam," *Current Digest,* January 19, 1966, pp. 3–4. This article cited the US press and statements in Washington as the authority for these numbers.

[6] M.P. Isaeev and A.S. Chernishev, *Sovetsko-v'etnamskie otnosheniya,* (Soviet-Vietnamese Relations), (Moscow: Thought Press, 1975), pp. 190–191. "Pravda Scores Chinese Attitude on Help to Vietnam," *Current Digest,* January 19, 1965, pp. 3–4.

[7] Paul Wohl, "Moscow wins round in Hanoi," *Christian Science Monitor,* December 27, 1965, p. 5.

[8] John Hughes, "Moscow-Peking Rift Divides Hanoi Rule," ibid., February 4, 1966, p. 1; "The news-briefly," ibid., March 28, 1966, p. F; "Agonizing, Not Arrogant," ibid., May 14, 1966, p. E.

[9] "Soviet Delegation Leaves for Democratic Republic of Vietnam," *Current Digest,* January 26, 1965, p. 25.

[10] Ibid.

the key arms negotiating sessions with the North Vietnamese throughout the war. A speech by Shelepin at the conclusion of the Soviet visit called for unity of action in the socialist camp and promised stepped up economic and military support.[11]

Given the nature of the American commitment, the Soviets realized that a very large and increasingly costly effort would be required if the level of violence were to be successfully forced upward. The Soviets acknowledged this fact, and their intention to pay the price, by announcing publicly an increased defense budget for 1966 directly attributable to the Vietnam war.[12]

Meanwhile, to encourage the United States to mire itself in a major Asian ground war, the Soviet Union continued to refrain, as the Chinese pointed out, from actions that could threaten the United States in other regions of the world. This so-called moderate attitude led many scholars, journalists, and Johnson administration officials to delude themselves that Soviet supplies to Vietnam were really a ploy to gain influence and cause Hanoi to somehow moderate its policy.[13] Since the Soviets were anxious to discount Chinese accusations that their aid to Vietnam was far from commensurate with Soviet capabilities, the supply effort was accompanied by a press campaign designed to show just how massive the effort truly was.[14] Eastern European newspapers, correspondents, and even Radio Odessa extensively reported on the extraordinary Soviet shipping effort from the Black Sea—providing unusually rich details for intelligence analysts.[15] In addition, the inclusion of Dimitri Ustinov in arms negotiations with the North Vietnamese was an indication of the seriousness with which the Soviets approached the whole affair. Indeed, there was some public discussion in the United States about Ustinov's role as "Mr. Military-Industrial Complex" for the Soviet

[11] "Rech' tovarishcha A.N, Shelepina," (Speech by Comrade A.N. Shelepin), *Pravda,* January 10, 1966, p. 3.

[12] "Garbuzov's Supreme Soviet Report on 1966 Budget," *Current Digest,* January 5, 1966, pp. 3–9.

[13] Zbigniew K. Brezinski, "Peace, Morality, and Vietnam," *The New Leader,* April 12, 1965; "Refutation of the New Leaders of the CPSU on United Action," *Peking Review,* November, 12, 1965, pp. 10–21; Donald S. Zagoria, *Vietnam Triangle* (New York: Pegasus, 1967), p. 49; Saville R. Davis, "Soviets watched for Hanoi clues," *Christian Science Monitor,* January 8, 1966, p. 1; William I. Stringer, "Soviet secret diplomacy rivals that of US," ibid., January 4, 1966, p. 4; *Pentagon Papers,* Book 6, "The Air War in North Vietnam," Volume I, p. 24. (Hereafter referred to as "Air War-Vol. I").

[14] See "Focus on red bloc," *Christian Science Monitor,* January 5, 1966, p. 1, for reports of Soviet accusations of Chinese interference with Soviet rail shipments.

[15] Paul Wohl, "How the Soviets ship arms aid to North Vietnam," ibid., January 14, 1966, p. 12.

Union and the significance of his participation in the negotiations.[16] All this suggests that it should not have required a brilliant intelligence effort on the part of the United States to have established the connection between Soviet actions and United States difficulties in Vietnam. Nevertheless, a November 1965 Defense Intelligence Agency document completely failed to differentiate between Soviet and Chinese policy when it reported to Secretary McNamara that North Vietnam's "limited industry made little contribution to its military capabilities. The great bulk of its military equipment...had to be imported. This was no particular problem, since both the USSR and China were apparently more than glad to help."[17] Despite clear evidence that the North Vietnamese were being supplied by the Soviet Union, and without those supplies the North Vietnamese simply could not match the United States on the battlefield, many scholars and administration analysts still saw increasing Soviet influence in Hanoi as a hopeful sign. The United States made gestures such as extending a bombing pause past the Shelepin-Ustinov trip to Hanoi[18] and sent elder statesman Averell Harriman on a personal mission to Moscow in December 1965.[19] "It has been made clear to us over a long period of time that the Soviet government hopes there can be a peaceful settlement," said McGeorge Bundy.[20] Vice-president Hubert Humphrey openly expressed the desire that the Soviet Union would exert a moderating influence on North Vietnam.[21]

The Soviets, while never stating their aim was anything other than unequivocal support for North Vietnam, were delighted by US misconceptions and were careful to foster the futile American hope for Soviet help in ending the war. The Kremlin, refraining from threats elsewhere in the world, projected a moderate image whenever possible, for example, by inviting Indian and Pakistani leaders to Tashkent for negotiations that achieved a cease fire in the war between their two countries. Of course there were other reasons for hosting these talks, but the Chinese were certainly correct to view the "Spirit of Tashkent" as a publicity effort designed,

[16]Paul Wohl, "Soviet Hanoi mission watched for clues," ibid., January 10, 1966, p. 4.

[17]*Secret History*, p. 469.

[18]Saville R. Davis, "Soviets watched for Hanoi clues," *Christian Science Monitor,* January 8, 1966, p. 1. See "Johnson Administrations's Big Conspiracy," *Peking Review,* January 14, 1966, pp. 5–9, for the Chinese view that the bombing pause and Shelepin's visit were pre-coordinated between the Soviets and Americans.

[19]See "Whom is the Soviet Union Taking United Action With?" *Peking Review,* February 4, 1966, pp. 10–13, for a Chinese view of the Harriman Moscow visit.

[20]Ibid.

[21]Ibid.

in part, to impress the United States with Soviet flexibility and reasonableness on regional conflicts, including Vietnam.[22] Although the "Spirit of Tashkent" might have been a more effective propaganda tool if Indian Prime Minister Lal Bhadur Shastri had not chosen to die during the negotiations, a cease-fire was agreed to.[23] While the Soviet answer to Averell Harriman's personal diplomacy was "No, we won't intercede on your behalf with the North Vietnamese," Harriman came away with a definite, if imprecise, impression that the Soviets shared US concerns over the war in Vietnam and desired peace in the region as ardently as the United States.

The Soviets sought to support this "Spirit of Tashkent" image by giving interviews to the US media. For example, a senior East European diplomat told an American reporter that there had been a North Vietnamese request to the Romanians to act as intermediaries in settling the Vietnam conflict. Allegedly, during a visit to Bucharest, Brezhnev encouraged the idea. The logic at this point was that Romanian leader Ceausescu would try to interest Zhou Enlai during a June visit to Romania.[24]

One would be hard pressed to find another example in a free society of intelligence efforts, academic research, and news reporting so far off the mark. Initially, the United States failed to believe that the Sino-Soviet rift was real. Once the exchanges between China and the Soviet Union were acrimonious, the United States accepted the split between the two powers but, apparently taken in by Chinese rhetoric, especially the rhetoric of the Cultural Revolution, was somehow convinced that the source of North Vietnamese intransigence was China, rather than North Vietnam's chief ally and arms supplier, the Soviet Union. In the American view, Mao was the source of communist "radicalism" and the "export of revolution" when all material evidence showed that the Chinese were unable to export anything of real value. The prime US strategic objective for fighting in Vietnam was to "contain" Chinese communist expansion while the prime Chinese objective—at least by Mao Zedong—was to contain Russian expansion.[25] And the prime Soviet objective was to re-install pro-Soviet leaders in China.

---

[22]"Whom is the Soviet Leadership Taking United Action With?" *Peking Review,* February 4, 1966, pp. 10–13.

[23]"Opening of the Ayub-Shastri Meeting in Tashkent," *Current Digest,* January 16, 1966, pp. 3–6.

[24]David K. Willis, "Hanoi dove flutters in Romania," *Christian Science Monitor,* June 2, 1966, p. 1.

[25]For additional evidence that the predominate US government and academic view was that the source of conflict was "radical" China and the "moderate" influence was the Soviet Union see William H. Stringer, "Soviet secret diplomacy rivals that of US," ibid., January 4, 1966, p. 41.

23d Party Congress Meets in Moscow

Soviet diplomatic pressure on China mounted in the first half of 1966, building to a peak in March and April during the 23d Party Congress of the Communist Party of the Soviet Union (attended by North Vietnam, boycotted by China). Brezhnev chose the signing of a Soviet-Mongolian Friendship Treaty in January 1966, an act which itself was a strategic threat to China, to signal the start of a new offensive: "Despite the absence of a common frontier and Vietnam's remoteness from the Soviet Union, our country is giving the Democratic Republic of Vietnam ever-increasing aid in repelling the American aggression. This aid embraces all spheres of our cooperation—military, political, and economic."[26] Later, in February, the Soviet Union hailed the sixteenth anniversary of the Soviet-Chinese friendship treaty. An official article pointed out that Soviet support had been crucial before and after the communist victory in China and had been central to the protection of China as a communist regime. Soviet enterprises in China were alleged, with some justification, to be the backbone of Chinese industry. The Kremlin went on to charge, a bit defensively, that "through no fault of our own, difficulties have arisen, but we have exerted and are exerting great efforts to overcome difficulties and normalize relations." The Soviets, according to Moscow, had undertaken increased efforts at improving Sino-Soviet relations since the fall of Khrushchev. The conflict in Vietnam made it especially urgent that all socialist countries unite to prevent the United States from capitalizing on the difficulties that had developed between China and the Soviet Union.[27]

Later, at the 23d Party Congress, Brezhnev made foreign policy his major theme. The first topic he addressed was the especially important place that "belongs to efforts to strengthen solidarity of the socialist commonwealth." The reason solidarity occupied such an important position was the Vietnam conflict and Brezhnev suggested top-level meetings in Peking or Moscow to resolve the Sino-Soviet dispute.[28] Finally, to underscore the primacy of the issue, the 23d Party Congress approved a series

---

[26] "Brezhnev at signing of the Soviet-Mongolian Treaty," *Current Digest*, February 9, 1966, pp. 1–3.

[27] "In Friendship Lies Great Strength," ibid., March 9, 1966, pp. 19–20.

[28] "Brezhnev's Report to the 23rd Party Congress I," ibid., April 13, 1966, pp. 5–24. The suggestion of top-level meetings was especially important because, at the right moment, given the American buildup, a top level Soviet-Chinese meeting might be the one big propaganda coup that would give the Liu-Deng group victory.

of measures for overcoming difficulties with China along with pledges of political and material support for Vietnam.[29]

In early 1966, the Soviet Union had achieved many of its most important foreign policy objectives. The United States was being drained by an ever-escalating conflict in Vietnam and a powerful group in the Chinese leadership that favored better Sino-Soviet relations used the American presence in Southeast Asia to further its interests. By June 1966, however, the Great Proletarian Cultural Revolution and a US reevaluation of its course of action in Vietnam provoked another round of Soviet policy reappraisal. This time the Kremlin developed a menacing, heavy handed strategy that was dangerous indeed. The Soviets began a large military buildup on China's northern border that obviously was deployed for offensive rather than defensive action.

---

[29] "Congress Resolution Approves Brezhnev's Report," ibid., May 4, 1966, pp. 3–7.

10

Mcnamara Changes His Mind

Major Events

- *October 1965*—Li Zongren returns to China.
- *February–June 1966*—Increasing US offensive activity in South Vietnam. Most activity in populated areas of Quang Ngai, Binh Dinh, Phu Yen, Hau Nghia, and Binh Duong.
- *February 8, 1966*—McNaughton and William Bundy draft "1966 Program to Increase the Effectiveness of Military Operations and Anticipated Results Thereof." Projected troop strength at the end of 1966 is 429,000 with the US killing the enemy at a rate as high as their capability to put men in the field.
- *March 1966*—United States decides to permit scholars and journalists to visit China. Mao responds.
- *April 1966*—United States accelerates troop deployments to Vietnam. Troop strength goal is 384,000 by the end of the year. McNamara presses military to find a way to increase this number
- *May 1966*—US Operation Paul Revere thwarts enemy monsoon offensive.
- *June 1966*—Vice-president Humphrey again signals changing US attitude toward China in West Point graduation address. Zhou Enlai equates importance of struggle against "Soviet Revisionism" with importance of struggle against "US imperialism."
- *June 1966*—Enthoven-Army plan increases end-of-1966 strength to 391,000. Mid-1967 target is 431,000. Plan approved by McNamara.

* *June 18, 1966*—CINCPAC submits to JCS "Calendar Year 1966 Adjusted Requirements and Calendar Year 1967 Requirements." Troop strength for the end of 1966 is projected to be 395,000. Mid-1967 target is 436,000.
* *July 15, 1966*—McNamara reports to president that he is "happy to report" that troop strength would reach 395,000 by the end of 1966.
* *August 5, 1966*—JCS formally transmits June 18 CINCPAC statement of requirements to Department of Defense.
* *August 5, 1966*—McNamara memorandum to JCS refers to June 18 statement and demands a line-by-line justification for any additions to the force structure in Vietnam. Wants to send the minimum required.
* *September 1966*—South Vietnam elects constituent assembly.
* *September 1966*—Chinese Foreign Minister states that China is not opposed to Sino-American negotiations to resolve Vietnam conflict. Chinese ambassador in Warsaw issues statement appealing for confidentiality in Sino-US talks in Warsaw.
* *October 1966*—National Intelligence Estimate 11-8 estimates that Soviet Union would double the size of its ICBM force in 1967.
* *November 5, 1966*—McNamara submits memorandum for the president which recommends that the United States institute a troop ceiling in Vietnam of 470,000 and gird for a protracted war. Military victory would be abandoned as a goal for the committed forces. The president approves the recommendation.
* *November 1966*—US and South Vietnamese forces win major victory in largest operation of war to date—Operation Attleboro.

From June 1966 to August 1967, two diverging trends in the US war effort appeared with profound implications for Soviet strategy. First, the United States began to win the war on the battlefield. Second, Secretary of Defense McNamara decided that the United States no longer should try to win the war.

McNamara reduced his strategic goals. He felt the United States should now strive for something less than an independent, non-communist South Vietnam and recommended, as a result of this conclusion, that the United States place an upper limit on its troop levels. He believed this troop ceiling should be low enough that it could be reached and sustained without having to resort to mobilization. This decision to end the open-ended commitment and deescalate was designed to lead, ultimately, to a US withdrawal and to passing of responsibility for the conflict to the Army of the Republic of Vietnam. Although President Johnson did not give final approval to this course of action until August 1967, McNamara's about-face in 1966 represents the beginning of the US strategic decision to abandon military victory in Vietnam as an objective. The United States would not make the decision public until after the 1968 Tet Offensive, however, and this delay would lead to a Soviet decision based on an incorrect assessment of American intentions.

As late as July 1966, McNamara was still pressing the military to accelerate the pace of the US buildup in South Vietnam. In early August, however, he told the Joint Chiefs of Staff that the United States wanted to send only the minimum requirements to Vietnam and that any future recommendation to add soldiers would have to justified "line by line." By October 1966, he had prepared a formal recommendation to the president that the United States set an upper ceiling on its Vietnam force of 470,000 soldiers and abandon the effort to reach the so-called "crossover point" at which enemy losses would exceed his ability to provide replacement men and/or materiel. McNamara recommended that the president consciously choose not to win—a sudden and complete reversal of his position throughout the first year of US ground force commitment. Until this flip-flop, he had been the source of intense and continuous pressure on the military to put more soldiers into Vietnam in 1966 than the military felt it could physically manage to deploy.

What caused McNamara's—and, ultimately the president's—change of heart?

There appear to be at least three important factors. First, improvements in North Vietnam's military capability made it clear that US troop levels required to achieve Phase II and Phase III objectives would have to be much larger than planned and, more importantly, even if the United States made this effort, the goals would not be reached until after the 1968 elections. Second, a massive military spending campaign initiated by Brezhnev and Kosygin began to redress the Soviet strategic nuclear disadvantage far more rapidly than anticipated by the United States. US intelligence concluded this in mid- to late 1966 and this probably affected administration thinking. Third, the exchange of overtures for improved US-Chinese relations reached a peak by mid-1966 and these signals suggested that improving relations with China could be a heretofore overlooked option. This meant that the US perception of China, the object of US containment policy, had changed significantly. The United States no longer perceived the threat of Chinese expansion as the principal threat to its interests in Asia and this undercut the logic of fighting a war to contain Chinese communism.

American Troops Begin to Win the War in 1966

The United States rapidly implemented the April 1966 presidential decision to accelerate the buildup in Vietnam and troop strength reached 300,000 by August.[1] The surge in American power started to have telling effects on the battlefield. US offensive operations picked up momentum throughout 1966. By early 1967, North Vietnamese and Viet Cong main force units had been forced into jungle sanctuaries away from large population centers and the support of Viet Cong local forces. The move to border regions and to sanctuaries in Laos and Cambodia was necessary to reduce North Vietnamese and Viet Cong losses both in men and materiel. When NVA or VC units moved out of sanctuaries, they were exposed to destruction by the overwhelming ability of the American forces to mass rapidly.[2]

Although largely anecdotal, a series of documents captured from the Viet Cong and North Vietnamese and published by the Joint United States Public Affairs Office in Saigon provides striking insight to the growing US battlefield successes. For example, the captured diary of a North Vietnamese soldier who infiltrated South Vietnam with his unit in August 1965 reveals a tale of increasing hardship, frustration, and disillusionment until the diary was seized by US forces in January 1967.[3] Two documents captured from the North Vietnamese Army's 95th Regiment reveal a continuous stream of casualties and failures throughout 1966 and into 1967. According to one dated May 13, 1967, "previously, we controlled 220,000 inhabitants in the Phu Yen liberated area and 40,000 in areas of mixed control. This is a total of 260,000 out of the 360,000 inhabitants in the entire province. At present, we control only 20,000 inhabitants or 1/10 of the old figure."[4] According to the other, discussing battles in the fall and winter of 1966, "we failed to maintain the initiative during the last phase of the campaign."[5] This collection of documents, captured from a variety of different North Vietnamese and Viet Cong units, supports the American view that 1966 was a year in which US forces progressively seized the initiative from the enemy.

---

[1] "Army buildup continues," *Christian Science Monitor,* August 2, 1968, p. 10 and Sharp and Westmoreland, *Report,* Section II, p. 127.

[2] Ibid., p. 115; *Pentagon Papers, Book 5,* "Volume I: Phase II," pp. 55, 62–68, 81–82; ibid., "Volume II: Program 5," pp. 1–2.

[3] *Viet-Nam Documents and Research Notes,* Nos. 1–50, Oct. 1967–Jan. 1969, (Saigon: Joint United States Public Affairs Office, 1969), Document No. 1.

[4] Ibid., Document No. 2.

[5] Ibid.

The United States concentrated on protecting the populated areas around Saigon and the coastal lowlands in the northern provinces. As a result, the major battles of 1966 were fought in these areas. The largest was northwest of Saigon in Operation Attleboro in which 22,000 American and South Vietnamese troops defeated a reinforced North Vietnamese division.[6] Numerous other offensive operations and spoiling attacks put the United States solidly in control of the initiative and demonstrated that the North Vietnamese could not afford to stand and fight against US forces.[7] By 1967, the North Vietnamese progressively avoided large unit battles and concentrated in border areas where sanctuary in Laos, Cambodia, and North Vietnam was readily available.[8]

Separation of the NVA/VC main forces from large population centers contributed to increasing South Vietnamese political stability and the Thieu-Ky regime began to solidify. One external sign of this improvement was the September 1966 election of a constituent assembly to draft a new constitution.[9] The polling, in which 81 percent of all eligible South Vietnamese voters participated, created a 117-member body to prepare for the restoration of civilian government in 1967. An October 1966 report to the president by McNamara provides more evidence of US tactical success. "We have done somewhat better militarily than I anticipated," said the defense secretary. "We have by and large blunted the Communist military initiative—any military victory in South Vietnam the Viet Cong may have had in mind 18 months ago has been thwarted by our emergency deployments and actions."[10] With nothing but good news from the battlefield and with every prospect of victory McNamara decided to abandon the effort.

McNamara Turns About-Face, April–November 1966

In late 1965 McNamara had reacted to the growing North Vietnamese military threat by pressuring his generals and admirals to accelerate the US

[6]Sharp and Westmoreland, *Report,* Section II, pp. 113–122; William C. Westmoreland, *A Soldier Reports* (New York: Doubleday & Company Inc., 1976), p. 180.

[7]See Gravel, Vol. IV, pp. 332–335. Operation Hastings in July 1966 defeated the NVA 325B Division in I Corps, which was followed by Operation Prairie that inflicted heavy casualties on two other enemy divisions. An earlier spoiling attack near the Cambodian border, Operation Paul Revere kept the enemy from mounting a monsoon offensive.

[8]Sharp and Westmoreland, *Report,* Section II, p. 114.

[9]Saville R. Davis, "Next Vietnam step watched," Christian Science Monitor, September 13, 1966, p. 1; Sharp and Westmoreland, *Report,* Section II, p. 127.

[10]*Pentagon Papers,* Book 5, "Volume I: Phase II," pp. 81–82.

military buildup. The service chiefs could find no way to speed the process any further without calling up the reserves or extending terms of service, which McNamara, citing domestic political constraints, refused to do. In April 1966, McNamara, having demanded that the military build up to a strength of 429,000 by the end of the year, acquiesced to a lower goal of 384,000 (70 maneuver battalions). Nine more maneuver battalions would arrive in January 1967 and strength by June 1967 was scheduled to reach 425,000.[11] McNamara, breathing fire and smoke in his determination to prosecute the war, accepted this "slower" rate of buildup only because it was imperative that there be *some* agreement with his military leaders that permitted rational planning for deployments. Decisions already taken (the initial 175,000 Phase I forces, the 112,500 Phase II forces, and the 41,500 Phase II initial add-on forces) had set the schedule for units arriving in Vietnam through mid-1966, with the United States sending soldiers to Vietnam as fast as it could.[12] Discussions within the administration in January, February, and March 1966 had no impact on deployments already under way. However, the specifics of what would happen beyond mid-1966 remained to be worked out and by April it was necessary to move beyond debate and issue orders. McNamara, still furious with the "slow" pace of the buildup, was forced to give way to his professional soldiers, although he did so with ill humor and little grace. He followed up his acquiescence with a demand for an explanation as to why the military could not do a better job in building up more quickly.[13]

McNamara directed Assistant Secretary of Defense Alain Enthoven to work with the army to try to develop a faster deployment schedule. The result of this pressure was an army plan, approved in June, for accelerated deployment of two brigades of the 9th Infantry Division. The new schedule achieved moderate success in meeting McNamara's demands and the new end-of-1966 target became 391,000 soldiers—with a June 1967 figure of 431,000. Total maneuver battalions would be 79 by the end of 1966 (as

[11]Ibid., p. 39. There is some inconsistency about the McNamara target troop strength. See *Gravel,* Vol. IV, pp. 309–318. CINCPAC recommended and McNamara accepted a target of 443,000. The JCS said that this number could not be attained without mobilization. During subsequent discussion, the target number changed. In one JCS document the assumption was that the target was 413,000. At another point, McNamara's guidance was taken to be 429,000 by the end of 1966. This number is consistent with a McNaughton-William Bundy memo from February 1966 that projected 429,000 as the desired and expected number. The point is that all these targets exceeded the 384,000 that the JCS said was possible.

[12]Ibid., p. 22. This is a Westmoreland memorandum on the limitations of the pace of the buildup.

[13]Ibid., pp. 39–40.

opposed to 79 by the end of January 1967) and 82 by the end of June 1967.[14]

In July, McNamara wrote approvingly to the president of the new, accelerated schedule for US units headed for Vietnam:

> I am happy to report that this effort has been successful, and we will be able to provide more troops and equipment during the remainder of this calendar year than we had thought possible last spring.... To illustrate the degree of acceleration already achieved, we now plan to have 79 Army and Marine Corps maneuver battalions in South Vietnam by December 1966, as compared to the 70 battalions we thought could safely be deployed only four months ago. We now expect to have 395,000 personnel in South Vietnam by the end of this year compared to 314,000 estimated last year.[15]

In other words, on July 15, 1966, McNamara reported to the president that he hoped to have 395,000 troops in Vietnam by the end of the year, (compared to the slightly lower Army-Enthoven figure of 391,000 developed in June; the higher numbers probably came from a June 18 statement of requirements from CINCPAC.) McNamara portrayed the nine-battalion increase as an important achievement in the prosecution of the war.

In military planning, the normal sequence is to determine the requirement, or optimum force structure, to include logistic support, and follow this with consideration of any existing constraints. Then, and only then, can staffs develop the actual size of the force to be deployed. Since the Enthoven-Army plan accelerated deployment of actual forces, the cart was before the horse. On June 18, 1966, Admiral Sharp, US CINCPAC, submitted the follow-up paperwork for decisions already approved, which bore the title "Calendar Year 1966 Adjusted Requirements and Calendar Year 1967 Requirements."[16] CINCPAC's 1966 year-end troop strength was projected to be 395,269. CINCPAC referred to a "rounding out" of forces—which may have accounted for the difference between the Enthoven-Army figure of 391,000.[17] At any rate, McNamara used the 395,000 figure in his report to the president in mid-July.

[14]Ibid., p. 48.
[15]Ibid., p. 49
[16]Gravel, Volume IV, p. 324.
[17]Ibid., p. 325.

At this point, it is necessary to present some explanation of military terminology, because the administration's troop strength numbers are confusing. Without such an understanding, it is easy to read the *Pentagon Papers* and other documentary sources and conclude—as many have erroneously done—that McNamara's about-face was nothing more than a case of a defense secretary learning to say "no" to his subordinates' unreasonable requests for resources. In fact, the military made no request that would have required a response. The June 18, 1966, statement of requirements—to which McNamara would react in August as if it were a sudden, unexpected request for a vast increase in forces, and to which he said "no"—was entirely consistent with earlier plans, even though it refers to troop numbers substantially higher than 395,000. The June 18 statement of requirements was not, as many have alleged, a troop request.

The basis of many explanations, including mine, is the *Pentagon Papers*. In the *Pentagon Papers* discussion of this issue, under the subheading "CINCPAC's 18 June Request," the first line says "However, even before the Secretary of Defense published Program No. 3, CINCPAC had submitted his Calendar Year 1966 adjusted requirements and Calendar Year 1967 requirements." This would appear to support the other positions on the issue. However, the subsequent data presented by the *Pentagon Papers* analyst does not support the contention. The analyst reports that "The requirements for 1966 had been adjusted to 474,786, *bringing the year-end totals for 1966 and 1967 to 395, 269 and 436, 506.*" (Emphasis added.) "The requirements for CY 1967," he continued, "were basically considered to be rounding out of forces." After all the deployments on the plan were carried out, according to the analyst, the strength in Vietnam would be 90 maneuver battalions and 542,588 personnel.[18]

While it is easy to understand how a reader could be confused from these figures, it is difficult to believe that defense analysts or, for that matter, the

[18]Theis, pp. 136–137; Herring, p. 152; Schandler, pp. 39–40; *Pentagon Papers,* Book 5, "US Ground Strategy and Force Deployments, 1965–1968," pp. 52–55. Some examples from major works illustrate this point. Wallace Thies, in *When Governments Collide,* argues that McNamara's turnaround was in response to a JCS request for a troop strength of 688,500. George Herring, in *America's Longest War,* explains that in June 1966, the president approved a force level of 431,000 to be reached by mid-1967. However, Herring also says "While the deployments were being approved, Westmoreland was developing a request for an increase to 542,000 troops by the end of 1967." Herbert Schandler, in *The Unmaking of a President,* says that even before the April figures had been published by the Department of Defense, the military commanders (on August 5, 1966) submitted new requirements for 1967. They considered, says Schandler, the additional troops to be "rounding-out" forces to give a balanced additional capability of 542,588 by the end of 1967. The 436,506 figure, as it turned out, was actually intended to be the June 1967 troop strength.

secretary himself, did not understand them. Recall that the original JCS position on what was possible by the end of 1966 had been 384,000. There was great interaction and exchange of information among General Westmoreland, Admiral Sharp, the individual military services, and the Joint Chiefs of Staff. Indeed, General Westmoreland has been cited several times in this work expounding on the logistic limitations that would delay the rate of buildup. The military had been consistent in saying that a more rapid buildup was not feasible without a reserve callup. Under great pressure, the army, with Assistant Secretary Enthoven's help, finally agreed that a level of 391,000 was possible, and after Westmoreland and Admiral Sharp had a go at it, the number was finally 395,000. The question we must ask ourselves appears to be, "Is it conceivable that in the middle of this discussion, the military suddenly, with as weak a reason as 'rounding out of forces,' proposed that the end-of-1966 strength should be 474,786?" The answer, of course, is "no," and it is here that we must have some understanding of military terminology.

The key words to understand are "required" and "authorized." For a military unit to be 100 percent capable of mission accomplishment, let us assume that it should have 500 soldiers. Because of constraints, it may not be possible to staff the unit fully, but if the shortages are carefully chosen, the unit can still function with a strength of 400 soldiers. Put in military jargon, this could be stated as "the unit has 500 required, 400 authorized." The optimum requirement is 500, but everyone knows that there will only be 400 living, breathing people in the unit. When the military position in the debate with McNamara over end-of-1966 troop strength was 384,000, that number was the authorized or actual predicted troop strength. The *required* or optimum strength listed in the Tables of Organization and Equipment for the units that comprised the 384,000 force was 443,000. The June 18, 1966, statement of *requirements* put *required* strength for the end of 1966 at 474,786.[19] This does not mean that Admiral Sharp expected 474,786 soldiers to be in Vietnam by the end of 1966. On the contrary, *authorized* or actual strength was to be 395,269. *Required* strength had changed from 443,000 to 474,786. When CINCPAC's statement was prepared, it was against the backdrop of McNamara's exasperation with the military for failing to be able to build up to an actual, or *authorized,* force level of 429,000 by the end of 1966, and was worked out with the knowledge that the Army and Enthoven had managed to nudge the 384,000

[19]Ibid., p. 53.

figure up to 391,000 and put nine more battalions in the field. Indeed, almost a full month after the June 18 document arrived in Washington, McNamara would use the 395,000 figure—not the 391,000 number—and report it as an achievement to the president. CINCPAC's end of 1967 *required* strength was 542,588, while *authorized* strength was to be 436,406. CINCPAC's statement *did not change the figures already approved.*[20]

Further evidence that CINCPAC did not change the already agreed-upon size of the force is provided by the number of maneuver battalions. The Enthoven-army formula was 79 by the end of 1966, precisely the same figure used in the June 18 CINCPAC statement of requirements. Moreover, *the Enthoven-army troop levels fell short of McNamara's desired troop strength.* (The accompanying chart may help resolve some of the confusion.)

	Army-Enthoven	June 18 CINCPAC	July 15 McNamara Report
End 1966 Troops	391,000	395,296	395,000
End 1966 battalions	79	79	79
Mid-1967 Troops	431,000	436,406	not mentioned

Three weeks after proudly telling President Johnson that he was going to be able to put 395,000 soldiers into a war zone by the end of 1966, McNamara "reacted" to the June 18 statement of requirements as if it were a new policy which he opposed and he demanded a line by line justification for every soldier added.[21] "It is our policy," he wrote in a memorandum to the Joint Chiefs on August 5, "to provide the troops, weapons, and supplies requested by General Westmoreland.... The latest revised CINCPAC requirements, submitted on 18 June, subject as above, are to be accorded the same consideration.... However, I desire and expect a detailed, line-by-line analysis of the requirements to determine that each is truly essential to the carrying out of our war plan. We must send to Vietnam what is needed, but only what is needed."[22] From August 1966, Secretary McNamara began to build a case for a troop ceiling and a reduction of US goals in Vietnam. Although many scholars have attributed McNamara's "disillusionment" to endless military requests for troop increases, the truth is otherwise.

[20]Except, of course, as noted, the difference between 391,000 and 395,000. This led, naturally, to a difference of 1967 figures of 431,000 versus 436,000.

[21]Ibid., pp. 53–54.

[22]Ibid.

There was no civilian-military split on the desired size of the force; there *was* disagreement over the rate of the buildup to the desired size; it was Secretary McNamara who desired that the rate of buildup be more rapid; and the June 18 statement of requirements from CINCPAC did not propose any substantial change to the ultimate size of the force or rate of buildup from figures that already had been approved.[23] Robert NcNamara, pure and simple, had changed his mind.

In October 1966, McNamara prepared a formal recommendation to the president that the United States establish a troop ceiling of 470,000. Moreover, in so doing, he set the stage in this recommendation for the United States to change its strategic objective from ensuring an independent non-communist Vietnam to ensuring only that the South Vietnamese had a reasonable chance to choose their own form of government. The elimination of "non-communist" was intended to pave the way for Viet Cong participation in a South Vietnamese coalition government.[24] McNamara won his point and the president approved the recommendation. Although the military would make a futile attempt to overturn the decision, the ultimate acceptance of the shift in national objectives is reflected by Westmoreland writing in 1968 about 1967.

> I had, by this time, refined my original concept of a three-phase war to one of four phases, two of which had already been completed. I envisioned 1968 to be the year of the third phase, in which we would continue to help strengthen the Vietnamese Armed Forces—turning over more of the war effort to increasingly capable and better armed forces. In the fourth—and decisive—phase, I could see the US presence becoming superfluous as infiltration slowed, the Communist infrastructure was cut up and a stable government and capable

[23]See Gelb and Betts, p. 132, Herring, p. 176, Komer, p. 144, and Schandler, p. 41, for the conventional interpretation that McNamara became disillusioned. While these scholars do not emphasize the change as much as I do, please note they do not disagree that there was a change. Gelb and Betts come closer to me than the others on the significance of the change. They attribute the change to disillusionment that resulted from a study concluded in the summer of 1966 that said the bombing of North Vietnam had no measurable direct effect on North Vietnam. For another angle, see Harrison Salisbury, *A Time of Change, A Reporter's Tale of Our Time* (New York: 1988), pp. 122–123. Salisbury says the first sign that McNamara was turning around came on July 4, 1966. In the wake of some highly successful air strikes against heretofore off limits oil storage facilities, McNamara surprised his military executive officer by expressing irritation over the strikes and the "escalation" they represented.

[24]*Pentagon Papers*, Book 5, "US Ground Strategy and Force Deployments, 1965–1968," pp. 82–93.

Vietnamese Armed Forces carried their own war to a success-ful conclusion.[25]

This is a remarkable change. Phase III originally had called for the final defeat of the Viet Cong by US forces. Now, US forces would turn over the war and become "superfluous." The beginning of this change was August 1966. The supposed catalyst for McNamara's change, according to the *Pentagon Papers,* was a June 18 document, a document that allegedly was not forwarded to McNamara till August 5.[26] In order for us to believe this we have to be able to accept certain unbelievable assumptions. For instance, we have to accept that this request from the commander fighting the war, a request that was allegedly such a startling bombshell, arrived at the Pentagon on June 18, and the Joint Chiefs of Staff concealed it from the Department of Defense until August 5. This would also mean, since McNamara responded on August 5, that he received, analyzed, and responded to this "stunning" request in less than one day. Further, we know that the figure the army and Enthoven worked out for 1966 was 391,000 with 79 battalions, which was an increase from the approved April figures of 384,000 and 70 battalions. On July 15, 1966, the figure McNamara reported to the president as an achievement was 395,000 and 79 battalions. The June 18 statement proposed 395,296 and 79 battalions. Where did McNamara get the 395,000 figure, if not from CINCPAC's statement? The difference is slight, but it is a difference and it means McNamara was aware of the June 18 statement of requirements by at least July 15—and he approved of the strength figures for 1966 contained therein.

Is there a justification for alleging the CINCPAC statement of requirements provoked McNamara to decide to abandon the effort to achieve military victory? The answer must be no. Did McNamara begin to advocate precisely that course? Yes. Moreover, even if CINCPAC's statement had been a request for a troop increase, it would not explain the about-face between July 15 and August 5. McNamara seized on the CINCPAC statement of requirements as a pretext to begin the process of ending the US open-ended commitment to South Vietnam. The question, then, is why, and the answer is not that Robert McNamara became disillusioned with the war.[27]

---

[25]Sharp and Westmoreland, *Report,* Section II, p. 136.

[26]Gravel, Volume IV, p. 325.

[27]Most advocates of the "disillusioned" thesis claim that lack of results from the bombing caused McNamara's disillusionment. While many in the bombing business would argue that the multitude of political restrictions on the bombing hampered effectiveness, in any case it does not follow that the solution to problems with bombing the North is to limit the number of soldiers in the South.

Was McNamara 'Disillusioned?'

The "McNamara became disillusioned" explanation of McNamara's change of heart received new life after McNamara's testimony at the Westmoreland versus CBS libel trial. Central to accepting this explanation is a blind belief that the ultimate North Vietnamese victory was inevitable because the United States had no hope of winning the hearts and minds of the South Vietnamese people and the leadership of the government of South Vietnam was hopelessly corrupt. Indeed, two CIA reports that allegedly influenced McNamara made these arguments. Blind acceptance of the premise is revealed in a book about the trial published in 1987. "If the CIA was right (and history has proven it so)," alleges this book, "then the United States was incapable of beating the VC/NVA on the ground or in the air— no matter what the Joint Chiefs of Staff said."[28]

History has not proven it so. The fall of South Vietnam only shows that a large, well-supplied tank and motorized force can usually beat a smaller, less well-supplied tank and motorized force. The tanks that broke into the presidential palace in Saigon represented a purely military solution. Moreover, the book's argument highlighted a part of the CIA analysis which charged that because of the larger American logistic tail, the North Vietnamese were even with or ahead of the United States in actual numbers of fighters in the field.[29] But both the CIA and the authors misunderstand military terminology by making a faulty distinction between the combat maneuver forces and the "indirect combat support, logistics, construction, engineering, security, and other support task units."[30] They used entertaining descriptions of air-conditioned clubs, PXs, and mobile laundries to dramatize this claim. But in the US Army "combat" refers only to infantry and armor units. "Combat support" refers to field artillery, air defense weapons used as ground weapons, attack helicopters, and combat engineers (driving huge plows into enemy fortifications.) The CIA and the authors who relied upon their work ignored the bulk of our firepower and how we fight. American military men gave up on human wave assaults right after Pickett's charge at Gettysburg. Field artillery is known as the "greatest killer on the battlefield." It was American technology that made the American advantage firepower and mobility. It would have been senseless not to use it.

---

[28]Bob Brewin and Sydney Shaw, *Vietnam On Trial, Westmoreland vs. CBS,* (New York, 1987), pp. 114–115. (Hereafter referred to as Brewin and Shaw).

[29]Brewin and Shaw, p. 114.

[30]Ibid.

A mobile laundry falls under a classification known as "combat service support." "Combat support" units, on the other hand, shoot at the enemy and kill his people and break things. The CIA was wrong. More importantly, the first CIA report that allegedly disillusioned McNamara was not completed until August 26, 1966—after McNamara "responded" to the CINCPAC June 18 Statement of Requirements.[31]

During the 1984 Westmoreland-CBS lawsuit for libel, McNamara testified that he concluded that the war could not be won militarily and that there also needed to be a political track to war. The press reported that his testimony suggested that he may have felt this way as early as 1965. One source called this "quite a revelation."[32] However, a close inspection of McNamara's deposition and his testimony reveals that he was consistently evasive about dates, always adding that his memory was imprecise. The only precise answer to the question of his change of mind was "certainly during the period of 1967 and after."[33] Moreover, it is important to understand what McNamara meant by saying there needed to be a political as well as a military track for US policy. Nobody, civilian or military, ever disputed the need for an effective pacification effort, though there were disagreements over allocation of resources. It is not startling that early on McNamara felt that pacification was important. But McNamara's testimony shows that "political solution" meant a deal with North Vietnam. He testified, by way of amplification on "political solution," that in 1967 Henry Kissinger was working as a private citizen for the administration as a go-between for direct contact with the North Vietnamese. This initiative had little to do with the hearts and minds of the people of South Vietnam. The trial documents do not support the suggestion that McNamara may have been "disillusioned" during the first half of 1966. In fact, the contemporaneous record in the *Pentagon Papers* confirms he was continuing to press the military for a faster buildup of forces.

Why?

Perhaps the best place to begin an investigation of why McNamara reversed his position is in his own justification of his recommendations to

---

[31]The second "disillusioning" CIA report was not until May 23, 1967.

[32]Brewin and Shaw, pp. 102–103.

[33]*Trial*, cards 331, 947, and 948. The deposition is on card 331 and his trial testimony is on cards 947 and 948.

the president for a troop ceiling and reduced strategic goals. Following a trip to Vietnam in October 1966, McNamara prepared a memorandum for the president in which he discussed US tactical successes. "We have done somewhat better militarily than I anticipated," he said. But he added, "My concern continues, however, in other respects. This is because *I see no reasonable way to bring the war to an end soon.*" (McNamara's emphasis.) Accordingly, McNamara had some "recommended actions" for the president. "Specifically," he said, "we must *improve our position by getting ourselves into a military posture that we credibly would maintain indefinitely—a posture that makes trying to 'wait us out' less attractive.*" (McNamara's emphasis.) Among several recommendations to achieve this, the first and most important was to "stabilize US force levels in Vietnam." Troop strength "should level off at the total of 470,000." This would be sufficient to defeat the enemy in large unit operations and keep main force units from interrupting pacification. Although it was possible that 470,000 American soldiers could break the enemy morale in the short term, it was not likely and "I believe also that even many more than 470,000 would not kill the enemy off in such numbers as to break their morale so long as they think they can wait us out." He also proposed that the president push for negotiations.[34]

McNamara followed his recommendations with a gloomy but telling prediction. "The prognosis is bad," he wrote, "that the war can be brought to a satisfactory conclusion within the next two years." Addressing himself to this point he expressed the view that "the solution lies in girding, openly, for a longer war and in taking actions immediately which will in 12 to 18 months give clear evidence that the continuing costs and risks to the American people are acceptably limited, that the formula for success has been found, and that the end of the war is merely a matter of time."[35] Or, stated a little (very little) differently, the solution was to convince the American voter before the 1968 election that there was a light at the end of the tunnel.

McNamara gave his memorandum to the Joint Chiefs of Staff for comment before it became a formal proposal to the president. The *Pentagon Papers* describes the military opposition to a troop ceiling as "predictably rapid and violent." It was neither. With regard to the 470,000-man figure, the JCS "wished to 'reserve judgment' until they reviewed the revised

[34]Gravel, Vol. IV, pp. 348–352.
[35]Ibid., p. 353.

programs being prepared during the CINCPAC planning conference." How can this be considered a "rapid and violent" response to McNamara's proposed memorandum for the president? The *Pentagon Papers* further says that the military disagreed with McNamara's "guarded assessment of the military situation, which in their eyes had 'improved substantially over the past year.' " But McNamara did not have a "guarded assessment of the military situation." McNamara's comment on the *military* situation was "We have done somewhat better militarily than I anticipated." This is not at variance with the JCS finding that the military situation "improved substantially." In fact, the military situation actually *had improved.* And the military establishment made no specific military counterproposal to the 470,000-man troop ceiling until March 1967.[36]

A quick look at the results of the October 20, 1966, "CINCPAC Planning Conference" proves that the military was not violently at odds with the administration and, by the way, further confirms the earlier explanation of the difference between "required" and "authorized" troop strength. The results were presented as follows:

	Requirements	*Capabilities*	
	US Maneuver Battalions	*Maneuver Battalions*	*Personnel*
End CY 66	82	79	384,361
End CY 67	94	91	493,969
End CY 68	94	94	519,310
End CY 69	94	94	520,020[37]

Notice that the "requirement" for end-of-1966 maneuver battalions is 82 while the number for maneuver battalions is 79 in the capabilities column. Notice also that 79 is exactly the number reported to the president by McNamara in July as an achievement, and that the capabilities column, despite the pressure and promises, had settled back to about 384,000, or the original end-of-1966 figure approved in April. The Enthoven-army figure for *mid-1967* had been 431,000. The *end-of-1967* figure (493,969) is not out of line and the final 520,000 figure to be achieved *three full years* in the future. The meaning of this is clear. Over time, the force that had been planned would be filled out to its optimum strength. This is consistent with General Westmoreland's contention about his position at the end of

---

[36]Ibid., pp. 356–357, discusses the JCS response. See Pentagon Papers, "Volume II: Program 5," p. 61, for the first specific military counterproposal to the 470,000 figure on March 18, 1967.

[37]Gravel, Volume IV, p. 359.

1966. His ultimate goal was a balanced force of "about 500,000 men."[38] Military expectations had not changed from April 1966. What had changed was McNamara's position. Instead of constant pressure to build up more rapidly, the secretary was now attempting to curtail the buildup. Had this CINCPAC conference published the above figures in April, it is likely that McNamara's only comment would have been to criticize the 384,361 figure as being too small.

Once the JCS had commented on McNamara's recommendation, Mc-Namara took his proposal to the president on November 4, giving the military a new program on November 11, 1966, that set a 470,000-man ceiling. As part of his explanation to the military he wrote:

> We have no prospects of attriting the enemy force at a rate equal or greater than his capability to infiltrate and recruit, and this will be true at either the 470,000 US personnel or 570,000.... By 4th quarter 1965 estimated enemy losses (killed, captured, military defectors) reached 2,215 per week. The weekly average for CY 66 has remained about the same, although enemy losses increased to 2,330 per week in the 3rd quarter and to 2,930 in October.... The enemy loss rate was apparently not affected significantly by the greatly increased friendly activity during 1966 which included: 44% increase in battalion days of operation; 25% increase in battalion sized operations contacting the enemy; and 28% increase in small unit operations accompanied by a 12% increase in contacts.... It is impossible to predict the point at which we can expect to attrite enemy forces at the rate he introduces new ones.[39]

Here is war-by-bean-counting at its worst. In McNamara's memorandum to the president recommending the troop ceiling he had argued that the United States was doing better militarily than he had anticipated. Only a few weeks later, in explaining the 470,000 troop ceiling to the JCS, he had argued that the United States was doing worse militarily than it should. This contradiction only makes sense when taken in the context of McNamara's reference to time and the poor prospect of bringing the war to a "rapid" conclusion. If we look closely at the numbers, we can see, first

---

[38]Westmoreland, *A Soldier Reports*, p. 194.

[39]Ibid., p. 110. See also p. 105 for McNamara's argument that US force increases would damage South Vietnam's economy.

of all, that in the third quarter enemy losses increased significantly and in the month preceding the memorandum had jumped by 32 percent (2,930 per week is 32 percent higher than 2,215). These casualty figures were not good enough for McNamara because the increase in the rate of killing had not been directly proportional to the increase in US troop strength. This point was highlighted by the disparity in the increase in operations and the increase in contacts. Battalion-days of operation increased 44 percent while contacts increased only 25 percent. Small unit operations increased 28 percent while contacts increased only 12 percent. Of course, these figures were good news, not bad. The building US military momentum was increasingly forcing the enemy to avoid large unit battles and to locate away from major population centers and near sanctuaries in North Vietnam, Laos, and Cambodia. McNamara, at least indirectly, acknowledged this by saying the lack of a rate of killing directly proportional to the amount of effort was partially due to "increasing enemy reluctance to fight large battles."[40] But this on-the-field good news was immediately transformed into a strategic disaster through numbers crunching and the political calendar. American successes led the enemy to avoid battle to reduce his casualties. This, combined with increased Soviet logistic support, meant that the rate of killing to achieve the mythical "crossover point" would not be reached soon, or more precisely, in time. The question is, in time for what?

Returning to McNamara's memorandum recommending the 470,000-man ceiling, we find clues to the time problem. His prognosis was that chances were bleak that the war could be brought to a "satisfactory conclusion within the next two years." He followed by saying the "solution lies in girding, openly, for a longer war and in taking actions immediately which will in 12 to 18 months give clear evidence that...the end of the war is merely a matter of time." Why did McNamara choose "two years?" Why not six months or even thirty months? The answer is that two years from November 1966 would be November 1968, or the next general election. McNamara told the president the prospects for victory in the next two years were bleak and said in regard to this grim fact "the solution" lay in "girding, openly, for a longer war...." The solution to what? Certainly not the war! He just said the United States was not going to win that soon. McNamara referred to the public relations problem of the Democrats appearing to be the masterminds of an increasingly costly war the United States did not seem to be winning at election time. He was proposing actions that

[40]Ibid., p. 111.

"will in 12 to 18 months," or just in time for the 1968 election campaign, make the administration look better.[41]

McNamara was hardly alone in this view. The *Pentagon Papers* analyst, who of course was a member of the Johnson administration, felt constrained to refer repeatedly to "political risks" when he gave an account of the president and McNamara reviewing the JCS comments on McNamara's proposals. Johnson and his defense secretary went over the document and comments at the president's ranch and approved the 470,000-man ceiling on November 5, 1966. At a ranch press conference, McNamara announced that troop increases would "be at a substantially lower rate." At this point, the *Pentagon Papers* analyst gives an analysis of the November 8, 1966, off-year elections (the results were mixed for the administration) quite self-consciously tying the election results to satisfaction or dissatisfaction with the administration's prosecution of the war. The analyst concluded by noting that "the 1968 Presidential race, potentially one debating our war policies, promised to be a more interesting and heated campaign than anyone had anticipated two years before."[42]

Another question that needs to be answered is why McNamara chose the 470,000-man ceiling. Apparently, the point at which the United States would be forced to mobilize or partially mobilize was roughly half a million. During two discussions with Westmoreland in October, it appears McNamara sought and received assurances from the general that a force of 470,000 would prevent defeat. The mobilization line was a "political sound barrier" that would not be broken.[43]

Although the president approved McNamara's proposal, the subject of whether this was a temporary or permanent troop ceiling remained open

---

[41]A minor but revealing point is McNamara's grammar. He wrote that the solution lay in "girding, openly, for a longer war." He separated the adverb "openly" with commas. There was no reason for this unless he wanted to call particular attention to it. In fact, it is evident that the purpose of all of this was to address the "open" or public relations issue.

[42]Gravel, Volume IV, pp. 362–363.

[43]Ibid., pp. 385–386. See page 360 for evidence that Westmoreland was hoping the figure would be slightly larger, in the 480,000–500,000 range. It was during McNamara's earlier trip to Saigon in October 1966 that McNamara probably first sought and received assurances on the 470,000 figure from Westmoreland, since he wrote his memo proposing the ceiling upon his return. The second meeting was in Manila at the end of October and involved a private meeting between the president and Westmoreland. The general evidently repeated assurances to the president, though he sounded out others in the party on the possibility of a slightly higher figure. See *Pentagon Papers,* Book 5, Phase II, pp. 61, 79–80, 83, 97. Westmoreland later went on record to say that the 470,000 level could avoid defeat, but it would lead to an unreasonably protracted war, perhaps five years. A protracted war, however, was precisely what McNamara had proposed and the president had approved.

for discussion. McNamara, probably anticipating some effort by the military to push the figure up, left some room for the number to increase as a sop to his service chiefs, who were still under the impression that the United States was seeking victory on the battlefield.

Since no course of action would win the war in any meaningful sense by 1968, the administration believed it was going into the 1968 elections susceptible to the accusation of having created a costly failure. Under these circumstances, would it be better not to win with a large or small effort? The answer McNamara gave was the latter. Given that the administration would have to admit that the United States had not won, it was better to have a smaller effort and scaled-down expectations. Thus, in McNamara's troop ceiling memo, the secretary discussed the pacification effort and said "This important war must be fought and won by the Vietnamese themselves." Moreover, he said of the war in general, "We should avoid any implication that we will stay in South Vietnam with bases or to guarantee any particular outcome to a solely South Vietnamese struggle." He recommended that the United States "develop a realistic plan for providing a role for the VC in negotiations, post-war life, and government of the nation." It would be early 1967 before the administration would reveal directly to the military its intention to abandon an independent, non-communist South Vietnam as a national goal, substituting in its place a rather hazy guarantee of "the inherent right [of the South Vietnamese] to choose their way of life."[44] It would be easier to admit not winning if the administration could claim it really had not been trying to win and everything was coming out as the leadership had planned all along. The *Pentagon Papers* explains McNamara's thinking on the troop ceiling this way: "The Secretary was thinking along different lines—if there was to be no quick 'successful' end to the war, why invest greater resources and run greater political risks to get there—still late."[45]

Why?—Part II

To be fair to Robert McNamara and the rest of the Johnson administration, there possibly were other reasons (besides political self-interest) to reconsider US objectives in Vietnam. There were strategic factors that also encouraged McNamara to hold fast to his conclusion that the United States

[44]Gravel, Volume IV, p. 393.
[45]*Pentagon Papers*, Book 5, "US Ground Strategy and Force Deployments, 1965–1967," p. 99.

should not seek victory on the battlefield. If we look back at the exchange of signals between China and the United States, starting with the Li Zongren affair, there is evidence that the United States finally began to understand that improving relations with the People's Republic of China was a foreign policy option, and that this understanding crystallized in the American leadership in mid-1966. Li Zongren had appeared in public with Mao in October 1965 and in a press conference had stated his feeling that the responsibility for China and the United States not being on good terms was entirely that of the US leadership.[46] Although there is no evidence the United States understood Mao's gesture to be an overture at improved relations, US fear of Chinese intervention in Vietnam led to efforts to reassure China of limited US goals.[47] The fear of Chinese intervention became more acute once the decision to increase Phase II forces was taken at the end of 1965.[48] The public effort to reassure China that the United States did not intend to threaten the Chinese began in early March 1966 with the decision to permit American scholars and journalists to visit China.[49] This decision had been reinforced by congressional hearings, as noted earlier, that suggested there was a strong sentiment in academia and in the government for ending China's isolation.[50] Vice-president Humphrey lent his authority to the idea of reducing Sino-American tension by advocating "containment without isolation," also in March.[51]

Mao had responded immediately to these US signals by addressing the subject of the congressional hearings and the decision to allow an exchange of scholars and journalists. An editorial stated, "everyone knows the continued cause of strained relations has nothing to do with journalists and scholars — it is the hostile policy of the United States...primarily because the United States is forcefully occupying China's province of Taiwan."[52] The meaning here is clear: if hostile relations were the fault of the United States, the leaders of China would prefer good relations. Further, the problem was Taiwan, not Vietnam. Mao reinforced these signals, as noted earlier, with continuing statements repeating and clarifying the position. A statement by Zhou Enlai in April and again at the end of June contributed

---

[46] "Li Tsung-jen's Press Conference," *Peking Review,* October 1, 1965, pp. 22–27.

[47] *Secret History,* pp. 490–492.

[48] Ibid.

[49] "The news—briefly," *Christian Science Monitor,* March 11, 1966, p. 3.

[50] Richard L. Strout, "Isolation of Peking opposed," ibid., p. 3.; Saville R. Davis, "How US policy shifts on communist China," ibid., March 16, 1966, p. 1.

[51] "The news—briefly," ibid., p. 2.

[52] "Old Tune, New Plot," *Peking Review,* April 1, 1966, pp. 13–15.

to the effort.[53] It appears that, this time, the United States read the signals, and responded with Vice-president Humphrey once again suggesting the desirability of improved relations in his June 1966 graduation address at West Point.[54]

This time, Mao left no doubt about his intentions by responding to the June 1966 American overture several times in July 1966, and also by intensifying attacks against the Soviet Union, equating the seriousness of the struggle against Soviet "revisionism" with the struggle against imperialism.[55] Since imperialism had always been the main enemy, the elevation of Soviet "revisionism" to an equally evil status was an extraordinary shift that also meant that US-Chinese relations were possible. Finally, just days before McNamara's about-face in August, the Chinese responded to a Soviet propaganda attack against China about US-Chinese diplomatic contacts in Warsaw. The Chinese accused the Soviets of various crimes, but did not repudiate the diplomatic contact.[56]

McNamara's draft proposal for a troop ceiling was written in October 1966. In September, Chinese foreign minister Chen Yi had surfaced the idea that China did not want to clash with the United States and was not opposed to Sino-American negotiations to resolve the Vietnam conflict.[57] Subsequent Chinese press clarifications perhaps muddied the waters by noting that Chinese policy had not changed. Nevertheless, the Chinese did not repudiate Chen Yi's statement. Further, at the September 7, 1966, Sino-US diplomatic meeting in Warsaw, the Chinese ambassador issued a statement chiding the United States for releasing the content of the previous talks, thereby permitting, according to the Chinese, the Soviets to follow up with a propaganda attack against the US-Chinese dialogue. This time, therefore, the Chinese ambassador was issuing a statement with his own version of the talks—and he rejected improved Sino-US relations because

[53] "Premier Chou En-lai's Four-Point Statement on China's Policy Towards US," ibid., May 13, 1966, p. 5. The statement was issued on April 10. "Comrade Chou En-lai's Speech at Taiwan Mass Rally," ibid., July 1, 1966, pp. 25–30.

[54] "Vietnam policy explained to West Point graduates," Christian Science Monitor, June 21, 1966, p. 11.

[55] "Vice-Premier Chen-yi's Speech at the Peking Mass Rally," *Peking Review,* July 15, 1966, pp. 27–29; "Who is the Rumour Manufacturer," ibid.; "Vice Premier Tao Chu's Speech," ibid., July 29, 1966, pp. 13–15.

[56] "No One Can Block the Eyes and Ears of the Whole World," ibid., August 12, 1966, p. 31. (*People's Daily* article on August 3).

[57] "The news—briefly," *Christian Science Monitor,* September 9, 1966, p. 2; David K. Willis, "Peking contrasts carefully studied," ibid., p. 3; "On the Statement by Chen-Yi," *Current Digest,* October 12, 1966, p. 8.

of a lack of American sincerity.[58] The ambassador also announced that the next meeting would take place January 11, 1967. In other words, the Chinese wanted the talks to continue, and they were making a request that, in the future, the discussions should be confidential.

It appears that finally the administration understood that absolute Chinese-American hostility was not the only foreign policy course in Asia. Perhaps US long-term interests in Asia could better be secured through a good relationship with China than with expending the resources it would take to "win," under the administration's concept of "win."[59] If the purpose of fighting the war in the first place was to contain Chinese communism, and Chinese communism turned out not to be the threat it once was thought to be, the logic of fighting the war was undercut. This does not mean that the administration instantly thought in terms of the dramatic Nixon trip to China, because it would take some time to change a relationship that had been exclusively hostile for nearly twenty years. It does mean that the administration's perception of China as a threat underwent a fundamental alteration. A May 19, 1967, draft memorandum for the president prepared by Assistant Secretary McNaughton and circulated for comment under McNamara's signature reflected this directly. McNaughton wrote, "To the extent that our original intervention and our existing actions in Vietnam were motivated by the perceived need to draw the line against Chinese expansionism in Asia, our objective has already been attained.... Any decision the US takes at this time with regard to South Vietnam...must be predicated on these premises as to our long run interests in Asia."[60]

Although much of the evidence of the "China factor" is circumstantial, the Sino-American diplomatic exchanges were an important backdrop to McNamara's recommendations to the president. Presumably, if the United States still considered containment of Chinese communism as vital to US interests, it would limit the administration's ability to change goals, election or no election. It is apparent that the slow process of changing American perceptions of the Chinese threat began during 1966, as the administration's concern with the 1968 elections grew. This changing per-

---

[58]"Ambassador Wang Kuo-chuan's Statement on Sino-US Talks," *Peking Review*, September 26, 1966, p. 8.

[59]*Trial*, card 811. This is a draft memorandum for the president dated May 19, 1967. It was prepared by McNaughton and circulated for comment by McNamara. It says that "decisions to make great investments in men, money and national honor in South Vietnam make sense only in conjunction" with a broad range of other efforts in Asia. The memorandum did not go to the president as written, but it is indicative of McNaughton's and McNamara's thinking.

[60]*Trial*, card 811; Gravel, Vol. IV, p. 477.

ception permitted the administration to elevate the importance of the election in decisionmaking. The May 19, 1967, draft memorandum for the president shows conclusively and specifically that McNamara's and McNaughton's view of China had changed.

A second major strategic factor that probably reinforced McNamara's change of heart was the shifting strategic nuclear balance between the United States and the Soviet Union. Although Kennedy had made the so-called "missile gap" a centerpiece of his 1960 campaign, he quickly discovered as president that the United States had an overwhelming nuclear superiority. This became clear publicly after the Cuban missile crisis in 1962. Although it appears that Khrushchev was disinclined to commit the resources to change this situation rapidly, Brezhnev and Kosygin launched a massive military spending campaign designed to overtake and surpass the United States. A 1987 study by Robert Crawford demonstrates that Lyndon Johnson and his advisers believed in 1964 that the Soviets would not be able to achieve a so-called "assured destruction" posture until the early 1970s, which caused McNamara to freeze US ICBM deployments in 1965 at 1,054. American intelligence detected the buildup by mid-1966, but incorrectly analyzed the data, concluding that the Soviets had accelerated their Anti-Ballistic Missile program. However, a National Intelligence Estimate released in October 1966 demonstrated that earlier assessments had been wrong and the Soviets were in fact redressing the strategic nuclear imbalance far more rapidly than anticipated. In 1964, the United States had possessed a "first-strike" capability that would have prevented effective retaliation from the Soviet Union. By 1967, the United States had lost this advantage.[61] Given the trends in nuclear forces, the United States leadership had to feel that it could ill afford to commit the military resources to win in Vietnam. The war was consuming the military budget and the bulk of US power was committed to Asia. By increasing the effort in Vietnam, the United States would not be in good position to respond to crises and threats elsewhere. The intelligence estimate with this disturbing information became available to McNamara in October 1966, or precisely when he developed the formal proposal for a troop ceiling in Vietnam. This suggests that the shifting strategic balance also contributed to McNamara's change of heart.[62]

[61]Robert W. Crawford, *Call Retreat, The Johnson Administration's Vietnam Policy, March 1967 to March 1968* (Washington: The Washington Institute for Values in Public Policy, 1986), pp. 9–11.

[62]ibid., pp. 10–11. Crawford builds a compelling chronology, beginning with McNamara's late September 1967 public acknowledgement that a change in the strategic nuclear balance was inevitable.

In any event, the military did not view the troop ceiling as appropriate. Whether they approved of the original plan to win by confining the ground war to South Vietnam and killing as many North Vietnamese as possible as fast as possible, at least the ultimate goal was to "win." They immediately recognized the troop ceiling idea for what it was—a recommendation to continue fighting without trying to win. As a result, the military attempted in the spring of 1967 to overturn McNamara's ceiling. The numbers would be adjusted, but by August 1967, military efforts would, once and for all, fail.

$$\boxed{11}$$

Soviet Response

Major Events

- *June 1966*—Soviet press begins close and continuous coverage of Cultural Revolution in China.
- *July 1966*—Conference of the Political Consultative Committee of the Warsaw Pact and meeting of Council for Mutual and Economic Assistance. Purpose: better coordination and division of labor in implementing January 1966 Soviet-North Vietnamese aid agreement.
- *July 1966*—Chinese Foreign Minister Chen Yi publicly blasts Soviets for military buildup on Chinese border.
- *August 1966*—11th Plenum of Chinese Communist Party ratifies 16-point program on Cultural Revolution.
- *September 1966*—Chen Yi does not preclude Sino-American negotiations to resolve Vietnam question. Mao is forced to use PLA troops to curb excessive violence in Cultural Revolution.
- *October 3, 1966*—Soviet Union and North Vietnam conclude new arms agreement which increases Soviet assistance for Vietnam.
- *January 1967*—Mao begins large-scale commitment of PLA to Cultural Revolution. Soviet troop deployments to Far East accelerate.
- *March 1967*—Soviets accuse Mao of aligning with the United States.
- *July 1967*—Bloody Wuhan incident. Soviets detect dissatisfaction in Chinese Army.
- *August 1967*—Soviet press reports that new US troop increases would force the United States to mobilize. Soviet press stresses signs of dissaffection in Chinese Army. Le Than Nghi arrives in Moscow to negotiate Tet logistic agreement.
- *September 23, 1967*—New Soviet-Vietnamese logistic agreement—far more extensive than any before.

- *October 1967*—Sharp increase in Soviet shipping to Vietnam begins—tied to September 23 agreement.

Developments in the last half of 1966 suggested a combination of disturbing trends for the progress of Soviet strategy. On the battlefield the North Vietnamese were losing the war. This meant, as some American public statements suggested, that the United States might be able to level off its troop strength in Vietnam, achieving its objectives without mobilizing and without appearing to threaten China's national security. These factors were especially alarming in the context of events within China. Mao had launched the Cultural Revolution, which was an attack upon those in the Chinese leadership favorably disposed to closer ties with the Soviet Union. And the Soviets had detected Mao's signals—even before the United States understood them—that China desired improved Sino-American relations. The Kremlin followed the exchange of Chinese-American diplomatic gestures closely and was fully aware that the stage was set for confidential Chinese-American negotiations in Warsaw in early 1967. All of these signs meant their strategy was in jeopardy.

With regard to the war effort, the Soviets decided to give further assistance to North Vietnam. They hoped to slow American progress on the battlefield, create a more violent conflict, force the United States to pour in more men and materiel and increase pressure on China to return to the Soviet camp. In July 1966, Moscow attempted to increase the efficiency and effectiveness of the January 1966 Soviet-North Vietnamese aid agreement. When this proved insufficient, they concluded a new arms agreement with the North Vietnamese in October 1966 which again stepped up the flow of Soviet military supplies.

With regard to China, the Soviets monitored the Cultural Revolution carefully and continued with propaganda designed to aid the Liu-Deng group. It did not take them long to detect what turned out to be the decisive element in the struggle—the Chinese military held the balance of power. The PLA, behind Defense Minister Lin Biao, supported Mao, but Mao's hold on the army was tenuous. While an escalating conflict to the south had to worry China's military leaders, the Soviets decided to generate a second national security threat in the north. Some modest Soviet troop transfers to the Sino-Soviet border region already had occurred, but the buildup continued throughout 1966 and accelerated in 1967. Although a Soviet invasion force on the Chinese border may not seem a good way to improve Sino-Soviet relations, the Soviet goal at this stage was to defeat Mao in the power struggle. The Cultural Revolution was distracting the military's attention toward domestic affairs. The Kremlin most likely felt that an external threat to China would remove the PLA from the internal power struggle and allow Liu and Deng to triumph. Diplomacy could always achieve the desired improvement in Sino-Soviet relations in the wake of Mao's defeat. Moreover, if Soviet strategy were to fail and China established good relations with the United States, a strong Soviet force in Asia would be a prudent hedge against the possibility of a hostile China aligned with the United States.

The Soviets Watch the War with Concern, Increase Supplies

While the Soviet Union expends considerable effort on espionage, there is no evidence that the Russians were aware of McNamara's transformation from a hawk to a dove in 1966. Most likely, Soviet analysis of US intentions was based on what the United States did and said publicly. Certainly, the Soviets watched American success in the ground war in 1966 with alarm. At the time McNamara privately recommended a troop ceiling, US strength in Vietnam had reached only 325,000 men. The largest predicted number for mid-1967 troop strength under any US plan had been 436,000. McNamara's 470,000-man ceiling, to be reached by the end of 1967, *exceeded* this figure by 36,000 and represented a 40 percent increase over the 325,000 troops already in Vietnam in the fall of 1966. The Soviets, during 1966 and 1967, saw US actions as perfectly consistent. The US was determined, in Moscow's view, to throw as many troops as it could into the battle without mobilizing—which was fine with the Kremlin, so long as North Vietnam did not actually lose the war. US strength was drained and China was pressured to return to the Soviet bloc. Official US statements that the Vietnam war would be long were almost assuredly interpreted to mean that the United States was firmly committed to settling the issue on the battlefield and suggestions in the press that troop strength ultimately would level off most likely were seen as a sign of American confidence in its military performance.[1]

---

[1]For an example of "leveling off" suggestions see Saville R. Davis, "Vietnam War Trend Sets Stage for Peace," *Christian Science Monitor,* February 3, 1967, p. 3. This story reveals that McNamara in alleged "private suggestions" to congressmen expressed the view that US forces could be leveled off with less manpower than originally scheduled.

The Soviet "solution" to its Vietnam problem was to beef up the North Vietnamese military.

The renewed Soviet logistic effort began in mid-1966 with a "Conference of the Political Consultative Committee of the Warsaw Pact."[2] Complementing this was a meeting of Communist parties and governments of the Council for Mutual and Economic Assistance in Bucharest.[3] The purpose of these meetings was to work out better coordination and division of labor among East bloc nations in implementing the January 1966 aid agreement. The Soviet Politburo subsequently ratified the work conducted at these sessions, which, according to Soviet sources, concerned "all necessary measures...in support of the heroic Vietnamese people, including measures linked with economic and military assistance to repulse US aggression, with due account of the needs arising from the new phase of the war in Vietnam."[4]

The "new phase of the war" was increasing US military strength and success on the ground. The purpose of this mid-1966 coordination was to supply more efficiently "assistance in the volume and form agreed upon" and did not result in an increase in aid. By September 1966, however, it was apparent that additional assistance would be necessary if the American forces were to be denied victory. As a result, Hanoi's chief aid negotiator, Le Than Nghi, journeyed to Moscow and "exchanged information on the implementation in 1966 of earlier Soviet-Vietnamese agreements and noted with satisfaction that they were being successfully fulfilled." Moreover, the delegation "discussed ways and means of expanding and strengthening economic cooperation...and further Soviet assistance towards enhancing the defense capability of the DRV." On October 3, 1966, the Soviets and North Vietnamese concluded an agreement to increase economic and military aid.[5] The declaration at the end of the visit affirmed Soviet determination to satisfy economic and defense requirements "with due account of the needs arising from the new phase of the war in Vietnam."

---

[2]Paul Wohl, "Hard line sounded by Moscow," ibid., July 9, 1966, p. 2; "Zayavelenie v svyazi agressiya SShA vo V'etname," (Statement in connection with US Aggression in Vietnam), *Pravda,* July 8, 1966, p. 1. Eric Bourne, "Soviet bloc hints Hanoi aid if US keeps bombing North," *Christian Science Monitor,* July 12, 1966, p. 4.

[3]Kotov and Yegerov, *Militant Solidarity,* p. 121.

[4]Ibid., and "The news-briefly," *Christian Science Monitor,* July 13, 1966, p. 2.

[5]Kotov and Yegerov, *Militant Solidarity,* pp. 129–139. See also "Further Strengthening of Friendship and Cooperation," *Pravda,* October 4, 1966, pp. 1, 3.

The Soviets Eye the Cultural Revolution

During the Cultural Revolution, the Soviet press routinely reported events in great detail and with an accuracy that suggests they had well placed connections inside China. On June 5, 1966, *Pravda* noted that the Chinese Communist Party's Central Committee had appointed Li Xuefeng to replace Peng Zhen as head of the Peking City Party Committee.[6] Later in June, *Pravda* pointed out, with no small measure of concern, that Chinese newspapers had started to demand that all who opposed the thought of Mao Zedong should be overthrown. Moreover, commented another Soviet article, "a number of party and propaganda organizations are being reorganized and leading party, state and YCL [Young Communist League] cadres, editorial boards of newspapers and magazines and officials and professional-instructional staffs of higher educational institutions are being replaced."[7]

The Liu-Deng group's resistance to Mao was significant, but Mao won an important, if narrow, victory over Liu Shaoqi at the August, 1966, 11th Plenum of the Central Committee of the Chinese Communist Party. The Central Committee Plenum ratified a sixteen-point program on the Cultural Revolution designed to undermine the resistance by Mao's opponents at all levels. The focus of the Cultural Revolution was the levers of power, the "Party and government leadership organs." The ultimate purpose of the Cultural Revolution was the purge of "those powerholders within the Party who take the capitalist road"—Liu Shaoqi, Deng Xiaoping, and their supporters.[8]

The Soviet press was quick to point out the anti-Moscow flavor of the 11th Plenum, noting that "it regards all who do not agree with the general line of the CPC as modern revisionists."[9] The whole event was seen as part of Mao's efforts to avoid closer contact with the Soviet Union and indeed the Soviets accurately quoted the Plenum's resolution that "there can be no joint actions with them [the Soviets].... The struggle against imperialism

[6]"Reorganization of Peking City Committee of Communist Party of China," *Current Digest,* June 29, 1966, p. 39.

[7]"Velikaya Kul'turnaya Revolyutsiya v Kitae," (On the Great Cultural Revolution in China), *Pravda,* June 26, 1966, p. 4.

[8]Thornton, *China,* pp. 285–289; "Communique of Eleventh Plenary Session of the Eighth Central Committee of the Communist Party of China," *Peking Review,* August 19, 1966, pp. 4–8; "Study the 16 points, Know Them Well and Apply Them," ibid., p. 21.

[9]"11th Plenary Session of Central Committee of Communist Party of China," *Current Digest,* September 14, 1966, pp. 3–5.

presupposes a struggle against modern revisionism."[10] The Soviets interpreted this as a clear policy statement of China's uncooperative role in Southeast Asia and discussed other "crude slanderous attacks directed against the Soviet Union and its aid to Vietnam."[11]

After the 11th Plenum, Mao appeared at a mass rally and accepted an armband from a student group calling itself the "Red Guards," thereby legitimizing the new entity.[12] "Since the 11th Plenary session," reported *Pravda*, "Peking has been going through unusual days.... Young people and juveniles in semi-military uniforms with red armbands on left sleeves in the streets...[are] members of red guards...a new organization of Peking students."[13] Quickly, numerous bands of students moved out to attack "old customs, habits, thoughts and culture."[14] Soviet reporting described the targets as "politics, ideology, organizations and the economy," but went on to explain that the ultimate purpose was nationalist and anti-Soviet.[15] Mao's "clique" encouraged these young people and summoned other students from various parts of China to Peking to receive instructions before moving back to the countryside. The attacks, Moscow predicted, would move from Peking to outlying areas where Mao's opponents controlled the Party and government structures.[16]

There was resistance as the Red Guards started to assault leaders in the provincial party apparatus. Many pretended to cooperate with the Red Guards but issued confusing modifications to instructions published by the Cultural Revolution Group in Peking—even, on occasion, creating rival groups of Red Guards that mixed workers and students. This tactic provoked a warning from Mao:

> In order to shift the targets for attack, besides continuing to incite students to struggle against each other, they [Mao's opponents] have also stirred up a few workers and peasants to struggle against the students.... Diehards who take the capitalist road...identified the leadership of their own units

[10]Ibid.

[11]Ibid.

[12]"Chairman Mao Joins a Million People to Celebrate the Great Cultural Revolution," *Peking Review*, August 26, 1966, pp. 3–8.

[13]"Pekin vo vremya Kul'turnoi Revolyutsii," (Peking During the Cultural Revolution), *Pravda*, August 26, 1966, p. 4.

[14]Thornton, *China*, p. 292.

[15]"Pekin vo vremya Kul'turnoi Revolyutsii," (Peking during the Cultural Revolution), *Pravda*, August 26, 1966, p. 4.

[16]Ibid., and "How the Cultural Revolution in Peking is Proceeding," *Izvestia*, August 27, 1966, p. 2.

with the Party's Central Committee and the entire Party....
They have raised slogans such as "defend the Party Committee in your own locality, and of your own department...." In
some places a small number of workers, peasants and cadres
were hoodwinked and deceived and took part in the struggle
against the revolutionary students.[17]

The Soviets correctly analyzed events, and gave what support they could
to Liu and Deng. "In the first days...," noted *Pravda,* "groups of Red
Guards acted without apparent guidance. Afterward they were commanded
by adults in civilian clothes.... Red Guards are meeting spontaneous resistance.... An announcement...speaks of Red Guards beaten up in Chung
wen Borough.... Eight Red Guards were killed in Peking...The August 27
newspaper *Hei Lu Chiang Jih Pao* (*Black Devil River Daily*), in Northeast
China, called to aim the spearhead of Cultural Revolution directly at the
Province Party Committee."[18] The Soviets were fully aware that the Red
Guards were organized and sanctioned by Mao to attack the provincial
party and government structures and that leaders in the provinces loyal to
Liu and Deng fought back.[19]

Viewing the Cultural Revolution with concern, the Soviets began building up Soviet troop strength in Mongolia and the Far East, developing an
invasion force on the Chinese border. Initially the troop shifts were gradual
rather than dramatic. Still, Chinese intelligence detected the movements by
mid-1966 and Chinese Foreign Minister Chen Yi blasted the Soviets
publicly in July 1966, accusing them of threatening China and staging
provocations on the Sino-Soviet border.[20] Mao's reaction to the Soviet

[17]"Workers, Peasants and Soldiers Must Firmly Support the Revolutionary Students," *Peking
Review,* August 26, 1966, pp. 18–19.
[18]"Kul'turnaya Revolyutsiya v Kitae prodolzhaet," (The Cultural Revolution in China Con-
tinues), *Pravda,* September 3, 1966, p. 3.
[19]"Khung Ueiping prodolzhaet Kul'turnuyu Revolyutsiyu," (Hung Weiping continue the Cultural
Revolution), ibid., September 16, 1966, p. 5; "Soviet Views of Developments in China," *Current
Digest,* October 12, 1966, pp. 3–9; "Victoriously March Forward Along the Road of Mao Tse-tung's
Thought," *Peking Review,* August, 26, 1966, pp. 16–18; "What are Sung Shih, Lu Ping and Peng
Pei-yun Up To In The Cultural Revolution?" ibid., September 9, 1966, pp. 19–21; "Comrade Lin
Piao's Speech," ibid., September 23, 1966, pp. 10–11.
[20]"Vice Premier Chen Yi's Speech at the Peking Mass Rally," ibid., July 15, 1966, pp. 27–29.
For other evidence of the Soviet buildup see "Moscow watches Siberian border," *Christian Science
Monitor,* June 6, 1966, p. 1. See especially John Hughes, "Rising tension seen on Sino-Soviet border," ibid., January 26, 1967, p. 2. This article discusses a visit by the Soviet Chief of Strategic Rocket Forces to the Far East and Soviet supplies to Mao's opponents. It also discusses Chen Yi's charges
in July 1966 that the Soviets transferred troops from East Europe to the Sino-Soviet border.

troop movements was to make additional overtures to the United States for improved Sino-US relations. Chen Yi, in a discussion with a Japanese goodwill group in September, made a truly remarkable statement when he observed that China "does not necessarily preclude the idea of negotiations with the United States for the purpose of resolving the Vietnam question," which would remove the Soviets entirely, and the North Vietnamese largely, from the equation.[21] Chen Yi also argued that China did not have the strength to attack the United States and dismissed the possibility that the United States would attack China. Although the Chinese ambassador in Warsaw cautioned the United States not to get the wrong idea from Chen Yi's remarks, he did not "clarify" Chen's statement.[22] The Soviets, as could be expected, sharply attacked the Chinese in their press, charging them with collusion with the United States. "Peking," said an obviously concerned *Izvestia*, "still maintains contact with Washington on the Ambassadorial level in Warsaw."[23]

Publicly, the Soviets began to appeal directly to the Liu-Deng group. *Pravda*, while it justified its criticism of high level Chinese who were anti-Soviet, expressed the hope that "sooner or later healthy forces will come around" to help the Soviets meet the US threat in Asia.[24] The Soviets also noticed that, in September 1966, Mao was forced to use regular PLA units to curb excessive Red Guard violence in Canton. In the wake of the these events, reports from travelers and new regulations emphasizing obedience to Mao suggested that resistance to Mao and Lin Biao existed in the army.[25] Soviet articles took note of these developments and the importance of the

[21]"Zayavlenie Shen i," (Statement by Chen Yi), *Izvestia*, September 22, 1966, p. 2; David K. Willis, "Peking contrasts studied carefully," *Christian Science Monitor*, September 9, 1966, p. 3.

[22]"The Chinese People, Armed with Mao Tse-tung's Thought, Do Not Fear US Intimidation or Believe Its Lies," *Peking Review*, September 16, 1966, pp. 7–10, and "Ambassador Wang Kuo-chuen's Statement on Sino-US Talks," ibid., p. 8. See also "The news-briefly," *Christian Science Monitor*, September 9, 1966, p. 2. Recall that these overtures were mentioned in Chapter 10. Note that they occurred in September, only a month prior to McNamara's draft memorandum in which he proposed a troop ceiling.

[23]"Zayavlenie Shen i," (On the statement by Chen Yi), *Izvestia*, September 22, 1966, p. 2.

[24]"Soviet Views of the Developments in China," *Current Digest*, October 12, 1966, pp. 3–9.

[25]"Hold Fast to the Main Orientation in the Struggle," *Peking Review*, September, 23, 1966, pp. 22–23. This cautions against losing sight of the main targets in the Cultural Revolution; "An Army and a People Equipped with Chairman Mao's Thinking on People's War are Invincible," ibid., pp. 29–30; "Carry the Mass Movement for the Creative Study and Application of Chairman Mao's Works to a New Stage," ibid., October 14, 1966, pp. 5–8; "The Army and People Throughout the Country are Determined to Master Mao Tse-tung's Thought," ibid., October 21, 1966, pp. 11–12; "The news-briefly," *Christian Science Monitor*, September 20, 1966, p. 2; "Red Guards, farmers clash," ibid., September 23, 1966. p. 16; "China warns troops," ibid.

PLA in the Cultural Revolution. *Pravda* especially highlighted resistance to Mao in the Army and linked it to the continuing political strength of the Liu-Deng group.

> Reports coming in from various parts of China say that Communists and non-party people who uphold Marxism-Leninism and who advocate friendship with the USSR and other socialist countries, are in all strata of the Party and also in the State apparatus and in particular in the Army and organs of state security. Therefore, Mao Zedong's group is trying to discredit the backbone of the Party and State cadres and to split and undermine the force of the Party. Leaders of the Mao group—Chen Po-ta, Chiang-ching, Kang Shen—try to make it seem that the masses want to overthrow Liu and Deng. Columns of marchers are headed by representatives of the Army, without whom not one question involving the economy, culture or politics is now decided.... Mao's campaign more and more resembles a reactionary military coup.[26]

When violence escalated in Sichuan, *Izvestia* reported on the resistance of the provincial organization to the Red Guards and noted that "Mao's partisans have not gained the support of the Army units."[27] However, according to *Pravda,* Mao sought to use those loyal to him in the Army to form a high command for the Red Guards to gain better control over their attacks. "Military commanders and garrisons of the PLA," said a worried Soviet commentator, "are being invited to serve as instructors in Red Guard headquarters."[28]

A Violent Struggle Breaks Out in China in 1967

Mao's difficulties were just beginning, however, as his ad hoc organization of Red Guard students proved impossible to control. He simply could not direct neat, clean "surgical" operations against specific opponents.

[26]"Obstanovka v KNR nakalyaetsya," (Conditions in the CPR Heat Up), *Pravda,* April 14, 1967, p. 5.
[27]"Zalpy po Khunveibinam," (Salvos at the Hung Weiping), *Izvestia,* June 28, 1967, p. 2.
[28]"Soviet Views of the Developments in China," *Current Digest,* October 12, 1966, pp. 3–9.

Moreover, Liu and Deng, by creating rival groups of Red Guards, generated an astonishing amount of confusion. More often than not, public security forces committed to bring order out of chaos sided with Mao's opponents. In early 1967, an angry but frustrated Mao acknowledged the resistance he was facing:

> Responsible people in the party had earlier tried to put forth the bourgeois reactionary line to counter Mao's correct line.... [They] tried to suppress the Cultural Revolution and reversed black and white, right and wrong.... They encircled and suppressed revolutionaries, clamped down on different views.... At that crucial moment the Eleventh Plenary Session of the Eighth Central Committee was convened and presided over by Chairman Mao.... [The Plenum] drew up decisions on Cultural Revolution and exposed the reactionary line which shielded the person in the Party in authority taking the capitalist road.... However, the very few persons who persist in the bourgeois reactionary line are not reconciled to their defeat.... [They] resort to a variety of tricks [and] use their influence in the Party.... The most important plot of these persons is to incite the masses to struggle against each other.... [They] have some people hoodwinked.... [They] provoke conflicts in which coercion or force are used to create confusion. They label revolutionaries with the bourgeois reactionary line.[29]

The "person in the Party in authority taking the capitalist road" was, of course, Liu Shaoqi. The tactic of creating rival Red Guards and issuing modifications to the Cultural Revolution Group's instructions forced Mao to increase PLA involvement to the extent of using regular army corps in the Cultural Revolution.[30] Mao let it be known in a January 1967 *Liberation Army Daily* article that he intended to have the army support the Red Guards in seizing power.

> It is entirely justified for the revolutionary rebels to seize power.... The PLA is a pillar of the dictatorship of the

---

[29]"Carry the Great Proletarian Cultural Revolution Through to the End," *Peking Review,* January 1, 1967, pp. 8–15.

[30]Thornton, *China,* pp. 300–302.

proletariat. The PLA must support the revolutionary rebels. Even though they may be just a minority temporarily, we must support them without the slightest hesitation. In the new situation... it is not possible for the People's Liberation Army to refrain from intervening.... The question is not whether or not to intervene, but which side to stand on.... [The PLA] must support the proletarian left.... Political power grows out of the barrel of a gun.... The People's Army must defend power with a gun.[31]

China was in chaos. Some army commanders obeyed instructions from political cadres who turned out to be Mao's opponents. Some used their own command authority or their political discretion to reject PLA involvement in the power struggle. Mao, through Lin Biao, began staging frequent purges of army commanders who resisted the Maoist line.[32]

An additional problem with the Red Guards soon became apparent. The youths did not possess the necessary administrative skills to govern when they successfully seized power. As a result, military leaders found themselves more and more involved in municipal administration.[33] By August 1967, Mao had committed twenty of thirty-seven regular army corps to internal police and administrative duties.[34]

The Soviets Analyze the Struggle

The Soviets viewed developments in the Chinese power struggle with a mixture of hope and alarm. The brutality of the conflict and the direct references in the Chinese press to the "person in the Party in authority" told the Soviets that there would be no middle ground, no compromise between the warring factions. One side was likely to win and the other to perish. The uncompromising and violent assault by the Red Guards against the

---

[31]"The People's Liberation Army Firmly Backs the Proletarian Revolutionaries," *Peking Review*, January 27, 1967, pp. 10–11.

[32]Thornton, *China*, pp. 302f.; For evidence of confusion and some difficulty within the Army see "Get Rid of Self-Interest," *Peking Review*, February 10, 1967, pp. 2–21, which cautioned units not to stockpile ammunition while sitting on the sideline awaiting the outcome of the struggle. See also "Cadres Must Be Treated Correctly," ibid., March 3, 1967, pp. 5–9, which cautioned against attacking the wrong cadres.

[33]Thornton, *China*, pp. 305–309.

[34]Ibid., p. 321.

Liu-Deng group was a grave concern to Moscow. Signs of resistance, however, gave the Soviets reason to hope for an outcome favorable to their interests. Since the PLA held the balance of power, the Kremlin was particularly sensitive to the slightest indications of dissatisfaction among military leaders.

In early 1967, as Mao began to commit regular Army corps, *Pravda* reported that "organizers of the so-called Cultural Revolution are relying on detachments of Red Guards, the Army and state security agencies."[35] Mao, said Moscow, had concentrated his main attack upon party cadres, "seeing in them the main obstacle to the implementation of [his] special course in both domestic and foreign policy." The Red Guards had assaulted the Central Committee's Sichuan Party Province Committee, distributing materials specifically attacking Liu Shaoqi and Deng Xiaoping.[36]

Throughout the first half of 1967, the Soviets built a case for isolating China within the socialist world. Mao was using the army to defeat true communists, charged the Kremlin. He was building a military-bureaucratic dictatorship, changing the nature of Chinese society internally, and realigning China internationally with capitalism. As a result, the Soviets implied, they would once again be justified in organizing a conference of socialist countries to excommunicate China from the communist movement. More ominously, China's overtures to the West warranted military preparedness on the Sino-Soviet border. The Soviets also rebuked Mao for his virtual betrayal of Vietnam. Until 1967, the Soviets had gone to great pains to show how Mao's policies had interfered with the socialist camp's efforts to aid Vietnam. Now Moscow accused Mao of aligning himself deliberately and overtly with the United States and giving the Americans free reign to do whatever they wanted as long as they did not actually attack China.

In March 1967, the Kremlin accused China of making a deal with the United States that would permit an American victory in Vietnam.[37] In July, the Soviets charged Mao with constituting a threat to socialism. "If a military-bureaucratic dictatorship establishes itself in China," said *Izvestia*, "it will fundamentally change the character of rule in the country."[38] Brezhnev lent the authority of his name to the campaign by giving a speech

---

[35]"Novie Zig zagi Kul'turnoi Revolyutsii v Kitae," (New Zig Zags of the Cultural Revolution in China), *Pravda*, January 8, 1967, p. 5.

[36]Ibid.

[37]I. Gavilov, "Kapitalisti na dolyu," (Capitalists on the Dole), *Izvestia*, March 31, 1967, p. 2.

[38]L. Delyusin, "Ugroza sotsializmu v Kitae," (A Threat to Socialism in China), *Izvestia*, July 4, 1967, pp. 2–3.

condemning the "great power anti-Soviet policy" of Mao and indicated that the Cultural Revolution "has entered a dangerous new phase.... What a blow to all genuine communists in China." By way of justification, Brezhnev maintained "the CPSU will continue its policy of friendship and solidarity with the CPC and the CPR. By exposing the present Peking leadership's ideology and policy, which have nothing in common with Marxism-Leninism, we are thereby waging a struggle not against the CPC, not against China, but for the CPC, for its return to the path of internationalism, for its solidarity with fraternal parties."[39] The Russian leader concluded by talking about alleged pressure from other communist parties to convene an international conference of communist parties—the thinly veiled mechanism to threaten Mao with excommunication. Brezhnev approved of the idea but felt additional preparatory work would be necessary.[40]

On the issue of Chinese-US rapprochement, *Pravda,* on July 23, commented that "enemies of communism place their principal stake on the kindling of nationalism, which they would like to use in setting the socialist countries against one another."[41] The United States, in the Kremlin's view, was excited about Mao's independent course from Moscow and the evidence of Chinese nationalism. The consequences of the "fuss being made by international reaction over the schismatic line of Mao" was American aggression in Vietnam. The United States "would never have dared to launch such a cynical escalation of the war in Vietnam were it not for the course pursued by Mao."[42]

After Chinese mobs created a disturbance at the Soviet embassy in Beijing and harassed a planeload of Soviet "experts" enroute to Vietnam, *Izvestia* reported a major battle in China to which "Army troops were dispatched and helped the rebels take control" of an embattled settlement.[43] Mao, according to these reports, had dispatched "storm troopers supported by the Army to launch violent repressions against good communists" who

[39]"Rech' tovarishcha L.I. Brezhneva," (Speech by Comrade L.I. Brezhnev), *Pravda,* January 14, 1967, p. 1.

[40]Ibid.

[41]"Yedinstvo—istochnik nashei sili," (Unity—Source of Our Strength), *Pravda,* July 23, 1967, p. 4.

[42]Ibid.; "Ob antisovetskoi politike Mao Tse-Duna i ego gruppi," (On the Anti-Soviet Policy of Mao Tse-tung and his Group), ibid., February 16, 1967, p. 3; "S kem v kompanu?" (In League With Whom?), *Izvestia,* March 30, 1967, p. 2.

[43]"Eshche odna provokatsiya," (Still Another Provocation), *Pravda,* February 3, 1967, p. 5; "Smut'yani beschinstvuyut," (Rebels Run Rampant), *Izvestia,* February 5, 1967, p. 5.

resisted.[44] A Soviet "legal expert" added his opinion that Chinese party and state institutions were changing fundamentally and the "Army is the main component of the apparatus of state power."[45]

According to Moscow, internal changes led directly to changes in foreign policy. "It is no accident," the Soviets alleged, "that interest in China has risen so much at present in the circles of imperialist reaction. Prospects of rapprochement with China are being discussed with increasing persistence. Many facts attest that such intentions are meeting a response from Mao's group—a reorientation of China's economic ties from the socialist to the capitalist world is taking place."[46] Moreover, the Soviets alleged that US officials openly agreed with the Russian view that Mao's policies served American interests.[47]

On Vietnam, the Soviets, in addition to charging the Chinese with refusing to cooperate, alleged increasing interference with Soviet supplies. Quoting *Newsweek* to emphasize the Sino-American connection, *Pravda* reported Chinese actions disrupting rail shipments.[48] *Izvestia,* citing *Le Monde,* reported similar events.[49] A lengthy article in *Literary Gazette* expressed Moscow's view that radical rhetoric by Mao was in reality a signal to the United States to pursue military victory—so long as US soldiers stayed away from Chinese territory. "Peking gave Washington the following idea at the highest level," said *Literary Gazette,* "don't stop the war—just don't come too close to our borders."[50] "Peking," reported *Pravda,* "has not denied reports in the foreign press about tacit China-US agreement in

[44]"Ob antisovetskoi politike Mao Tse-Duna i ego gruppi," (On the Anti-Soviet Policy of Mao Tse-tung and his Group), *Pravda,* February 16, 1967, p. 3.

[45]"A Jurist Examines Legal Institutions in Mao's China," *Current Digest,* August 30, 1967, pp. 3–7.

[46]"Ob antisovetskoi politike Mao Tse-Duna i ego gruppi," (On the Anti-Soviet Policy of Mao Tse-tung and his Group), *Pravda,* February 16, 1967, p. 3.

[47]Ibid.

[48]I. Ivanov, "V nogu s pentagonom," (In Step with the Pentagon), *Pravda,* February 15, 1967, p. 2

[49]V. Matveyev, "Beshenye diktuyut," (Madmen Give the Orders), *Izvestia,* February 15, 1967, p. 2.

[50]"Top Secret: People From Peking and the Boys From Langley," *Current Digest,* May 24, 1967, p. 16. This reflects a Soviet argument that has remained consistent into the 1980s. See D.M. Pospelov and E.D. Stepanov, *Pekin protiv V'etnama,* (Peking Against Vietnam), (Moscow: Thought, 1983), pp. 32–51. In this work, the authors accuse the Chinese of making improvement of Sino-US relations a cornerstone of Chinese policy "since the beginning of the 1960s." At the same time, according to this book, the Chinese saw Vietnam as a good test case for the theory of people's war and opposed all efforts at a peaceful solution while making a lot of radical sounding noise. This alleged radicalism was a smokescreen because it included "self-reliance" by the North Vietnamese. It was really a means of reassuring the United States that China would do nothing as long as China was not attacked.

Vietnam."[51] China had refused to allow the Soviets to put bases on Chinese soil to supply Vietnam with heavy weaponry and had denied the Soviets free access to one of China's southern ports for transhipment to Hanoi.[52]

A *Pravda* series entitled "Events in China" provided weekly and, at times, more frequent insights into the Cultural Revolution. Liu and Deng's resistance, according to the Kremlin, prompted Mao to seek to destroy the existing party apparatus and replace it with something new. He directed the formation of Revolutionary Committees at all levels dominated by Red Guards loyal to himself, although *Pravda* observed with some satisfaction in July 1967 that Mao had "so far managed to establish Revolutionary Committees in only four provinces and two cities."[53] Since the youthful Red Guards did not possess the administrative experience, the Soviets noted, army representatives stepped in to govern and played the leading role in the Revolutionary Committees that had been established. The daily newspaper in Hunan, Moscow pointed out, had failed to appear for ten days in June. When the paper again was published, it charged that the editorial office had been seized and the print shop destroyed by persons incited by officials of the Province Party Committee (in other words, by the old apparatus, not the new Revolutionary Committee). It was returned to Maoist control only with the aid of soldiers.[54]

The Soviets Decide on the Sino-Soviet Border and Support for the Tet Offensive

Although the situation was complicated by the summer of 1967, an analysis of the Soviet press shows that the Soviets had arrived at three important conclusions. First, Liu and Deng's supporters in the Chinese power struggle were holding their own against Mao.[55] Second, successful resistance to the Red Guards (and the Red Guard's inability to govern when they seized power) had compelled Mao to commit a large portion of the PLA to the Cultural Revolution.[56] Third, and most importantly, the

---

[51]Boris Strel'nikov, "Eskalatsiya bezrasudstva," (Escalation of Recklessness), *Pravda,* March 16, 1967, p. 3.

[52]Ibid.

[53]"Sobytiya v Kitae," (Events in China), *Pravda,* July 4, 1967, p. 5,

[54]Ibid.

[55]"Sobytiya v Kitae," (Events in China), *Pravda,* July 12, 1967, p. 5. This article discussed attacks on Liu, but noted "there is no official confirmation concerning Liu's removal."

[56]Thornton, *China,* p. 321.

increasing involvement of the army had not met with the universal approval of military leaders and, indeed, the Soviets had detected growing signs of dissatisfaction.

In July, *Izvestia* saw hopeful signs in a bloody incident in Wuhan:

> Maoist attempts to get on top of the situation in Wuhan have failed—the troop units quartered in Hupeh did not support Mao in the effort to remove Chen Tsia-tao and Wang Jen-chung, the Party and administrative leaders of the province.... *Liu's supporters are not only holding their positions, but are offering increasingly energetic resistance....* The main reserve of the Cultural Revolution—*the Army—is becoming less and less obedient to Mao Zedong.* The line which even those military units loyal to Mao Zedong do not want to cross in the struggle is becoming more and more clearly defined. Frequently troops take a cautious, wait-and-see position and often they side with Mao's opponents. The Wuhan events...are graphic evidence of the disloyalty of a substantial part of the Army to Mao's group.[57] (Emphasis added).

In August, *Pravda* reported that "the [Chinese] military uses force of arms and plays a dominant role in Mao's committees.... However, lately resistance to Maoism has begun to develop even in the Army, where another purge is now being carried out."[58]

In the Soviet view, there was discontent among the group holding the balance of power, the military, and Liu and Deng still represented a viable alternative for military leaders, should they decide to shift allegiance. Brezhnev confirmed this Soviet understanding with a speech in September 1967. "The events in China," said the Kremlin leader, "attest not only to the ideological-political fall of the Mao Zedong grouping, but also to the strength of the resistance to its policy by broad strata of the working people, *numerous cadres of the Party and state, and the best representatives of the armed forces.*"[59] (Emphasis added.) It was imperative for the Soviet Union

---

[57]"Konvul'sii 'Kul'turnoi Revolyutsii'," (Convulsions of the "Cultural Revolution"), *Izvestia,* July 28, 1967, p. 2.

[58]I. Aleksandrov, "Vopreki interesam kitaiskogo naroda," (Contrary to the Interests of the Chinese People), *Pravda,* August 16, 1967, pp. 4–6.

[59]"Rech' tovarishcha L.I. Brezhnev," (Speech by Comrade L.I. Brezhnev), *Pravda,* September 8, 1967, pp. 2–3.

to drive a wedge between the Chinese military leadership and Mao Zedong. The Soviets arrived at this conclusion at the same time the North Vietnamese requested Soviet support for a new initiative in the war, a massive, coordinated, countrywide ground offensive to take place during the Lunar New Year holiday in 1968—the Tet offensive.

The Soviets Apply Military Pressure to China, North and South

The outcome of the Chinese power struggle, complicated though it had been, now boiled down to one decisive factor—the allegiance of the leadership of the People's Liberation Army. Soviet actions suggest that they felt external military pressure would most likely squeeze the PLA out of the Cultural Revolution. The Kremlin attempted to generate this pressure in two ways. In the north, the Soviets accelerated their military buildup on the Sino-Soviet border. In the South, the Soviet Union agreed to pay the bill for the Tet offensive.

Evidence of Soviet intentions in the Far East surface early in 1967 with a visit by the Commander of Soviet Strategic Rocket Forces.[60] Western observers began to note increases in Soviet force structure in the Far East.[61] The buildup was acknowledged by Secretary McNamara in open testimony before Congress late in January 1967.[62] To add to the growing sense of military pressure, Soviet diplomatic sources in February leaked a story that the Soviet Union had informed Warsaw Pact allies of plans to withdraw 50,000 troops from Eastern Europe to transfer to the Chinese border.[63]

Soviet military transfers to the Far East in 1965 and 1966 had been very gradual, only two or three divisions over the twelve to fourteen already present. Beginning in 1967, however, the pace accelerated and by 1969 there were twenty-five to twenty-seven Soviet divisions in the Far East. Contrary to Soviet "news leaks," the buildup did not involve a transfer of forces from Eastern Europe. The new deployments resulted from a shift of forces within the Soviet Union and from mobilization of additional resources. American intelligence detected the acceleration and it became public

[60]John Hughes, "Rising tensions seen on Sino-Soviet border," *Christian Science Monitor,* January 26, 1967, p. 2.

[61]"Pravda pushes attack against Peking leaders," *Christian Science Monitor,* January 21, 1967, p. 2.

[62]Neal Stanford, "World impact read in Sino-Soviet clash," ibid., January 30, 1967, p. 4.

[63]"The news-briefly," ibid., February 4, 1967, p. 2.

knowledge in September 1967 with reports of the restationing of Soviet troops in Outer Mongolia "within the last few months."[64]

The Soviets coupled the troop transfers with a new aggressiveness by their border forces. This included a decision to provoke incidents and to respond to minor Chinese harassment with force, and, more importantly, to publicize the whole process. In mid-July 1967 a border incident resulted in a lengthy *Pravda* article on the fortitude and courage of Soviet border guards defending the eastern frontier against Chinese Red Guards. The article was a means of conveying a not-so-veiled threat to China. "Let us recall," said *Pravda,* "how many conflicts have been avoided," implying that the Soviets in the future would not be so patient.[65]

The Soviets revealed their own thinking on the matter, and brought the rest of world's attention to it, when they ridiculed the argument that Soviet actions were designed to pressure China militarily in conjunction with the US armed forces in Vietnam. In August 1967, *Pravda* citing the growing isolation of China, referred specifically to the military pressure on two fronts by talking about "a ring around China." The ring existed, said Moscow, but what made the concept ridiculous was the goodwill and non-aggressive policy of socialist countries. Despite the Soviet military buildup, the Soviets could not be considered a threat. This was small comfort for the Chinese. The article stated: "A military psychosis was whipped up in every way possible in the country under the pretext of a war peril threatening China. The Peking leaders even went so far as to circulate absurd, slanderous allegations about the existence around China of some 'ring' supposedly created from the threat of attack not only on the part of imperialism but of—socialist countries."[66]

Meanwhile in Vietnam, the October 1966 Soviet-North Vietnamese arms agreement failed to blunt US progress. The North Vietnamese, with their NVA regular and VC main force units forced away from population centers, lost their access to recruits, food, intelligence, servants, and other resources that the population in the South formerly supplied. The Soviets indirectly acknowledged this in their press accounts. "In view of the new

[64]Thomas W. Wolfe, *Soviet Power and Europe, 1945–1970,* (Baltimore and London: The Johns Hopkins Press, 1970), pp. 466–469.

[65]Konstantin Simonov, "Priznanie v lyubvi," (Confessions of Love), *Pravda,* July 19, 1967, p. 3.

[66]I. Aleksandrov, "Vopreki interesam kitaiskogo naroda," (Contrary to the Interests of the Chinese People), *Pravda,* August 16, 1967, pp. 4–6.

situation that developed in the second half of 1966," said *Pravda* in April 1967, "the high command of the patriotic forces has devoted a great deal of attention to strengthening the partisan underground organizations in occupied territory.... One of the chief tasks in the period immediately ahead is further development of political and armed struggle in occupied territory."[67] By mid-1967, the North Vietnamese concluded that they needed something dramatic to arrest pacification and South Vietnamese political progress. Their decision to launch the Tet offensive was prompted by an urgent need to undermine the faith of the people in the government's ability to protect them.[68]

Looking back, the mid-1967 date for the North Vietnamese decision can be discerned intuitively, since the planning and coordination for such a colossal effort required over half a year. After all, the casualties that resulted from earlier large-scale contacts with American forces had compelled the North Vietnamese to withdraw to sanctuaries. Planners in North Vietnam had to anticipate that widespread large battles would lead to extraordinary casualties and, more importantly from their point of view, extraordinary loss of materiel. Thus, the logistic needs were great. Without acquisition of the required support, the offensive could not occur. The Soviets agreed to support the offensive.

The chief North Vietnamese aid negotiator, Le Than Nghi, had worked out numerous agreements with Moscow. In August 1967 he included in his delegation Dinh Duc Thien, Chief of Logistics of the North Vietnamese Army, for the first time.[69] Le met with Brezhnev and Kosygin, which indicates that the negotiations had the blessing and involvement of the highest levels in the Soviet Union.[70] The presence of Dinh Duc Thien and the involvement on the Soviet side of future Defense Minister Dimitry Ustinov and chief of the Soviet military supply system Marshal Ivan Bagramyan provided the necessary military and technical expertise to translate strategic

[67]I. Shchedrov, "K yugu ot 17-i paralleli," (South of the 17th Parallel), *Pravda,* April 9, 1967, p. 4.

[68]Don Oberdorfer, *TET!,* (New York: 1971), pp. 42–76. This chapter is entitled "Decision in the North." As sources, Oberderfer used translated broadcast of Radio Hanoi, captured documents made available through the US-Vietnamese Combined Document Exploitation Center near Saigon, and personal interviews with high ranking Viet Cong who were captured or defected. He puts the decision to conduct the offensive in the summer of 1967. See also Dave Richard Palmer, *Summons of the Trumpet,* (New York: 1978), p. 225. Palmer agrees with Oberdorfer's date.

[69]Kotov and Yegorov, *Militant Solidarity,* p. 157.

[70]Ibid., and "Vstrecha s v'etnamskimi druz'yami," (Meeting with Vietnamese Friends), *Pravda,* September 13, 1967, p. 1. This article also reveals the involvement of future Defense Minister Ustinov.

intentions into concrete actions.[71] The talks undoubtedly worked out the amounts and types of supplies, delivery priorities, and schedules necessary to meet the Tet deadline. The discussions took six weeks, longer than any previous arms negotiation, from August 14 to September 23, 1967. On September 23, the Soviets and Vietnamese announced the largest and most extensive Soviet-DRV aid agreement to date. According to the announcement in *Izvestia,* "The Soviet Union will deliver to the Democratic Republic of Vietnam aircraft, anti-aircraft missiles, artillery and firearms, ammunition and other military supplies and also complete sets of equipment, vehicles, oil products, ferrous and non-ferrous metals, food, chemical fertilizers, medicaments and other items for the further enhancement of the DRV's defense capability and the development of its national economy.[72]

In the wake of the agreement, Soviet aid shipments to North Vietnam increased significantly. The Soviets publicly tied the increase to the September 23 arms deal. On November 14, 1967, for example, Radio Odessa announced that traffic between Black Sea ports and Haiphong had increased sharply.[73] Later, Soviet domestic broadcasts announced that ten new dry-cargo vessels had left Black Sea ports for Haiphong, promising to complete the trip ahead of time.[74] Radio Moscow reported in December that "weapons, ammunition, military equipment and medicines are the principal items of Soviet aid to Vietnam.... Military aid is being stepped up in accordance with an agreement of September 23, which stipulates that the Soviet Union will supply even more aid."[75]

While hindsight could suggest many reasons for the Soviet decision to pay the bill for the Tet offensive, circumstances in mid-1967 point directly to China. Logically, what could the Soviets have expected from a massive North Vietnamese attack? First, it was clear that American firepower and mobility were vastly superior to those of the North Vietnamese and Viet Cong and, in any event, the United States would not permit the defeat of a theater army. Therefore, the Soviets could not possibly have expected military victory for the North Vietnamese. Since the South Vietnamese

[71]Takashi Oka, "Moscow hits US bombing," *Christian Science Monitor,* August 25, 1967, p. 1. This article reports on consultations between Le Than Nghi and Marshal Bagramyan. The delegation from Hanoi arrived August 14. See also Paul Wohl, "Red bloc steps up Hanoi aid," ibid., January 25, 1968, p. 2. This article reports that Kosygin and Ustinov had played a major role in the September 23, 1967 aid agreement.

[72]Kotov and Yegorov, *Militant Solidarity,* pp. 156–157.

[73]Paul Wohl, "Red bloc steps up Hanoi aid," *Christian Science Monitor,* January 2, 1967, p. 2.

[74]Ibid.

[75]Ibid.

government had regained control of a great deal of the population, and by the Soviets' own admission much work needed to be done to build up the partisan infrastructure, the Soviets also could not have reasonably expected a general uprising.[76] The North Vietnamese wanted to deliver a blow to the South Vietnamese government's political progress—and this was surely a possibility, but not one that adequately explains the Soviet decision.[77] The usual thorough military analysis by the Soviets almost certainly predicted that the US forces would inflict terrible casualties on the attacking force. Moreover, the realization by American military leaders that they had seriously hurt the North Vietnamese and Viet Cong most likely would prompt requests for additional forces to exploit the victory. Since troop levels were approaching half a million, or near the point where a major increase would require some mobilization, and any new increase could be accomplished more rapidly with mobilization, the most likely American response would be to cross the mobilization barrier and send more units into battle.

 The Soviets demonstrated some awareness of the American troop strength debate and the administration's reluctance to cross the mobilization line, although they gave no indication that they considered the opposition to more troops to be strong. In August, *Pravda* noted a trip by Maxwell Taylor and Clark Clifford to Thailand and discussed the military-civilian debate over the numbers of soldiers to be deployed to Vietnam. "If Washington were to decide to satisfy Westmoreland's new request for manpower through its own human resources," said Moscow, "(and as is known he demanded that the number of American soldiers in Vietnam be brought to 600,000) the United States, as at least the *New York Times* affirmed,

---

[76]It could be argued that they hoped for a general uprising, but "hope" would not have justified risks and costs of this magnitude.

[77]A few words about the North Vietnamese and their expectations. Naturally, they did not go into this with a goal of suffering a costly failure. However, neither could they have expected victory over the American military force. If we look closely at their attacks, we see that they were not focused primarily on the Americans but against South Vietnamese military and political targets. If they succeeded in administering a devastating blow to the South Vietnamese military and political structure, even a victorious American military would be in the position of being the sole prop for a defeated regime. If they could have achieved this outcome, the costs would have been worth it. Also, a cynic might note that the attacking forces were primarily Viet Cong main force units and not North Vietnamese units. After Tet, any marginal semblance of independence from the North the Viet Cong may have had was gone, due to the massive casualties among the hard core Viet Cong. The North Vietnamese would have killed two birds with one stone. In the event, of course, though the South Vietnamese government was a little shaken, the South Vietnamese military responded with distinction and it may have been their finest hour.

would have to undergo a partial mobilization in the near future."[78] This, most likely, is what the Kremlin desired and expected—for mobilization would be a major shock likely to cause Chinese military leaders to demand removal of the PLA from the Cultural Revolution, which would mean defeat for Mao.

Circumstantial evidence strongly suggests that the Soviets paid the bill for the Tet offensive in the hope that a major US response could bring Liu and Deng to power. Most attempts by Americans to decipher Soviet motives in this area have been hopelessly prejudiced by subsequent events. But Moscow would have needed an almost mystical political foresight to have predicted the tremendous domestic American political fallout from the aftermath of Tet. More likely, Soviet planners war-gamed a number of possible outcomes, developed contingency plans accordingly for those outcomes, and only agreed to expend the resources and take the attendant risks after concluding that the more likely results were in their interests. The physical outcome of North Vietnamese plans would be a big battle that could reasonably be expected to set back South Vietnamese political stability and gains in pacification, but would result in terrible communist losses. Surely the Soviets expected this to generate requests from American field commanders to exploit the defeat of communist military forces and a Johnson administration eager to pour in men and materiel to win the war.

But, unbeknownst to the Soviet Union, the troop ceiling discussions were coming to a close inside the Johnson administration. Where the 470,000-man decision had left the principle of a ceiling open for discussion, if for no other reason than to convince US military leaders that their opinion was being heard, President Johnson would put the final stamp of approval on the concept of a troop ceiling (set at 525,000, not 470,000) almost simultaneously with the Soviet decision to support Tet.

The decision the Soviets were trying to prevent already had occurred.

---

[78]Oleg Kalkin, "S pustymi rukami," (Empty Handed), *Pravda,* August 3, 1967, p. 4. While no source short of an intelligence coup could ever demonstrate that the Soviets *wanted* US mobilization, this source demonstrates Soviet awareness that a large US troop increase would *require* mobilization. And it appeared at the same time that dissent in the Chinese military was appearing and being highlighted in the press—all of which coincided with the Soviet-North Vietnamese negotiations for the Tet offensive logistic support. Is it rational that the Soviets desired the dissent in the Chinese military to sway the power struggle against Mao? Yes. Is it rational that a Soviet evaluation of the possible outcomes of Tet would conclude that a likely outcome could be a major US troop increase? Again, yes. Given these factors, the Soviets decided to pay the bill expecting a US mobilization.

12

The Final Decision

Major Events

- *December 1966*—Formal JCS response to 470,000-man troop ceiling. JCS requests permission to change composition of force.
- *December 1966*—Congressional pressure on administration develops to do more to support the military in Vietnam.
- *January 1967*—US report shows enemy-to-friendly kill ratios over preceding six months up from 3.3 to 4.2. Enemy killed during January a new high (5,954).
- *January 1967*—Debate inside administration over draft National Security Action Memorandum exposes wide civilian-military split over fundamental US goals.
- *March–April 1967*—Military sends request for troops in excess of 470,000. (Desired range is approximately 570,000 to 670,000.) Request is circulated within the administration for comment.
- *May 1967*—Department of Defense Systems Analysis strongly recommends the 470,000-man ceiling be maintained.
- *May 19, 1967*—Assistant secretary of defense prepares draft presidential memorandum (circulated for staffing under McNamara's signature) in which a token increase in the troop ceiling is advocated but it is made clear that the issue of a troop ceiling is closed.
- *July 1967*—McNamara flies to Saigon and bargains with Westmoreland on final troop ceiling. The number is 525,000.
- *August 1967*—President approves final ceiling.
- *August 14, 1967*—The 525,000-man program is formally published by the Department of Defense. Negotiations begin in Moscow for the logistic support for the Tet offensive.
- *September 1967*—Administration pressures military to accelerate deployments before the March 12 New Hampshire primary.

Inside the Johnson administration, the promulgation of McNamara's 470,000-man troop ceiling on November 11, 1966 was known as "Program 4."[1] McNamara, abandoning the original objective—military victory—now sought to neutralize large North Vietnamese units and allow the South Vietnamese to conduct the war themselves. His strategy rested on the successful development of the South Vietnamese government and armed forces. McNamara argued that increased troop levels above the proposed ceiling would have a negative impact on the South Vietnamese economy, which in turn would hurt South Vietnamese stability.[2] Although it took some time for soldiers in the field to grasp fully the magnitude of the change, senior military leaders quickly understood what the secretary had proposed. They did not like it one bit and in the spring of 1967 made known their opposition formally by issuing a counterproposal. In the discussions that followed, the currency of debate was troop strength numbers but the real subject was strategy. Should the United States commit half a million of its soldiers to a war it had made a conscious decision not to try to win? In the end, the final number for the ceiling would be increased from 470,000 to 525,000, but the president rejected the military's position and upheld McNamara. The formal decision for deescalation came in August 1967.

Ironically, evidence of US ground success once again surpassed official expectations in early 1967. At the beginning of the New Year, American statistics showed enemy-to-friendly kill ratios improving from 3.3 to 4.2 during the preceding six months. The significance of this was even greater since US killed in action had doubled in the period, meaning a far greater number of enemy soldiers had perished.[3] Total enemy killed during January 1967 reached a new monthly high of 5,954.[4] These losses were seriously hurting the regular North Vietnamese units and documents captured by US forces clearly revealed that communist irregular forces also had declined. The Viet Cong's recruitment base had shrunk, according to North Vietnamese/Viet Cong estimates, by more than 1,000,000 people "lost" to South Vietnamese government control.[5] Communist-initiated action declined and the North Vietnamese were forced to supply replacements for

---

[1] *Pentagon Papers,* Book 5,"Phase II, Program 3, Program 4," p. 103.

[2] Ibid., pp. 81–89.

[3] *Pentagon Papers,* Book 5, "Program," pp. 1–4. I do not write easily about an improvement resulting from a doubling of Americans killed, but it is necessary to understand the mathematical precision with which McNamara's Defense Department viewed the war trends.

[4] Gravel, Volume IV, p. 408.

[5] Ibid.

Viet Cong units.[6] Pacification, dubbed Revolutionary Development by the Americans, was moving forward apace—as evidenced by North Vietnamese/Viet Cong efforts to interfere with it. In 1964 and 1965, the Viet Cong hardly bothered with pacification programs. In late 1966, they diverted a large number of assets to attack pacification cadre teams.[7] Moreover, the US logistic structure finally caught up with troop levels in 1967, as most facilities' construction projects were completed.[8]

The very success of the military effort, however, permitted the administration to adopt McNamara's about-face. Forces would be leveled off, the public would be prepared for a longer war, and the public explanation would tie all of this to the military success. Of course, rather than tell the public that military victory had been abandoned as a goal, the administration would simply announce that its objectives had been achieved, that the results of the war had been what was intended all along. Inside Vietnam, the ceiling meant US forces would have sufficient strength to combat larger enemy units in border sanctuaries but not enough to prosecute the guerrilla war aggressively. The result would be a protracted conflict by conscious design of the US leadership.[9]

Despite battlefield successes, the United States could not reach the so-called "crossover" point soon enough—or so McNamara believed after examining evidence of increasing North Vietnamese infiltration that accompanied the larger kill ratios.[10] The Soviet-East European meetings of mid-1966 and the October 1966 Soviet-North Vietnamese arms agreement had once again boosted North Vietnamese/Viet Cong military power at a critical time. General Westmoreland and the JCS, through January and Februrary 1967, argued against the McNamara troop ceiling, pointing out that the exploitation of battlefield success was a sound, elementary—indeed, rudimentary—military principle. However, under all scenarios and under any suggested force level, even if the crossover point were reached, clear victory could not be achieved before the end of 1968—and that was McNamara's key concern.

[6]Ibid.

[7]Ibid.

[8]Sharp and Westmoreland, *Report*, pp. 143–145, and Heiser, *Logistic Support*, p. 22. Heiser reports that "the period 1965–66 was characterized by 15 months of unprecedented growth and development."

[9]*Pentagon Papers*, Book 5, "Volume I: Phase II, Program 3, Program 4," pp. 125–127.

[10]*Secret History*, p. 525. John Dillin, "Infiltration escalates in Vietnam," *Christian Science Monitor*, November 26, 1966, p. 1.

Rostow Memorandum Exposes Split Over Goals

The discussions within the administration centered around a draft National Security Action Memorandum prepared by Walt Rostow at the president's request. This document, which was supposed to spell out strategic guidelines for 1967, was circulated within the government for comment and exposed wide disagreement between military and civilian leaders over fundamental US goals.[11] The military held fast to the position that the "national objective of the United States in South Vietnam (SVN) is an independent nation free of communist subversion and able to determine its own government and national aspirations."[12] The JCS position, clearly reflecting the views of Admiral Sharp and General Westmoreland, recommended that the NSAM contain "a clear, concise statement of national policy for Vietnam," and that it should stipulate that "actions taken to terminate hostilities shall be in accordance with our national objective to assist the government of Vietnam and its armed forces to defeat externally directed and supported communist subversion and aggression, and attain an independent non-communist society in South Vietnam.... "[13]

McNamara's position, represented by comments of Assistant Secretary McNaughton, reflected "a growing concern with our diminished prospects of early success."[14] McNaughton argued for a lesser goal of ensuring the South Vietnamese "the inherent right to choose their own way of life."[15] The *Pentagon Papers* explains McNaughton's comments (which were forwarded back to Rostow through McNamara) as "painstakingly developing alternatives to continued widespread US military involvement over time."[16]

Top US military leaders were stunned by this 180 degree turn—and at a loss as to what to do. The military leadership opposed the November 1966 troop ceiling, the implications of which it all too clearly understood, but, with the exception of a JCS message to McNamara which took issue with some of his logic, there was no immediate counterproposal. In fact, the official military response to the troop ceiling—issued December 2, 1966—

[11]Gravel, Volume IV, p. 392.
[12]Ibid., p. 395.
[13]Ibid., p. 396.
[14]Ibid., p. 393.
[15]Ibid.
[16]Ibid., p. 393.

requested only that the military be allowed the flexibility to substitute units in the programmed deployment so long as troop totals remained below the 470,000-man ceiling.[17]

Although the evidence is circumstantial, it appears that the military, once it realized that McNamara had lost the will to fight, gave up hope of convincing their civilian leaders with memos and meetings. Instead, they turned to allies on Capitol Hill to generate pressure from outside the administration. A December 1966 poll of nineteen senators, for example, revealed a consensus among them that the military needed more support. Senator John Stennis (D-Miss.) stated that General Westmoreland's request for troops should be met "even if it should require mobilization or partial mobilization." Stennis estimated that existing US troop requirements fell 100,000 shy of what was needed.[18] Initial military calculations in the wake of the troop ceiling were, in fact, that 570,000 troops would permit a continued quest for victory, and this figure was available only in classified documents. It strains credibility to believe that Senator Stennis accidently used the same estimate as the Joint Chiefs of Staff.[19] Congressional resistance led to press reporting that contained accurate "classified" military reports on requirements and discussed administration desires to level off troop strength.[20] The military, it seems, was appealing to Congress and the American people for consistency in the conduct of the war and US objectives.

On March 18, 1967, the military presented a formal alternative to the 470,000-man troop ceiling, probably hoping to provide a policy around which the loyal opposition in and outside the administration could rally. The proposal, developed by General Westmoreland, was structured to present the administration with two options on manpower for the war, one labeled "minimum essential force" and the other "optimum."[21] The JCS required additional details before forwarding the request and the final proposal at the end of March included a third option somewhere between the original two. The military called for boosting troop strength in Vietnam

---

[17]Ibid., p. 401.

[18]Ibid.

[19]Ibid.

[20]*Pentagon Papers*, Book 5, "Volume II: Program 5," p. 192. This discusses a *Washington Daily News* article that accurately discussed force levels and alternative courses of action. See also *New York Times*, January 16, 1967, and Ibid., January 18, 1967. For the counter argument and administration efforts to suggest battlefield success could permit troop strength to be leveled off, see Saville R. Davis, "Vietnam war trend sets stage for peace," *Christian Science Monitor*, February 3, 1967, p. 3.

[21]*Pentagon Papers*, Book 5, "Volume II: Program 5," p. 61.

from 470,000 to between 559,397 and 678,248.[22] According to Westmoreland, the 470,000-man ceiling would cause the war to drag on for another five years. The minimum essential force could win the war in three years while the optimum force could win in two.[23]

The military's position was subtle and clever. They ignored the Johnson administration's desire to abandon victory as a goal. They treated the 470,000-man ceiling as a plan to win the war in five years, while expressing their professional opinion that adding forces could bring the conflict to a victorious close in two to three years. Clearly they were hoping to use congressional and public opinion to reinvigorate the administration.

With the ball in the administration's court, there were a series of inter-agency reviews involving the State Department, Defense Department, and the National Security Council. Each agency's comments demonstrated reluctance to support increased troop strength, and instead presented alternatives—such as demanding more from the Vietnamese armed forces or changing tactics within Vietnam.[24] (In fact, the Pentagon Papers subheading for this episode is "The Stimulation of Inter-agency Reviews: A Proliferation of Alternatives.")[25] Although it was preordained that the troop request would be denied, the killing blow to the military's position was administered in May by the Systems Analysis Office of Assistant Secretary of Defense Enthoven. Enthoven's office expressed "surprise and incredulity" at the JCS's plan, treating it as something of an attempt at political sabotage—which, from the administration's perspective, it was. Everyone associated with Vietnam ground force policy on McNamara's staff, explained the Pentagon Papers, "believed that COMUSMACV [Westmoreland] had received the message during program 4 discussions [the 470,000 ceiling was program 4], that any troops were going to be difficult to come by and those that were forthcoming had to be completely and convincingly justified."[26] After criticizing the level of sophistication of the military's troop request, Enthoven recommended in May that the force levels should be only sufficient to "prevent military defeat in South Vietnam," and to "prevent excessive terrorism."[27] His final recommenda-

---

[22]Gravel, Volume IV, pp. 432–433. The minimum comes from my addition of the total minimum add-on of 80,576, a previously requested 8,821 increase to add a rifle company to existing battalions, and the 470,000 ceiling.

[23]Pentagon Papers, Book 5, "Volume II: Program 5," p. 61.

[24]Gravel, Volume IV, pp. 438–447.

[25]Ibid., p. 438.

[26]Ibid., p. 456.

[27]Ibid., p. 457.

tion was that the 470,000-man "ceiling be firmly maintained."[28] Neverthe-less, the military's ploy was beginning to have an effect. There was renewed political pressure from Capitol Hill to back the war effort and reports in the press that the administration was not doing enough to support General Westmoreland were causing embarrassing public discussions. Secretary McNamara therefore decided to throw the JCS a bone—to raise the troop ceiling but adhere to his "no-win" strategy. The Secretary charged the ser-vices to find ways to increase units in Vietnam without crossing the "per-sonnel sound barrier" of mobilization or calling up reserves.[29] McNamara, of course, beginning to address the political discontent brewing among his military subordinates, intended to portray any increases in public as an ex-ample of his wholehearted backing of General Westmoreland. The army replied that it could exceed its estimated ability to deploy forces by about six maneuver battalions. Assistant Secretary Enthoven, using the army's report, declared that the army could provide about 24,000 more troops than originally estimated.[30] This paved the way for a draft presidential memorandum prepared by Assistant Secretary of Defense McNaughton which, although it rejected the March JCS troop request, provided a smaller increase that would not require mobilization. McNaughton also testily recommended that it should be made clear to the military that the subject of troop increases was closed.[31] The JCS, naturally, recommended that the

[28]Ibid., p. 459.
[29]Ibid., p. 472.
[30]Ibid.
[31]Ibid., pp. 478–489. The complete draft presidential memorandum is available in *Trial,* card 955. The Brewin-Shaw book mistakenly says that this was a memorandum for the president from Mc-Namara, not realizing that it was a draft that was circulated for staff comment. It did not go to the president. The mistake is understandable, because McNamara introduced the memorandum into evidence and claimed it was a highly classified communication from McNamara to the president. The defense counsel had been challenging McNamara's credibility, arguing that McNamara's public comments do not support the contention that McNamara felt the war was not winnable. Moreover, the counsel wondered why McNamara had not informed the president of his views. McNamara of-fered his copy of the May 19 draft presidential memorandum (DPM) as proof he had informed the president. The *Pentagon Papers* makes it clear that the May 19, 1967 document was a DPM authored by McNaughton and that it was "floated" for comment on May 19. The document produced by Mc-Namara and introduced into evidence as exhibit 955 is indeed titled "Draft Memorandum for the President." It is dated 19 May 1967. Immediately after the date the following is typed: "(first r(h [*sic*] draft; data and "estimates" here have not been checked.)" It was signed by McNamara because it circulated outside the Department of Defense for comment—in other words, it went to State, NSC, etc. It did not go to the president. All quotes in the *Pentagon Papers* cited as coming from the 19 May McNaughton DPM can be found in the DPM introduced as exhibit 955. In McNamara's tes-timony he said of the DPM "and it was a memorandum from me to the President...." The attorney asked "When did you send that memorandum to the President?" McNamara answered "I believe I

draft presidential memorandum not be sent to the president.[32] After another round of interagency comment, McNamara flew to Saigon for a final discussion with Westmoreland in July 1967. Armed with the information that something on the order of 86,000 above the 470,000 ceiling could be achieved without mobilization, McNamara "bargained" with Westmoreland in Saigon, settling on a "compromise troop ceiling of 525,000."[33] Additionally, certain money would be made available to convert some personnel spaces in Vietnam to civilian hire, thus making more soldiers available for military operations.[34]

The president approved the final troop ceiling. In his tax and budget message to Congress on August 4, 1967, he announced plans to increase troop strength between 45,000 and 50,000, bringing the total to 525,000.[35] The press portrayed this as a compromise between military recommendations for an additional 70,000 men and McNamara's recommendations of an increase of 15,000–30,000.[36]

It is apparent that the president and McNamara intended the 525,000-man troop level to be a final troop ceiling, that the military's congressional gambit had failed.[37] The administration would continue to make its own fate in the next election a higher priority than the fate of the American soldiers engaged in combat in South Vietnam. The *Pentagon Papers,* with an unmistakable air of defensiveness, summed up Program 5, which was Johnson and McNamara's response to the JCS's proposal, this way:

> Its origins and its limits can be traced to one primary factor—
> that of mobilization. When the President and the Secretary of
> Defense, as well as other Congressional leaders and political-
> ly attuned decision makers in the government began to search

---

sent it May 19." This is incorrect. Since McNamara claimed over and over to have no specific recollection of any discussions with the president at any time (it seems he had no specific recollection of anything), it would strain credibility to suggest that the one specific thing he did remember about his service as secretary of defense was taking this draft to the president on May 19, 1967.

[32]Gravel, Vol. IV, p. 500.

[33]Ibid., p. 515, p. 523.

[34]*Pentagon Papers,* Book 5, "Volume II: Program 5," p. 209.

[35]Ibid., p. 527.

[36]Ibid.

[37]Herring, p. 179 and Gelb and Betts, p. 156. George Herring does not agree that "Program 5" was a troop ceiling, writing about it "No ceilings were set, however, and there was no reassessment of the search and destroy strategy." Once again, we see a military technique confused with strategy. Leslie Gelb and Richard Betts explain "Program 5" as "In the end McNamara and the President put another notch in the tradition of compromise and authorized an increase to 525,000 men."

for the illusive point at which the costs of Vietnam would become inordinate, they always settled upon the mobilization line, the point at which Reserves and large units would have to be called up to support a war which was becoming increasingly distasteful and intolerable to the American public. Domestic resource constraints with all of their political and social repercussions, not strategic or tactical military considerations in Vietnam, were to dictate American war policy from that time on.[38]

Shortly after the 525,000-man ceiling decision, the official military surrender to McNamara was conducted by Army Chief of Staff Harold K. Johnson, who suggested publicly in September that some troop *reduction* could be expected in eighteen months because of US successes.[39] The fundamental decision to abandon military victory as a national goal had been made, appealed, and upheld.

The public position, however, continued to be that the US commitment was open-ended. The troop ceiling was portrayed as another troop increase, with accompanying *suggestions* that it would be the last, because of US progress on the battlefield. This obfuscated the decision and led the Soviets to believe that the troop ceiling was open to discussion and the American objective remained victory. Increasingly, the administration would "gird for a long war" publicly in order to gain approval for its policies at the polls. The administration would say that the Vietnamese ultimately had to win themselves, that the costs and risks for the American people were acceptably low, that the formula for success had been found, and that victory was only a matter of time. However, this was a gradual process and not clear in mid-1967.

The Soviets embarked on the negotiations with the North Vietnamese to support the Tet offensive believing that the issue of US troop strength in Vietnam was still under debate. It is no small irony that the Soviet-North Vietnamese negotiations began August 14, 1967, the same day that Program 5—the 525,000-man troop ceiling—was formally published inside the Johnson administration. The final decision the Soviets hoped to prevent, a leveling off in the American presence on China's southern border, already had been made.

[38]Ibid., pp. 527–528.
[39]George W. Ashworth, "Possibilities sighted of Vietnam troop cuts," *Christian Science Monitor,* September 5, 1967, p. 3.

Once More It Looks Like an Unlimited Commitment

The American press made a contribution to the Soviet misreading of US policy by staying remarkably well informed of some of the classified details of the lengthy troop ceiling discussions that followed the March 1967 troop request. For example, an article in the *Washington Daily News* in June 1967 surfaced the problem of force levels in Vietnam and their relationship to mobilization. The author stated that military estimates for required troop strength called for 200,000 to 250,000 more troops, which would bring totals to about 700,000. The reporter wrote that this increase could not be achieved without at least partial mobilization. He noted, correctly, that the White House wanted to avoid mobilization, especially before the 1968 elections. He put pressure on the administration by running interviews with military men in Vietnam citing personnel deficiencies by rank and skill and alleging that many units were operating below acceptable manpower levels. One disgruntled officer talked about the administration's desire to wait until the 1968 elections, saying "A lot of us are going to die before then."[40]

Later, in July, a *New York Times* article discussed the need for an additional 70,000-man force to allow the United States to retain the initiative in the war. It contained much accurate, allegedly classified information, including a discussion of a Westmoreland "minimum request" for 70,000 more soldiers that had been supported by the JCS. The author's charge that administration inaction was the result of a reluctance to order partial mobilization so angered the president that he ordered the secretary of the army to work with defense department public affairs officials to refute the story. However, the secretary of the army reported that much of the information was accurate, especially data on low troop strength in Europe (which supported the accusation that worldwide readiness had been sacrificed to conduct the war in Vietnam). He recommended that the most prudent course of action would be to ignore the article. The administration did not respond.[41]

The true US position must have been unclear to the Soviets in 1967, as in fact it was to most Americans. The Johnson administration clearly wished to avoid mobilization and hoped that troop levels could be capped. There was political pressure to increase troop strength, however, and no

---

[40]*Pentagon Papers*, Book 5, "Volume II, Program 5," pp. 192–193.
[41]Ibid.

indication that the US commitment had lessened. As internal administration debates were reconstructed in public, the Kremlin probably concluded that the bickering was over the levers of power rather than policy. According to the American press, McNamara and Westmoreland had argued over troop calculations and the president had split the difference between the two.[42] Ironically, certain administration actions served to confirm the Soviets' reading of the American scene. Smarting under charges that he had not supported Westmoreland adequately, President Johnson decided to accelerate the approved troop deployments, in the hope that this would result in some short-term, highly visible military successes prior to the March 12, 1968, New Hampshire primary election.[43] Since it would strain the ability of the military to get soldiers to Vietnam faster, the extraordinary logistic arrangements, closely covered by the press, would contribute to the public impression that everything possible was being done to support General Westmoreland.

On September 6, 1967, General Harold K. Johnson, acting chairman of the Joint Chiefs of Staff, informed the Joint Chiefs that the administration had asked him what could be done to speed up deployments.[44] The same people who had just denied the military's recommendation to deploy a larger force were now pressuring the military to take extraordinary measures to get the forces that had been approved into the field rapidly. The alleged purpose, as explained to General Johnson, was to meet the threat in South Vietnam's northern provinces. But these excuses were immediately transparent to the service chiefs when the administration asked General Johnson specifically (a) what could be done prior to Christmas? and (b) what could be done prior to the March 12, 1968, New Hampshire presidential primary election?[45] The urgency of the query to General Johnson is revealed by the three-day deadline the acting chairman gave the Joint Staff for a response. A memorandum compiled by the director, Joint Staff was given to General Johnson on September 9, 1967, and the general took it to the White House personally on September 12.[46]

---

[42]To understand how American policy could have been confusing for the Soviets to understand see George W. Ashworth, "More US Forces predicted for Vietnam," *Christian Science Monitor,* July 8, 1967, p. 3; Saville R. Davis, "Limited reinforcement of a limited Viet war," Ibid., July 15, 1967, p. 1.

[43]*Pentagon Papers,* Book 5, "Volume II: Program 5," p. 215.

[44]Ibid.

[45]*Pentagon Papers,* Book 5, "Volume II: Program 5," p. 215.

[46]Ibid., pp. 215–218. The Director, Joint Staff is a three-star position on the Joint Staff. He coordinates the work of the staff. He could be called the Chief of Staff for the Joint Chiefs of Staff.

In September 1967 the total number of troops authorized but not yet deployed was 62,132. Because most of these forces needed equipment before entering combat, which was not yet available, accelerated deployment proved infeasible, said General Johnson. After more study it was concluded that, through extraordinary measures, it would be possible to accelerate deployment of the 101st Airborne Division and the 11th Light Infantry Brigade. Deployment of the division early would cost an additional $15 million for air transportation, and the required non-divisional combat support elements that could not be deployed would have to follow later. Interim non-divisional support would be supplied by existing resources already in Vietnam. Moreover, the 101st Airborne Division would require an additional four weeks training in Vietnam before commitment. Similar problems accompanied accelerated deployment for the 11th Brigade. The president made no decision on General Johnson's recommendations but once again stressed his desire that the military devise ways to increase pressure on North Vietnam within existing policy limitations.[47]

Given more time for analysis, the army was able to devise less costly methods to achieve accelerated deployment of the 101st Airborne Division and the 11th Light Infantry Brigade. The secretary of defense approved plans for the 101st on October 21, 1967, and for the 11th Brigade on October 31.[48] Both could be deployed by Christmas and employed, after additional training, before the end of January 1968.

The administration also moved ahead with plans to "civilianize" many military manpower slots. The intent was to get more troops into the field without increasing the pressure to mobilize. The process involved identifying jobs being performed by soldiers that could be handled by civilians, hiring qualified personnel, and sending the freed-up soldiers into combat in Vietnam or for duty in other areas that had been drawn down to support

---

[47]Ibid. The Army classifies units in three categories: Combat, combat support, and combat service support. Infantry and tank units are examples of combat units. Artillery and combat engineers are combat support units. Quartermaster and maintenance units are combat service support units. Additionally, though a division is relatively self-sustaining, it requires support external to the division to sustain itself in combat for extended periods. An example of "non-divisional" support might be a maintenance and repair shop that would be able to conduct a major overhaul of a tank that had been damaged by a mine. Additionally, sometimes "non-divisional" artillery will be attached to a division to beef up its firepower. Many military terms like "attached," "assigned," "reinforcing," and "organic" have precise meanings that are unnecessary for the general reader to understand. Thus, though a purist might amplify on this explanation, this should help clarify General Johnson's recommendations.

[48]Ibid., pp. 218–221.

Vietnam. This gave the administration the ability to squeeze more forces out of the active military without having to call up reserves.[49]

On October 17, 1967, the Joint Chiefs submitted a list of proposed actions to the president to increase pressure on North Vietnam without exceeding the 525,000-man troop ceiling. It included a number of straightforward, potentially decisive military initiatives outside existing policy limitations such as mining North Vietnamese ports and removing restrictions on the bombing campaign. However, actions that were within policy limitations contained nothing dramatically new, and the president promptly rejected it saying that it was not what he wanted.[50] On November 7, 1967, the Chairman of the Joint Chiefs of Staff was directed to "take all feasible measures to deploy Program 5 forces at the earliest possible date."[51] Efforts continued, with an eye always on the approaching New Hampshire primary, to give the impression that all military requirements had been satisfied and to gain some dramatic battlefield success.

At a White House luncheon on November 8, 1967, the secretary of state recommended that the State Department and Defense Department prepare a "joint policy document which would govern political and military operations in Southeast Asia over the next four months."[52] Stated differently, this would be a plan of action focused on the New Hampshire primary—since it was four months and four days from the White House luncheon until this important vote. On November 27, 1967, the Joint Chiefs responded to this pressure by stating that there was nothing more they could do within current policy limitations.[53]

According to the public position of the administration, the United States was winning the war in Vietnam. The commitment to a 525,000-man force, coupled with accelerated deployment, was meant to insure that the United States retained the initiative. The North Vietnamese and Viet Cong, the administration line went, were willing to increase the level of conflict, but the latest troop decisions could more than cope with any escalation. General Westmoreland dutifully echoed this line in a statement at the end of the year, stating that signs of success were more encouraging than ever.[54] The

[49]Ibid., p. 218.
[50]Ibid., p. 223.
[51]Ibid.
[52]Ibid., p. 225.
[53]Ibid., p. 227.
[54]Beverly Deepe, "Westmoreland sights Viet victory," *Christian Science Monitor,* December 11, 1967, p. 1; "The news-briefly," Ibid., November 16, 1967, p. 2.

administration was hoping for good news from the front that would have a positive affect on the president's showing in the New Hampshire primary and further pave the way for the final public revelation that American goals had shifted and that the US was no longer seeking a military victory and a noncommunist South Vietnam. Lurking around the corner, however, was a shock that would undermine this strategy. The Tet offensive would lead the administration to develop a new explanation for the decision to deescalate. But it would not, as is commonly believed, change the strategic decision for a troop ceiling that had already been made, appealed, and upheld.

13

The Tet Offensive

Major Events

- *August 1967*—Chinese press attacks Liu Shaoqi as China's Khrushchev. He is accused of "illicit relations with foreign countries." Soviet press reports on dissent within Chinese military.
- *September 1967*—Acting PLA Chief of Staff Yang Chengwu is appointed as leader of the campaign to criticize Luo Ruiqing. North Vietnam and Soviet Union sign most extensive arms agreement to date.
- *September 1967–January 1968*—Soviet shipping to Vietnam takes quantum leap.
- *November 1967*—Soviets announce that consultative conference of communist parties will be held in Budapest in February 1968.
- *January 25–31, 1968*—Soviet-Indian talks conducted on Soviet aid for India.
- *January 30, 1968*—The Tet offensive begins.
- *February 1968*—Westmoreland responds to query from General Wheeler. Wheeler suggests it would be a good time to press for the addtitional forces required to win. Request is for 206,000 more men.
- *February 13, 1968*—President directs deployment of 11,000 "emergency" reinforcements over objections of Joint Chiefs of Staff who argue that there is no emergency.
- *Late February 1968*—Department of Defense recommends that the president reject any troop request other than token increases. McNamara leaves administration. Clark Clifford becomes secretary of defense. Soviets announce that international conference of communist parties will be in November–December 1968 with a theme of unity of action over Vietnam.
- *March 8, 1968*—President formally rejects 206,000-man request.

201

- *March 10, 1968*—206,000-man request is leaked to the press.
- *Mid March 1968*—Yang Chengwu turns against Mao.
- *March 12, 1968*—Eugene McCarthy makes strong showing in New Hampshire primary against president.
- *March 18, 1968*—Johnson meets with informal group of senior advisors—the "wise men."
- *March 22, 1968*—Johnson recalls Westmoreland from Vietnam and replaces him with Creighton Abrams. Westmoreland becomes chief of staff of army. Information provided to the press by the administration indicates he has been recalled because he had painted an overly optimistic picture of the war that had been exposed by Tet.
- *March 24–25, 1968*—Mao removes Yang Chengwu as PLA chief of staff.
- *March 31, 1968*—Johnson in televised address announces troop ceiling, bombing curtailment, and that he will not run for reelection in the fall.
- *April 1968*—Yang Chengwu criticized publicly.

The North Vietnamese planned to attack simultaneously more than 100 cities and towns in South Vietnam on January 30, 1968. The chain of command did not communicate successfully orders for a twenty-four-hour postponement to the entire attack force. As a result, the battle began at Nha Trang at thirty-five minutes after midnight on January 30, as originally planned. Coordination was not perfect, but in light of the difficulties of command and control of large formations under the best of conditions the initial attacks were remarkably well done.[1] Overall, the military effort would be a major disaster for the Vietnamese communists. Politically, they would achieve results beyond their expectations. This political success in turn meant that the original Soviet strategy would fail.

The Attack

On January 30 with Tet parties in full swing, a barrage of mortars and rockets slammed into Ban Me Thuet, a town of 65,000 in the central highlands. The barrage was followed by a ground assault by 2,000 soldiers.[2] The North Vietnamese had violated their agreement for a truce during the

---

[1]Dave Richard Palmer, *Summons of the Trumpet,* (New York: 1978), p. 237, (hereafter referred to as *Trumpet*); Don Oberdorfer, *TET!,* (New York: 1971), pp. 124–134.

[2]Oberdofer, *TET!,* p. 129.

holidays. Since a quick-thinking US military policeman had cleared the town of US soldiers at midnight, when the firecrackers and rifle firing accompanying the revelry began, the town turned into a nightmare of dead, wounded, and terrified Vietnamese civilians.[3] The communists scored the first victory in a series to be heralded by the American press.

Intelligence sources had caused General Westmoreland to be so apprehensive that he had encouraged President Thieu to abandon the scheduled holiday truce. Upon Westmoreland's urging, Ambassador Bunker recommended to Washington that the allied cease-fire be cancelled in I Corps (the northern part of South Vietnam). President Thieu agreed, but failed to issue the necessary orders.[4] The next day the North Vietnamese won another, far more important victory—a victory that would mean the failure of the Soviet Union's China strategy. At 2:45 a.m., members of the Sapper Battalion C-10 approached the front gate of the American Embassy in Saigon in a taxi. At 2:47 they opened fire and two US military policemen returned fire and closed the gate. The Sappers blew a hole in the wall with plastic explosives and entered the embassy, killing the two Americans at the cost of several of their own, including the platoon leader. They rushed the embassy, but Americans inside managed to shut the doors. Now without their platoon leader, the Viet Cong milled around firing occasionally until the last one was killed at about 7:00 a.m.[5] This would, in the mind of the American public, cancel all that American soldiers would achieve on the battlefield in the following days.

North Vietnam committed about 84,000 combat troops against 36 provincial capitals, 5 autonomous cities, 64 district capitals, and 50 hamlets. The 84,000 includes combat soldiers, not support troops. The total force was at least twice as large.[6] American and allied forces would inflict nearly 60,000 North Vietnamese and Viet Cong casualties, about the total number of US servicemen killed during the entire war.[7] By any military standard, the attacking force suffered a catastrophe.[8] Moreover, any hopes the North Vietnamese had for a general uprising were crushed. The main targets—the government of South Vietnam and its army—were preserved by the tenacious fighting of the South Vietnamese soldiers. The *Pentagon*

---

[3] Ibid.

[4] Ibid., p.132; Sharp and Westmoreland, *Report*, p. 158.

[5] Palmer, *Trumpet*, p. 241.

[6] Sharp and Westmorland, *Report*, p. 158.

[7] Oberdofer, *TET!*, dedication page, and Sharp and Westmoreland, *Report*, p. 161.

[8] Sharp and Westmoreland, *Report*, pp. 161–162; Palmer, *Trumpet*, p. 255.

Papers, looking back at the tumultuous event, noted that "the RVNAF held up against the initial assault with gratifying and in a way surprising strength and fortitude."[9] "Saigon's armed forces refused to fold," says another chronicler. "The citizens of the South...turned out to be overwhelmingly anti-communist.... In all, it was South Vietnam's finest hour."[10] But smoking fine cigars and sipping expensive brandy atop the Caravelle Hotel in Saigon was an army that no commander could conquer—the US press corps. General Westmoreland would command a large army in a desperate battle and win—only to be defeated by this brandy-sipping collection of journalists.[11]

Combat is loud, smoky, frightening, and confusing. Even a trained soldier at the point of contact may not be able to figure out whether he is winning or losing. The chain of command's job at the tactical level is to make order out of chaos and shift people, weapons, ammunition, and firepower as required. A soldier's ultimate duty is to conduct mindless violence at the risk of life and limb.[12] The reason nations have armies, after all, is to kill people and break things. A reporter suddenly thrust face to face with combat—especially if the fighting is a surprise—is likely to be convinced that disaster is upon him, just as soldiers in "rear" areas are easily overwhelmed by the sights, sounds, and smells of battle in front of them.[13] To an MP sergeant near the American Embassy, any Viet Cong presence is likely to suggest that all is lost. And the same "overweight and overwrought" sergeant can easily turn into a military spokesman for an equally overwrought reporter. Most in the American media did not intentionally misrepresent what they saw. They just did not understand what they were seeing. In the view of the press, there should not have been enemy rifle and artillery fire near the commanding general's headquarters if the war truly was being won. The fighting in Saigon was a shock. The ferocity of the fighting they witnessed was a shock. The instant, on-the-scene analysis by American reporters was completely off the mark.[14]

What actually happened was that a large North Vietnamese and Viet Cong army lost over half of its combatant strength in a short period of time.

---

[9]*Pentagon Papers,* Book 5, "Volume III: Program 6," p. 13.

[10]Palmer, *Trumpet,* p. 254.

[11]See Oberdorfer, *TET!,* pp. 178 and 183 for a description of reporters and the Caravelle Hotel.

[12]From many speeches by General John W. Vessey, Jr., former vice-chief of staff of the army and former chairman of the Joint Chiefs of Staff. General Vessey held every rank from private to general and received a battlefield commission at Anzio in World War II.

[13]Field soldiers have an acronym for "rear" soldiers known as REMF. It need not be explained.

[14]See Oberdorfer, *TET!,* pp. 1–40 and pp. 331–333, for an enlightening discussion of this issue.

In the ancient city of Hue, the communist forces systematically murdered 2,800 civilians during the twenty-six days they held the town. General Westmoreland would explain what was happening in Hue and his words would be reported. But above his explanation in the *New York Times* or the *Washington Post* would be a picture of Saigon police chief Loan shooting a Viet Cong prisoner in the head. Fifteen American soldiers would earn the Medal of Honor during Tet—but the most famous military man would be an unnamed major quoted as saying "it became necessary to destroy the village to save it." The famed television newscaster Walter Cronkite would decide to oppose the war. Modern electronics would allow the press to tell its errant, demoralizing story every night—and every night the most spectacular footage available would make its way into American homes.[15] No communist propagandist or psychological operator could have devised so thorough a campaign or have the resources to implement it.

US and South Vietnamese forces won a stunning military victory and the press reported it as a spectacular defeat.

Soviets Look for a Big Victory With Tet Offensive

Direct Soviet appeals in support of the Liu-Deng group were a double-edged sword. The Soviet propaganda that looked for "healthy forces" to emerge victorious in China allowed Mao to criticize his opponents for being in league with hostile foreigners. Yet Mao's public criticism also reflected concern that Soviet overtures to Liu Shaoqi and Soviet troop deployments against China were having an effect on the Chinese military leadership. In August 1967, as the Soviets and North Vietnamese began to negotiate the Tet logistic agreement, a joint editorial in *People's Daily, Red Flag,* and *Liberation Army Daily* appeared in which Liu Shaoqi was labeled another Khrushchev. The code for Liu was "the top Party person in authority taking the capitalist road" and he was accused of colluding "with the big conspirators, careerists and warlords Peng Teh-huai and Luo Ruiqing for 17 years in order to bring about the restoration of capitalism.... [They] engaged in

[15]Ibid., pp. 331–333 and p. 233, Illustrations 25 and 26 and pp. 246–251. See Gareth Porter, *A Peace Denied,* pp. 65–66, for the argument that the massacre in Hue never happened. Porter speaks in glowing terms of Wilfred Burchett and has a footnote for his view that the murders in Hue did not occur—he cites an earlier article by himself. He is in disagreement with every non-communist source.

activities to usurp Army leadership in a vain attempt to turn the Army into their tool."[16] However, the editorial also suggested that Liu's strength within the military was considerable. "We must be vigilant," said the editorial, "to make sure the gun is firmly in the hand of the proletariat—and prevent the revisionists from usurping military power."[17] A separate *Red Flag* article reflected similar fears by stating:

> For a fairly long historical period, the proletariat faces danger of losing the Army.... Peng Teh-huai and Luo Ruiqing were agents of the Top Party Person. In order to usurp military power, Lo and Peng made desperate efforts to oppose giving prominence to proletarian politics and to peddle revisionist trash imported from abroad.... Backed by the Top Party Person taking the capitalist road [they] cultivated their own private influence within the Army and...maintained illicit relations with foreign countries.[18]

Mao clearly used articles to quickly communicate his concerns and instructions to supporters. He would not have surfaced the issue of Liu Shaoqi's strength in the army unless he had reason to be worried. Numerous other articles also confirmed the existence of a serious struggle for the loyalty of the leadership of the People's Liberation Army.[19] Soviet strategy, it seems, was on solid ground. Liu was competing with Mao for the loyalty of the decisive group in the power struggle—the military leadership. That leadership was unhappy with Mao's large-scale use of the Army in the Cultural Revolution. In this context, the Soviet Union must have seen the large and expensive logistic effort to support the Tet offensive as a way of creating another powerful military force—an American retaliatory force—on the Chinese border, another potential threat for the Chinese generals to worry about.

There was plenty of evidence to convince the Soviets that their strategy was on the right track. A Maoist article quoted Liu as having said that China

---

[16]"Chairman Mao Tse-tung on People's War," *Peking Review,* August 4, 1967, pp. 5–13.

[17]Ibid.

[18]"The Proletariat Must Take a Firm Hold of the Gun," ibid., pp. 36–39.

[19]For example, "Nationwide Army Day Celebration," ibid., August 11, 1967, pp. 11–13; "Peng Teh-huai and his Behind the Scenes Boss Cannot Shirk Responsibility for Their Crimes," ibid., August 25, 1967, pp. 6–7; "The Great Chinese PLA—Reliable Pillar of Our Proletarian Dictatorship and Great Proletarian Cultural Revolution," ibid., pp. 36–39.

"should unite with [the Soviet Union], seek common ground while resolving differences and together oppose imperialism."[20] In other words, the external threat to China should take precedence over other issues, according to Liu Shaoqi. This argument had not fallen on deaf ears in the Army, as Mao's group was forced to admit. "It is inevitable," noted *Red Flag,* "that a few leading members of PLA units in some places suffered from certain shortcomings or made certain mistakes. Those Army cadres who made mistakes must become aware and immediately correct them."[21]

Mao was determined to purge army leaders opposed to him, but realized that he would have to move carefully. The smokescreen behind which he planned to carry out his objective was a campaign throughout the army "to criticize Luo Ruiqing" and especially end any lingering influence Luo had in the General Staff. The campaign, following guidance from Mao and Defense Minister Lin Biao, was under the direct leadership of the head of the Party Committee of the Headquarters of the General Staff, Acting PLA Chief of Staff Yang Chengwu.[22]

According to *People's Daily,* there was a "certain anarchist trend still alive in the Army, under the guise of ultra left but is really ultra right," and that Liu Shaoqi's forces were attempting to split the leadership of the army from Mao. A *People's Daily* article charged that there was an ongoing "futile attempt to split the leadership of Proletarian Headquarters headed by Mao Tse-tung and the PLA, the great pillar of the dictatorship of the proletariat."[23]

When Brezhnev made an appeal to "healthy forces" in China in September 1967, Mao used those comments as proof of Liu's collusion with the Soviets. A *People's Daily* editorial called Liu Shaoqi and Deng Xiaoping "China's Khrushchevs" and noted that Brezhnev had called them "outstanding representatives and eminent statesmen of the Party." Brezhnev, according to the article, wept and mourned over Liu and Deng's difficulties. "Brezhnev's shameful performance has once again divulged the open secret that China's counter-revolutionary revisionists and the Soviet revisionist renegade clique are just

---

[20] "Along the Socialist or the Capitalist Road?" ibid., August 18, 1967, pp. 10–18.

[21] "The Great Chinese PLA—Reliable Pillar of Our Proletarian Dictatorship and Great Proletarian Cultural Revolution," ibid., September 1, 1967, pp. 5–6.

[22] "PLA Men Criticize and Repudiate Conspirator Lo Jui-ching," ibid., September 8, 1967, pp. 10–11.

[23] "Hold to the General Orientation of Revolutionary Struggle, Unfold a Deep-Going, Revolutionary Campaign of Mass Criticism," ibid., September 15, 1967, pp. 8–9.

Tweedledum and Tweedledee.... Brezhnev...openly urges the Chinese...revisionists...to...come back."[24]

Although Yang Chengwu controlled and continued the campaign to criticize Luo Ruiqing in the Army General Staff, there was confusion in the provinces. In October, Zhou Enlai was critical of army units in Wuhan, prodding them to "do more ideological and political work so as to help promote the great alliance of mass organizations."[25] During severe disturbances in Wuhan, the army units interfered on the wrong side (from Mao's point of view). Moreover, there was evidence that the "mistake" was intentional and that some military leaders were tiring of criticism from Mao. "Some of our cadres," Zhou explained, "who have risen to high positions, have assumed arrogant airs, thinking that they are somebody and are becoming fond of telling people off."[26]

A Soviet assessment at the end of 1967 likely showed that the United States was accelerating its troop deployments to Vietnam, that the Chinese power struggle was still in doubt, that there was evidence of anti-Mao feeling in the army, and that the American threat in Vietnam was still a weapon that could be used to drive China back to the Soviet camp. The Soviets were rushing supplies to North Vietnam that would make the Tet offensive possible. With the offensive planned for the end of January 1968, the Soviets apparently hoped for a swift US response that would raise fears among the Chinese military. To maximize pressure on China at this moment, the Soviets decided to convene the long-awaited international conference of communist parties to excommunicate China from the socialist camp.[27] Amid a number of harsh editorials charging that Chinese actions damaged North Vietnam, *Pravda* announced on November 25, 1967, that "on the basis of bilateral consultations among parties who participated in the March 1965 meeting and in accordance with the wishes of the 1965 meeting—these parties deem it expedient to hold a consultative meeting in February 1968." The meeting would be in Budapest.[28]

In conjunction with the conference, and to emphasize the growing "ring"

[24] "Brezhnev's Anti-China Ravings," ibid., September 22, 1967, pp. 26–27.

[25] "Comrade Chou En-lai's Speech," ibid., October 20, 1967, pp. 8–12. See also "Closely Follow Chairman Mao's Latest Instructions, Realize the Revolutionary Great Alliance," ibid., September 29, 1967, pp. 7–9.

[26] "Comrade Chou En-lai's Speech," ibid., October 20, 1967, pp. 8–12.

[27] "O sozive konsul'tativnoi vstrechi kommunisticheskikh i rabochikh partii," (On the Calling of the Consultative Meeting of Communist and Workers Parties), *Pravda,* November 25, 1967, p. 1.

[28] Ibid. For charges against China see "Pyat'desyat let velikikh pobed sotsializma," (Fifty Years of Great Victories of Socialism), ibid., November 4, 1967, pp. 2–6.

around China in a way that would exploit the expected American reaction to Tet, the Soviets scheduled a visit by Kosygin to China's longtime enemy, India, from January 25–31, 1968. The talks would be about new Soviet aid to India.[29]

On the eve of the Tet offensive, the Soviets summed up their understanding of the situation in China in *Izvestia*. A few months ago, the article noted, Mao said the situation in China was exceptionally favorable. But "in the past few days the tone of the Maoist press and radio had changed noticeably.... It no longer talks about the favorable situation and virtually admits that a state of civil war exists." More ominously, the Soviets noted widespread and broadbased anti-Mao sentiment. "More and more often [the press] mentions those who are disposed to conduct a civil war.... Workers and peasants are told not to rebel but to do their daily work, devoting only their free time to the Cultural Revolution." The Soviets finished the analysis by focusing on the critical element—the army. "There are reports of armed clashes.... Peking press admits real battles have taken place.... In these conditions the chief bulwark of Mao Tse-tung and his supporters continues to be the Army."[30] In a few days, the Soviets hoped, the "chief bulwark" would crumble and defect from the Cultural Revolution.

Snatching Defeat From the Jaws of Victory

As the first onslaught in Vietnam was repulsed, it was evident to General Westmoreland that the South Vietnamese Army had bent but not broken. The pacification effort had received a setback and popular confidence in the ability of the government to protect citizens had been shaken.[31] General Wheeler cabled Westmoreland to ask if he needed reinforcements.[32] Indeed, this is the central question, the answer to which helps explain the Johnson administration's bizarre behavior in the aftermath of Tet. A simple "yes" or "no" to General Wheeler's query does not clarify matters. General Westmoreland did indeed *need* reinforcements, but why he needed them must be understood. He did not need emergency reinforcements to ward

---

[29] "Sovetsko-indiskoe kommyunike," (Soviet-Indian Communique), ibid., February 1, 1968; "India buying subs from Soviet Union," *Christian Science Monitor*, November 4, 1967, p. 1.

[30] "Narastayushchee soprotivlenie," (Mounting Resistance), *Izvestia*, January 19, 1968, p. 2.

[31] *Pentagon Papers*, Book 5, "Volume III: Program 6," pp. 12–13.

[32] Ibid.

off defeat. In fact, very early in the offensive the US command realized that the US and South Vietnamese forces were on the verge of an historic military thrashing of their enemy. If there was no need for reinforcements to help in the immediate battle, then why would General Westmoreland need help? The answer, in part, lay in the shock to the South Vietnamese population caused by Tet. Westmoreland needed to divert troops from the large unit war to protect pacification efforts.[33] The administration and military already had concluded that the troop ceiling would provide sufficient forces to prevent the enemy from operating a large-scale conventional war—but not enough to prosecute the guerrilla war aggressively. Tet called attention to that defect, and made the modest increase in the troop ceiling represented by Program 5 palpably unsatisfactory to a general on the verge of victory. A commander who hurts his foe is trained to exploit that success and press for a decisive outcome. The need to press offensive action, perhaps into sanctuaries in Laos and Cambodia, in the wake of the stunning enemy casualties conflicted with the need to protect a shaken population. Thus, in response to General Wheeler, General Westmoreland renewed his March 1967 request for a large enough army to end the war on the battlefield, a request the Johnson administration already had denied because of concerns over the upcoming elections.[34]

In the immediate aftermath of the initial assaults, the administration wished to present as positive an image as possible and give the appearance that its field commander had the full support of Washington. At the initiative of the secretary of defense, the administration decided to deploy one brigade of the 82nd Airborne Division and one Marine Regimental Landing Team to South Vietnam as reinforcements.[35] However, General Westmoreland did not need emergency reinforcements. By the time the emergency deployments were directed on February 13, 1968, it was clear to Washington leaders as well as the US command in Saigon that there was no danger of destruction or defeat of General Westmoreland's forces, or the government and armed forces of South Vietnam. There had been a great

---

[33]This situation resulted from the blow to the confidence of the people caused by the widespread fighting in allegedly secure areas. This works somewhat in the same way Stalin cowed the Soviet population with the collectivization of agriculture and the great purges. After such terror, it was unnecessary to resort to such extreme measures again. A little reminder here and there is all that is necessary. Likewise, in the wake of Tet, very minor and nearly unpreventable terrorist actions could have a great impact on the population.

[34]Ibid., p. 15.

[35]Ibid., p. 6.

battle and the United States had won. And McNamara and the president knew it. Moreover, the size of the reinforcing force was far too small to permit General Westmoreland to protect pacification while regaining the initiative with offensive operations. Accordingly, the *Joint Chiefs recommended against deployment* of this force, pointing out that it was too small to be effective in Vietnam but would significantly weaken the US strategic reserve.[36] But the administration deployed the force anyway and a haggard and troubled-looking president was filmed bidding farewell to Airborne troopers boarding their aircraft for Vietnam at the Green Ramp at Pope Air Force Base.

Since the military did not want or need these forces, the question is, Why did McNamara and the president send them? And why did they turn the deployments into a public spectacle of self-doubt and contrition? It certainly wasn't loss of public support—not at this stage. The American people rallied around the flag.

While "peace" candidate Eugene McCarthy made a strong showing against President Johnson in the New Hampshire Democratic primary in March 1968, three out of every five McCarthy votes were "hawkish" votes in favor of ending the war through escalation.[37] The American public was dissatisfied with the handling of the war, but it did not support a "softer" prosecution of the conflict.

Just after the beginning of Tet, opinion polls showed the largest margin in favor of escalation to that point in the war—58 percent in favor of escalation to 6 percent in favor of withdrawal. One study of this issue has concluded, "The evidence strongly suggests that the failure to escalate after Tet contributed to Johnson's popularity decline."[38]

During the first month and a half after Tet, public pressures for escalating the war, combined with military recommendations to increase troop strength and seize the initiative, left Johnson in a quandary. He had already made a decision to abandon victory and a noncommunist South Vietnam as an objective—although he had not bothered to tell the American public. That decision had been challenged by the military and reaffirmed by his administration long before Tet. He could reverse course, but that would mean persuading—or dumping—his most important advisors. It appears that Johnson briefly attempted to build a new consensus in his

---

[36]Ibid.

[37]Gelb and Betts, p. 172. Gelb and Betts establish a new and thoughtful basis for consideration of the consequences of Tet .

[38]Crawford, *Retreat,* pp. 3–4;

administration and political party in favor of renewed escalation. When this effort failed, he reaffirmed deescalation and withdrew from the coming presidential race.[39]

If the American public was confused, imagine what the Russians and Chinese were faced with from January to March 1968. It was clear that the administration knew that there was no military emergency and the enemy had suffered enormous casualties. The administration's public reaction to the sensationalized press coverage was to encourage the atmosphere of crisis engendered by it. The first mention of the so-called "psychological victory" for the Viet Cong came on February 1, 1968, from Secretary Mc-Namara in congressional testimony.[40] The president used the term the following day and Ambassador Bunker followed the next day by also declaring a psychological victory for the North Vietnamese.[41] The decision to send the unwanted and unneeded "emergency" reinforcements and the president's performance in seeing the troops off further contributed to the atmosphere of crisis generated by the spectacular battle footage on the nightly evening news. Later in February, still building the image of continuing crisis, the president dispatched General Wheeler to Vietnam for an assessment. He returned with General Westmoreland's request for an additional 206,756 soldiers by the end of 1968, though this request remained classified for the moment.[42]

Apparently, the president felt the crisis atmosphere would generate a "rally round the flag" sentiment within the administration, as it had among the general public. However, Johnson soon discovered otherwise. And then he, McNamara, McNamara's advisors—and a decade of historians—decided to make the military a scapegoat for dragging the United States into a major war. The Johnson administration "went public" with the argument that estimates provided by the military on the progress of the war had been overly optimistic; the risks and costs of victory, in the wake of Tet, now that the civilian leadership knew the truth, were unacceptable; and, therefore, the United States would cease escalating the conflict and seek a negotiated settlement.

Ironically, before this became clear the combination of public support for escalation and the administration's support of a crisis atmosphere suggested to the Soviets that a US mobilization was likely. Indications for this

[39]Ibid., pp. 16–24.
[40]Ibid.
[41]Ibid.
[42]Gravel, Volume IV, pp. 546–548.

hit a peak in early March, when Westmoreland's classified request for 206,756 troops appeared in the *New York Times*.[43]

Yang Chengwu Turns on Mao and the Soviets Smell Success

As the Tet offensive began, the Soviets claimed credit for preparing the North Vietnamese for the battle.[44] They also paid close attention to signs of any US response, taking every opportunity to stress the likelihood of new US troop commitments and the possibility of offensive action against North Vietnam. A *Pravda* article charged that "calls are being heard in Washington for 'resolute measures' against a sovereign Socialist state."[45] The next day *Izvestia* reported that "Tet has aroused a new fit of war fever" in the United States and implied that the United States was considering the use of tactical nuclear weapons.[46] The Soviets reported General Wheeler's trip to Vietnam, correctly charging that General Westmoreland favored a troop increase and expanded bombing. According to the story, General Wheeler returned to Washington carrying with him plans for escalating the war.[47] After General Wheeler returned and the president began to consider Westmoreland's still secret troop request, Johnson directed an internal "A to Z reassessment" of policy which Secretary of State Rusk revealed in congressional testimony.[48] The Soviets reported this, using the term "A to Z reassessment," and charged Rusk with being an advocate of escalation.[49] The same article reported General Westmoreland's request for an additional 206,000 men four days after it was revealed in the *New York Times*. This was followed by reports that South Vietnamese Vice-president Nguyen Kao Ky had offered to lead any attempt to invade North Vietnam. The Soviets suggested that "maybe this was not Ky at all, but words directed by Washington."[50] The article added that "for some time now there has

---

[43] "Westmoreland Requests 206,000 More Men, Stirring Debate in Administration," *New York Times,* March 10, 1968, p. 1.

[44] "Priznatel'nost' za poddgerzhku," (Gratitude for Support), *Izvestia,* February 8, 1968, p. 2.

[45] "My s vami, patrioti V'etnama," (We Are With You, Patriots of Vietnam), *Pravda,* February 10, 1968, p. 4.

[46] "Urok ne v prok," (Futile Lesson), *Izvestia,* February 11, 1968, p. 1.

[47] "Gotovyatsya plani rasshireniya agressii SShA vo V'etname," (The USA Prepares Plans for Expanding Aggression in Vietnam), *Pravda,* February 27, 1968, p. 5.

[48] *Pentagon Papers,* Book 5, "Volume III: Program 6," p. 16.

[49] Victor Maevskii, "Advokat politiki advantyurizma," (Advocate for a Policy of Adventurism), *Pravda,* March 14, 1968, p. 4.

[50] E Kobelev, "Valpi marionetki," (A Puppet Howls), *Pravda,* March 17, 1968, p. 5.

been ominous talk among American generals" about "the necessity for an American invasion of the DRV territory by ground forces."[51]

Simultaneously, the consultative conference of communist parties, which turned out to be a preparatory meeting for the formal "excommunication of China" conference, met in Budapest. On February 28, 1968, the head of the Soviet delegation, Politburo member and party theoretician M.A. Suslov, delivered a speech calling for the international conference to be held in November–December 1968 with a theme of unity of action over Vietnam.[52] Clearly, the power that refused to cooperate over Vietnam could not be a participant.

Meanwhile, in China, Mao proclaimed that the Tet offensive proved that people, not weapons, were important in war—meaning the Vietnamese did not need a unified socialist camp in order to win. Victory would be certain as long as the Vietnamese persisted in a protracted struggle.[53] At the same time, the Chinese press condemned the Budapest conference. The Soviets were charged with orchestrating the meeting to carry out international condemnation of China and Albania.[54]

There was, however, great pressure to acknowledge that a potential US threat to China existed. The Chinese press took note of the deployment of the "emergency reinforcements" and speculated that Johnson was preparing to call up the reserves and expand the war.[55] Indeed, much reporting in the US press supported this view. One February article cited the president as saying that the United States would build up "as rapidly as difficult circumstances permit" and added further that the president had not decided on an upper limit to troop strength.[56] Another reported that indications were strong that the JCS would ask for more troops and that it was expected that the plea would "meet with at least limited success." The size of the increase suggested in this article was an additional 100,000 troops.[57] The Chinese

---

[51]Ibid.

[52]"Rech' tovarishcha M.A. Suslova," (Speech by Comrade M.A. Suslov), *Pravda,* February 29, 1968, p. 4.

[53]"Victory Certainly Belongs to the Heroic Vietnamese People Persevering in Struggle," *Peking Review,* February 16, 1968, pp. 7–8; "A Quotation From Chairman Mao Tse-tung," ibid., p. 20.

[54]"The Counter-Revolutionary Budapest Meeting—A New Treacherous Step of Khrushchev Revisionists," ibid., March 1, 1968, pp. 13–14.

[55]"Ceaselessly Wiping Out the Enemy and Winning Greater Victories," ibid., March 8, 1968, pp. 21–22.

[56]Saville R. Davis, "Johnson opts for Vietnam buildup," *Christian Science Monitor,* February 29, 1968, p. 1.

[57]George W. Ashworth, "Gears turn for more G.I.'s in Vietnam," ibid., March 5, 1968, p. 1.

press announced that the United States was making a last ditch effort to avoid failure. It planned to pour in more troops and step up the bombing. It sought new appropriations, would soon call up the reserves, and would spread the war to Laos, Cambodia, and North Vietnam.[58]

Soviet pressure and the unclear signals from Washington had an effect on China. Chinese military leaders in February and early March had no idea whatsoever that President Johnson would give up on the war and his own reelection on March 31. On the contrary, with the prospect of a growing national security threat in the south and increasing isolation—and even hostility—from the Soviet Union, Yang Chengwu, acting chief of the General Staff of the PLA, You Lijin, political commander of the air force, and Fu Chongbi, commander of the Peking Garrison, turned against Mao. Fu Chongbi was especially important, since the palace guard plays a key role in any coup.

Precise timing is difficult to pinpoint. As late as February 19, 1968, Yang Chengwu and Fu Chongbi appeared in public at a reception for Mao and Lin Biao.[59] The PLA General Staff headquarters had convened a "Congress of Activists" for "The Creative Study and Application of Mao Tse-tung's Thought" in late January. This was part of the ongoing campaign to criticize Luo Ruiqing. The congress ended February 20, 1968. During the congress, the Tet offensive had been launched and the United States had hurried reinforcements to Vietnam amid signs that even larger deployments were forthcoming. At this gathering of military men, the risk of the apparent growing US commitment to Vietnam was evidently the subject of some discussion. This surely generated criticism of Mao's continued use of the PLA in the Cultural Revolution. At any rate, Yang, You, and Fu were still in their positions when the conference ended. Maoist loyalists must have reported the growing dissension because Mao moved very quickly against his former supporters. A press report on the congress on March 8, 1968, did not mention Yang Chengwu and indicated blandly that the evil influence of Luo Ruiqing was "further uprooted."[60] Since Yang was the acting chief of staff and the man designated by Mao to lead the criticism

---

[58] "Excellent Situation in Vietnamese People's War Against US Aggression and for National Salvation," ibid., March 29, 1968, pp. 21–22.

[59] "Chairman Mao and Vice-Chairman Lin Piao Receive Revolutionary Fighters," ibid., March 15, 1968, pp. 6–8.

[60] "PLA General Staff H.Q. Holds 4th Congress of Activists in the Creative Study and Application of Mao Tse-tung's Thought," ibid., March 8, 1968, pp. 9–12.

of Luo Ruiqing, it is impossible that his name would be omitted in this story unless he had already turned against Mao.

As March progressed, however, the United States did not seek to exploit its victory on the battlefield and signals increasingly indicated that it would not.[61] When the president finally announced the troop ceiling and curtailment of bombing, the "US threat" argument suddenly evaporated as a credible position in the Chinese internal debate. The Soviets glumly reported the purge of Yang Chengwu, Fu Chongbi, and You Lijin as a new "anti-party grouping."[62] Wall posters at the end of March in Beijing expressed support for the "wise decision" of Mao to replace Yang Chengwu with Huang Yangsheng. The move, according to the wall posters, came at a meeting of military commanders in Beijing on March 24–25.[63] Thus did Yang Chengwu become a "black boss" while his allies became "two-faced counter-revolutionaries." Tet had ratified the troop ceiling decision and the public announcement of it sealed the fate of Yang Chengwu and of Soviet strategy.

The United States Publicly Abandons Victory

In November 1967 President Johnson had announced that McNamara would be changing jobs from secretary of defense to president of the World Bank. The move came, according to one authoritative source, because of McNamara's close personal relationship with one of Johnson's Democratic political rivals, Robert Kennedy. Johnson was not about to enter a campaign with a member of the cabinet whose loyalty was suspect—especially one closely involved with the dominant issue in the upcoming campaign, the Vietnam War.[64] The new secretary would be Clark Clifford, who would be sworn in on March 1, 1968. Ironically, his first official act would be to prepare the recommendation for the president that spelled the end of Johnson's political career. A study group headed by Clifford recommended against any new escalation of the fighting and against meeting Westmoreland's request.[65] Moreover, it was clear that Johnson had done

---

[61]See George W. Ashworth, "US hard pressed to maintain Vietnam offensive punch," *Christian Science Monitor,* March 20, 1968, p. 3.

[62]"Sobytiya v Kitae," (Events in China), *Pravda,* March 31, 1968, p. 5.

[63]Ibid.

[64]Halberstam, p. 784

[65]Gravel, Volume IV, pp. 575–584.

nothing to line up congressional support for mobilization. On March 4, the same day Johnson received Clifford's recommendation, an article in the *Christian Science Monitor* reported that Westmoreland had asked for 100,000 new troops "and perhaps more." The article reported a rising tide of sentiment in the Congress against calling up more troops "when we have 225,000 in Europe."[66]

According to President Johnson's *Vantage Point*, he formally rejected the troop request on March 8, 1968.[67] Though there is evidence the president continued to wrestle with Westmoreland's proposal after March 8, the administration began preparing the public for the official announcement that America's open-ended commitment in Vietnam had ended. On March 8, Secretary Clifford began this process by hinting that troop increases would not be forthcoming in the near future, noting that the president was keeping an "open mind on the question of more troops," but that "it will be some time before any decisions are made."[68] This was accompanied by Senate debates which questioned the wisdom of troop increases. Senator William Fulbright (D-Ark.) indeed asked the critical question which the administration had intentionally permitted to go unanswered, which was, "Why is there a request for 200,000 troops if there was no defeat?" Fulbright cited the press for his information, saying that it had been reported that General Wheeler had returned from Vietnam with a request for between 100,000 and 200,000 soldiers.[69]

The implication that Tet had been a defeat unquestionably paved the way for the administration's new strategy, which was to make the military the scapegoat and Westmoreland the "fall guy." Since General Westmoreland had been brought back from Vietnam in 1967 and told to convey the message that US successes would ultimately permit a troop ceiling, this was grossly unfair to Westmoreland. Nevertheless, the general would be ridiculed for his pre-Tet optimism (although he certainly made good on his words by winning a crushing battlefield victory). As part of the speaking tour on which the light at the end of the tunnel became famous, Westmoreland told the National Press Club

[66]David K. Willis, "Viet troop drain revives NATO defense debate," *Christian Science Monitor,* March 4, 1968, p. 1. This is a good example of how important was the issue of mobilization. Congressmen were suggesting that they were willing to sacrifice the NATO alliance and send the rest of the regular army to Vietnam rather than pay the political cost of mobilization.

[67]Johnson, p. 402.

[68]"The news—briefly," *Christian Science Monitor,* March 9, 1968, p. 2.

[69]Richard I. Strout, "Viet issue escalates in Senate," ibid., March 9, 1968, p. 1.

in November 1967, "I see progress as I travel all over Vietnam."[70] In February 1968 a column by humorist Art Buchwald captured the essence of the Johnson administration's explanation of "defeat." "Gen. George Armstrong Custer said today in an exclusive interview with this correspondent that the battle of Little Big Horn had just turned the corner and he could now see the light at the end of the tunnel. 'We have the Sioux on the run,' Gen. Custer told me. 'Of course we will have some cleaning up to do, but the Redskins are hurting badly and it will only be a matter of time before they give in.'"[71]

The press leak about the troop request came on March 10. Although the size of the troop request, 206,000, was correct, the debate the request was supposed to have provoked already was over. The effect of the article was to provide ammunition to congressional opponents of the war and lend credence to Fulbright's question about "defeat." A few days later the president approved orders for deployment of the support troops required to back up the "emergency deployments" and a final increment of 30,000 more soldiers.[72] On March 18, the president assembled a group of trusted friends and advisors from outside the government to seek their counsel on Vietnam.[73] After dinner and briefings from administration officials, this group, by consensus, recommended to Johnson that he wind down the war.[74]

The *Pentagon Papers* points out that the written record is sparse after Secretary Clifford's March 4 recommendation that the troop request be rejected. The president says he made the decision to reject the troop request on March 8. The *Pentagon Papers* analyst, however, concludes that the issue was still in doubt when Johnson assembled his group of friends and advisors on March 18, though documents in the *Pentagon Papers* presented just prior to the discussion of this event demonstrate that Johnson had already decided to consider only a moderate increase of about 30,000. There was no written record of the meeting of friends and advisors and the Pentagon analyst noted "Whatever impact this group's recommendations

[70]Gelb and Betts, p. 317.

[71]Cited in Halberstam, p. 788.

[72]Gravel, Volume IV, p. 591.

[73]Ibid. The group included former Undersecretary of State George Ball; Arthur Dean, a Republican New York lawyer who was a Korean War negotiator during the Eisenhower Administration; Dean Acheson, Secretary of State for Truman; General Matthew Ridgway, former commander of United Nations forces in Korea; Cyrus Vance, former deputy secretary of defense; McGeorge Bundy, former national security advisor to Kennedy and Johnson; former Treasury Secretary C. Douglas Dillon; and General of the Army Omar Bradley.

[74]Ibid., p. 592.

and the direct briefings he had received had on the president was not immediately apparent in any decision which affected the deployment of forces."[75] Many writers and scholars have indicated that this meeting had a profound effect on the president because he discovered that, even among this group, there was no support for "hard line" or escalation.[76] It is more likely that, since there is evidence that consideration of any massive troop increase was already over, the president discovered that his own political position was untenable from this trusted group.

Although political appointees in the administration could hide behind the claim that they had been misled by an overoptimistic military, the president could not avoid his responsibility as commander-in-chief. The military rules regarding command apply to the president—a commander is responsible for everything his command does or fails to do. This responsibility cannot be delegated. Therefore, while blaming the military generally and Westmoreland specifically could get many off the hook, it could not exonerate the president for failure. Before Tet, the administration had planned on explaining its about-face by claiming "success" in meeting its original objectives. After Tet, it used "failure" as a reason for winding down the war. Once Johnson, for whatever reason, accepted the position that Tet meant failure, he was a political liability to the Democratic party. It is very likely that Johnson received the message from his friends and advisors that he should step aside if the Democrats were to have a chance in November. This could explain the "profound effect" on Johnson. Moreover, he needed to step aside in a way that would allow his successor a chance of winning, and this meant shifting the blame away from the administration by charging Westmoreland with the failure. In a move designed to imply that the American "setback" had been Westmoreland's fault, Lyndon Johnson recalled Westmoreland from Vietnam on March 22, 1968, and replaced him with General Creighton Abrams.[77] The background information the administration leaked to the press on Westmoreland's removal—which appeared on March 25—specifically referred to

---

[75]Ibid., p. 593.

[76]For example see Gelb and Betts, p. 176; Halberstam, p. 795.

[77]Ibid. General Abrams was not named Westmoreland's successor immediately. He consulted with the president in great secrecy on March 26, 1968, and apparently concurred on a final troop ceiling of 549,500. General Westmoreland was not "relieved," and became chief of staff of the army. His sudden removal in the wake of Tet and, more importantly, his 206,000-man troop request, conveyed the impression that he had been relieved.

Westmoreland's public optimism in the fall of 1967, an optimism, it is clear, he loyally expressed to pave the way for a policy he wholeheartedly disapproved of.[78]

The day following the meeting of the advisory group, press reports revealed that the president was considering a "moderate increase" in troop strength of about 35,000—a clear indication that the 206,000-man request had been rejected.[79] Other articles conveyed the same image as March progressed.[80] The president conducted a surprise meeting with General Abrams on March 26, 1968. Although the meeting was in great secrecy, apparently General Abrams agreed to a final troop ceiling of 549,500.[81] In other words, there would not even be a "modest" increase. The "emergency" reinforcements of 11,000 already had been deployed and only the required support for this force of about 13,500 would be added.

On March 31, 1968, the president announced the final troop ceiling in a televised address. He also ceased the bombing campaign against North Vietnam, with the exception of areas in the immediate vicinity of the DMZ. After a call for negotiations he concluded by saying "I shall not seek, and I will not accept, the nomination of my Party for another term as your President."[82]

The president of the United States announced to the world that the United States had half a million men in combat in Asia with no apparent purpose, direction, policy, strategy, or goal other than to keep from getting killed. He had relieved the old commander and ordered the new one not to try to win (but keep fighting), and, personally, the president himself was going to quit.

This was not America's finest hour.

Nevertheless, the unintended result was the total destruction of the expensive and extended Soviet strategy to exploit the "ever growing" American threat to China in Vietnam to restore the Sino-Soviet relationship. March 31, 1968, in this context was a strategic watershed that ushered in a period of serious Soviet reassessment.

---

[78]George W. Ashworth, "Command change: new path?" *Christian Science Monitor,* March 25, 1968, p. 1.

[79]"The news—briefly," *Christian Science Monitor,* March 19, 1968, p. 2.

[80]George W. Ashworth, "US hard pressed to maintain Vietnam offensive punch," ibid., March 20, 1968, p. 3;

[81]Gravel, Volume IV, p. 593.

[82]Ibid., pp. 596–602.

14

Soviet Reassessment

Major Events

- *April–June 1968*—Soviet press shifts from stressing US threat to China to accusing China of moving toward Sino-American rapprochement. Mao is charged with trying to change the basic nature of China's communist society.
- *May 1968*—US diplomatic sources report Soviet diplomatic offensive to improve relations with countries on China's periphery.
- *May 13, 1968*—Paris Peace talks begin.
- *Spring 1968*—Prague Spring receives criticism. China is criticized using the same terminology.
- *July 4, 1968*—Soviet-North Vietnamese aid agreement is signed in Moscow. No increase in logistic support is indicated.
- *August 1968*—Soviets invade Czechoslovakia. National mobilization exercise preceding the invasion also brings forces in Far East to war footing.
- *September 1968*—Mao terminates the Cultural Revolution and deploys PLA to Sino-Soviet frontier.
- *October 1968*—Liu Shaoqi is formally expelled from the Chinese Communist party. Deng Xiaoping is not.
- *November 1, 1968*—Johnson announces a complete halt to the bombing of North Vietnam.
- *November 4, 1968*—Richard M. Nixon is elected president of the United States.
- *November 25, 1968*—Soviets and North Vietnamese sign new aid agreement which increases Soviet military assistance.
- *November 26, 1968*—Chinese Foreign Ministry suggests Sino-American talks in Warsaw for February 1969.

After Johnson's March 31, 1968, announcement that he would not seek a military solution to the war, the Soviet Union could no longer hope for a growing American military presence in Vietnam that would in turn threaten China. Moreover, the course of future US policy was unclear. Johnson had withdrawn from the presidential race and the outcome of the elections, now half a year away, were unknown. The Soviets therefore continued to honor previous arms agreements, in order to keep pressure on the United States and make troop withdrawals difficult, but, pending a new analysis of the outcome of the November elections, they did not initiate or agree to changes in the logistic support for North Vietnam. Elsewhere, Moscow was more aggressive. The Kremlin accelerated its own deployment of forces to Asia, continued to press for a communist conference to excommunicate China, and sought to improve relations with countries that ringed China. Ominously, the Soviet Union invaded Czechoslovakia in August 1968 telling the world that it had a right to interfere in the internal affairs of wayward socialist states whose ideological development had gone astray. This gave a whole new meaning to the diplomatic plan to excommunicate China and, as Soviet criticism of China resembled Soviet criticism of Czechoslovakia, generated real—and well founded—fears that Moscow planned to use its military to install a friendly pro-Soviet regime in the Far East.

The military strength the Soviets deployed to Asia made Soviet threats of invasion credible. This, as it turned out, forced Mao to end the Army's involvement in the Cultural Revolution and deploy it along the Sino-Soviet border. Although Liu Shaoqi was formally expelled from the Communist party, the Kremlin got some of what it wanted. Survival of an anti-Mao group was assured. The old party cadres headed by Deng Xiaoping remained alive—albeit discredited. However, Soviet pressure set the stage for the very action the Soviets had been trying to prevent—formal Sino-US rapprochement. The Nixon administration was able to seize the moment and fully develop the contacts initiated by the Johnson administration.

The Soviets Seek Alternatives

Initial Soviet reaction to Johnson's March 31, 1968, speech was muted. Moscow reported the substance without much comment, though the Soviets tried to overemphasize the slight increase in troop strength. On April 2, *Izvestia* printed a story called "Johnson's Surprise," which referred to the president's decision not to seek reelection. But the story focused on the 13,500-man deployment of support troops, the small callup of reserve units, and the budget increase tied to the war.[1] Other articles in early April similarly focused on these minor details while the Kremlin leadership hurried to analyze the implications of the US decision.[2]

Meanwhile, the Soviets continued to publicize their continuing assistance to North Vietnam, with emphasis on the obstacles China placed to effective aid. *Pravda* published stories of Vietnamese gratitude for Soviet help while *Izvestia* told of two Soviet ships, the *Razdolnoye* and the *Komsomolets Ukrainy,* in Vladivostok taking on cargoes for Vietnam. The ships, according to the article, faced a difficult voyage. In the past "difficult" had referred only to "stormy seas" or the "fiery skies" of Vietnam. Now, "unfortunately, voyages to China have also become difficult."[3]

Later, a major article charged that Mao hampered socialist countries' efforts to give economic and military aid to Vietnam. The Soviets also charged—although the logic is a bit murky—that the Chinese were opposed to peace talks between the United States and North Vietnam because the Chinese saw the protracted war as a buffer between aggressive US forces and the territory of China.[4] By June, the Soviets were openly admitting the failure of their attempt to use the American military presence in Vietnam to force China back into the Soviet camp. As a key part of this, Soviet propaganda no longer mentioned the US threat to China and instead raised the specter of a Sino-American alliance. In early June, *Pravda* took note of statements by Undersecretaries of State Eugene Rostow and Nicholas Katzenbach that were "assessed as a definite step toward rapprochement with Peking." Rostow had mentioned that the United States was ready to welcome Chinese scholars and journalists and was prepared to review embargoes on export of certain goods to China. Katzenbach had announced to the Washington Press Club that the State Department had no

[1] "Syurpriz Dzhonsona," (Johnson's Surprise), *Izvestia,* April 2, 1968, p. 2.

[2] "Prizivayut rezervistov," (Reserves Are Called Up), ibid., April 3, 1968, p. 1; Gennady Vasilev, "Prekratit' agressii," (Cease Aggression), *Pravda,* April 7, 1968, p. 5.

[3] P. Demidov, "Pozornaya provokatsiya kitaiskikh vlastei," (Disgraceful Provocation by Chinese Authorities), *Izvestia,* April 13, 1968, p. 3. This is a story of two Soviet ships detained in a Chinese port. See also "Sessiya natsional'nogo sobraniya DRV," (Session of the National Assembly of the DRV), *Pravda,* May 25, 1968, p. 5. This article is a good example of publicizing Soviet aid.

[4] B. Zanegin, "Proval vneshnepoliticheskogo kursa Pekina," (The Failure of Peking's Foreign Policy Course), *Izvestia,* May 23, 1968, pp. 2–3. See also "Tragediya u reki zhemchuzhnoi," (Tragedy on the Pearl River), ibid., July 2, 1968, p. 2, for evidence of Chinese interference with rail movement of Soviet supplies to Vietnam.

objection to inviting Chinese representatives to participate in various conferences in the United States.[5]

A fundamental shift in the foreign policy orientation of China, according to the Soviets, would confirm that Mao had changed the very nature of the regime. In other words, a Maoist China was no longer a socialist state on the progressive path of Marxist-Leninist history. However, there were still true communists in China who were the legitimate spokesmen of the workers. Since the interests of the workers in China were universal and since Mao was turning China into a threat to socialism, the socialist commonwealth had the right to assist the "healthy forces" in China to regain their rightful positions.

In addition to claiming a right to intervene in China—whether by an armed invasion, covert aid, or propaganda—Moscow clearly believed it had to move quickly to prevent socialist heresies from spreading. As a result, it appears that one key foundation of Soviet policy in Asia would be a Soviet version of "containment of China." There was a renewed Soviet effort to create the so-called "ring" around China by improving relations with countries on China's periphery. US diplomatic sources, in May 1968, reported a Soviet "diplomatic offensive in Malaysia, Singapore and the Philippines along with stepped up aid to Pakistan and India and a staggering boost in trade with Japan." Moreover, there was an increasing Soviet naval presence in the Pacific and Indian Oceans. Despite the militant anticommunist policy of Indonesia, the Soviet Union maintained reasonable relations with that country.[6] Soviet Foreign Minister Andrei Gromyko, in an address to the Supreme Soviet in June, reported that "relations with India, Pakistan and Burma grow stronger every year." Moreover, said Gromyko, the Soviet Union "maintains good relations with Cambodia, Laos, Ceylon, Nepal" and looked forward to improving relations with Afghanistan. Gromyko noted achievements in economic relations with Japan and, though there were difficulties connected with the US use of Japanese bases to support the war in Vietnam, the Soviet Union favored strengthening political relations with that nation.[7]

---

[5] "US line on Peking relaxes," *Christian Science Monitor,* May 24, 1968, p. 1; "Sobytiya v Kitae," (Events in China), *Pravda,* June 5, 1968, p. 5.

[6] John Hughes, "Soviet shadow spreads into Southeast Asia," *Christian Science Monitor,* May 21, 1968, p. 1; John K. Cooley, "USSR, China vie in South Asia," ibid., June 20, 1968, p. 1.

[7] "O mezhdunarodnoi polozhenii i vneshnoi politike Sovetskogo Soyuza,"(On the International Situation and the Foreign Policy of the Soviet Union), *Pravda,* June 28, 1968, pp. 3–4.

China had a longstanding hostile relationship with India that made close Soviet-Indian ties especially threatening. The Chinese took note of the Soviet effort by adding India to the list of usual threats to China—Soviet revisionists, US imperialists, and Mongolian revisionists—and declared that Chinese Sinkiang and Tibet were of extreme strategic importance. Later the Chinese charged that the goal of US-Soviet strategy was to encircle China and set up bases for a ring of aggression against China.[8]

As the Soviet diplomatic offensive with non-socialist nations progressed, so did efforts to consolidate condemnation of China by socialist countries. The ultimate goal remained a conference of communist parties that would excommunicate China. The Kremlin had difficulty in orchestrating the meeting and the date would be postponed several times as countries like Rumania refused to cooperate.[9] However, in April, a lengthy theoretical article by a Soviet scholar argued that "Maoists...use falsified dialectic to justify splitting activity in the world communist movement and to justify crushing the CCP [Chinese Communist Party]." As a result of this problem, wrote the author, Mao was guilty of heresy, he threatened world communism, and an international conference of Communist parties in November or December would be necessary.[10]

In May, the meeting in Budapest finished its work and issued a communique setting November 25, 1968, as the date for the conference, with a final preparatory meeting scheduled for September. Moscow claimed that fifty-four Communist parties had participated in the sessions so far and that fifteen more would join the November event.[11] Brezhnev echoed this line in July in a foreign policy speech which called for a united front and hailed the coming conference of more than sixty Communist parties.[12] The Soviet invasion of Czechoslovakia in August 1968 would delay the date for the conference, but Soviet efforts to organize the conference began shortly after the tanks rolled into Prague. The preparatory meeting set for September actually

---

[8] "Speech by Comrade Huang Yung-sheng," *Peking Review,* December 13, 1968, pp. 7–9; "Renegade Feature of Soviet Revisionists Once Again Exposed," ibid., December 27, 1968, pp. 21–22.

[9] "Rech' glavi delegatsii KPSS tovarishcha M.A. Suslova," (Speech by the Head of the CPSU Delegation M.A. Suslov), *Pravda,* February 29, 1968, p. 1.

[10] G.P. Fedoseyev, "Leninizm—marksizm XX veka," (Leninism—Marxism of the XX Century), *Pravda,* April 22, 1968, p. 2.

[11] "Kommunike o zasedanii komissi po podgotovke mezhdunarodnogo soveshchaniya kommunisticheskikh-rabochikh partii," (Communique on the Meeting of the Preparatory Committee for the Internationalist Conference of Communist and Worker's Parties), ibid., May 4, 1968, p. 1.

[12] "Rech' tovarishcha L.I. Brezhneva," (Speech by Comrade L.I. Brezhnev), ibid., July 4, 1968, pp. 1–2.

convened in November in Budapest and established a new date, May 1969, for the conference.[13] (In the end, the results were inconclusive.)

After Tet, the Soviet Union evidently decided to maintain but not increase its supply effort to North Vietnam. Brezhnev in a July 4, 1968, speech noted "we shall continue to give struggling Vietnam the necessary aid in its struggle."[14] The same day, North Vietnamese chief aid negotiator Le Than Nghi signed a new aid agreement in Moscow. Unlike the protracted talks for the Tet offensive that took from August 14 to September 23, 1967, these negotiations took little more than a week.[15] If there had been significant changes and complex issues, the sessions would have lasted longer. Moreover, the communique in September 1967 had stated that aid would increase and listed the types of supplies in some detail. According to the July 1968 communique, which was simple and bland, "the Soviet Union has helped and shall continue to help strengthening the defense capability of the fraternal Democratic Republic of Vietnam."[16]

Soviet Military Threat Brings an End to the Cultural Revolution

The Soviet Union viewed the "Prague Spring" as a threat and invaded Czechoslovakia. According to Moscow, Czechoslovakia's Communist party leader Alexander Dubcek was guilty of altering the basic nature of the socialist country of Czechoslovakia. The Kremlin launched an extraordinary press campaign to criticize Dubcek before the invasion. Simultaneously, the Soviets accused the Chinese of the same crimes and built up military strength in the Far East. The combination of the propaganda and the actual military buildup, once Moscow sent its troops into Czechoslovakia, put extraordinary pressure on Chinese leaders—who had more than half of their armed forces committed to internal duties more appropriate for police and local militia. However, the Chinese response only partially suited Soviet objectives.

Alexander Dubcek's experiment with pluralism in Czechoslovakia was the object of extensive Soviet criticism in 1968. Moscow claimed that true communists and the working class in Czechoslovakia were alarmed over

[13] "Kommunike," (Communique), ibid., November 22, 1968, p. 1.

[14] "Bratskaya pomoshch'," (Fraternal Assistance), ibid., July 7, 1968, p. 1; "Soviet pledge," *Christian Science Monitor,* July 6, 1968, p. 2.

[15] "Bratskaya pomoshch'," (Fraternal Assistance), *Pravda,* July 7, 1968, p. 1.

[16] Kotov and Yegerov, *Militant Solidarity,* pp. 179–180.

attacks by internal anti-socialist forces, who were in league with external anti-socialist forces. For example, in early July *Pravda* reported Soviet rallies in which the Soviet people shared the anxiety of communists and the Czech working class over the "incessant attacks by anti-socialist and anti-Soviet elements on the socialist system, on the leading role of the Czechoslovak Communist Party, [and] on the friendship of our peoples."[17] A few days later *Pravda* repeated the charges and connected Soviet support with "healthy forces" inside Czechoslovakia.[18]

When Soviet and other Warsaw Pact forces invaded in August, the official Soviet explanation was that these "healthy forces" had appealed for help against "counterrevolutionary forces hostile to socialism." This affected the vital interests of the Soviet Union and other socialist countries and was in accord with the right of self-defense.[19] The "socialist gains of Czechoslovakia," said a Tass statement, "as a socialist state linked by alliance commitments to our country and other fraternal countries *is not merely the CCP's [Czechoslovakian Communist Party] internal affair.*"[20] (Emphasis added.) The Soviets then made the charge of collusion with external forces. "Alignment with NATO," said Tass, "these are words that the counterrevolution has not yet uttered. But they are on its mind."[21]

These charges against the Dubcek regime provide an important backdrop for the truly menacing propaganda the Kremlin directed against Mao's leadership.[22] According to the theoretical journal *Kommunist:*

> Events in China cause growing alarm among Marxist-Leninists.... The very existence of the Communist Party in China...has been threatened. The danger of a change in the nature of authority in the country has now clearly emerged, and so, consequently, has a real threat to the socialist gains of the Chinese revolution.... *The events in China are more than*

[17] "Podderzhika brat'yev po klassu," (Support for Class Brothers), *Pravda,* July 7, 1968, p. 4.

[18] I. Aleksandrov, "Ataka protiv sotsialisticheskikh ustoev Chekhoslovakii," (Attack Against the Socialist Foundations of Czechoslovakia), ibid., July 11, 1968, p. 4. For another reference to "healthy forces" see Takashi Oka, "How far will Moscow push?" *Christian Science Monitor,* July 19, 1968, p. 1.

[19] "Zayavlenie *Tass,*" (*Tass* Statement), ibid., August 21, 1968, p. 1.

[20] "Zashchita sotsializma —vysshyi internatsional'nyi dolg," (Defense of Socialism—The Highest Internationalist Duty), ibid., August 22, 1968, pp. 2–3.

[21] V. Zhuravsky and V. Mayevsky, "Otpor vragam," (Rebuff to Enemies), ibid., August 27, 1968, p. 4.

[22] See Thornton, *China,* pp. 332–333 for a discussion of the relationship between the Czech invasion and the threat to China.

its internal affair. The policy of Mao Tse-tung's group is doing great harm to the cause of socialism and revolution the world over.... It is leading to...its transformation into a force hostile to the Soviet Union and other socialist countries.[23] (Emphasis added.)

Later, *Izvestia* reported that the Chinese communist "party organization is actually destroyed—but millions of Party members and lower workers remain—it is namely these who nourish growing resistance to Mao."[24] The Soviets followed by accusing Mao of portraying the Soviet Union as more of an enemy to China than the United States: "If a socialist country weakens ties with the socialist commonwealth, it damages the common cause as well as itself.... If a socialist state, including a great power, openly struggles against the socialist common-wealth, the leaders of such a country are essentially passing sentence on their own policy."[25] *Literaturnaya Gazeta* joined the attack by accusing China of seeking an alliance with the Federal Republic of Germany.[26] In June, *Kommunist* followed up by stating that "there are healthy forces in the Party's ranks, and given proper conditions, they can return China to the correct path of socialism." *Pravda* again picked up the "healthy forces" theme in late June, explaining that Soviet policy was to give "practical internationalist assistance to the forces in China that have remained true to Marxism-Leninism and that, together with the entire Chinese people, will sooner or later put an end to the ruinous policy pursued by Mao Tse-tung's clique."[27]

A critical part of the Soviet justification of the Czech invasion was the accusation that alignment with NATO had been Dubcek's intention. Two days after the Soviets surfaced this specific allegation, *Pravda* accused China of the same crime. Chinese protests against the invasion of Czechoslovakia "further affirms that on the fundamental questions of the international situation and the struggle between the forces of imperialism and socialism, Mao's group is in the leading ranks along with the countries of

---

[23]"*Kommunist* Magazine Explores Origins of Maoism," *Current Digest,* May 29, 1968, pp. 3–7.

[24]"Rastet soprotivlenie maoistam," (Resistance to Maoism is Growing), *Izvestia,* May 16, 1968, p. 4.

[25]B. Zanegin, "Proval vneshnepoliticheskogo kursa Pekina," (Failure of the Foreign Policy Course of Peking), ibid., May 23, 1968, pp. 2–3.

[26]"'Ernst Henry' Warns of a Bonn-Peking Alliance," *Current Digest,* June 12, 1968, pp. 7–10.

[27]V. Pasenchuk and V. Viktorov, "Antinarodnyi kurs pekinskikh pravitelei," (Antipopular Course of the Peking Rulers), *Pravda,* June 22, 1968, pp. 4–5.

NATO and the most evil enemies of socialism."[28] When Chinese Foreign Minister Chen Yi condemned the Soviet invasion, the Soviets accused him of trying to justify the fact that China and imperialists had interpreted the Czech invasion the same way.[29] Mao, according to the Soviets, "had virtually joined hands with the West's most reactionary anti-Soviet forces." Anti-Sovietism made Mao a "natural ally" of imperialism. Peking's leadership had taken under its wing "counterrevolutionaries" who were "encroaching on socialist gains in Czechoslovakia."[30] The Soviet people deeply sympathized "with their brothers who came to grief.... We are convinced that the healthy forces in the CPC [Communist Party of China] enjoy the support of the working class, of the best people in the Army and of all progressive working people in the CPR [Chinese People's Republic]." Finally, *Izvestia* predicted—and it took little imagination to see how— "China will emerge from these trials with honor and return to the family of socialist countries."[31]

The Chinese press noted the accelerated Soviet military buildup in the Far East and increasing Soviet willingness to create border incidents. In September, the Chinese charged that in the immediate aftermath of the Czech invasion, Soviet violations of Chinese airspace increased. "It is rare," said a Chinese protest, "that in the short space of 21 days, so many concentrated, barefaced and flagrant military provocations should have been conducted. In particular, it should be pointed out these intrusions took place around August 20, when the Soviet Union invaded Czechoslovakia. It is in no way accidental."[32] In October, new Chief of the General Staff Huang Yangsheng, charged that "of late, the Soviet revisionist renegade clique...has sent large numbers of troops to reinforce its forces stationed along the Sino-Soviet and Sino-Mongolian frontiers and has intensified armed provocations against China."[33]

A Soviet invasion appeared imminent. The problem facing the Soviets was not conquest of 700 million unified people. Mao's hold over the countryside was tenuous. Anti-Mao (though not necessarily pro-Soviet)

---

[28] "Sobytiya v Kitae," (Events in China), *Pravda,* August 29, 1968, p. 5.

[29] "Isteriya klevetnikov," (Hysteria of Slanderers), *Izvestia,* September 13, 1968, p. 2.

[30] G. Dmitriev, "Pekinskie protivniki sotsialisticheskogo demokratii," (Peking Opponents of Socialist Democracy), *Izvestia,* October 10, 1968, pp. 3–4.

[31] A. Ter-Grigoryi, "Devyatnadtsat' let spustya," (Nineteen Years Later), ibid., October 1, 1968, p. 1.

[32] "Soviet Military Aircraft Intrusion Into China's Airspace Protested," *Peking Review,* September 20, 1968, p. 41.

[33] "Comrade Huang yung-sheng's Speech at Peking Mass Rally," ibid., October 11, 1968, pp. 7–9.

forces existed in great strength.[34] The chances of finding well-known Chinese who would cooperate in return for being restored to power were great. The Soviets had built the same case against Mao's leadership that it had built against Dubcek. Given the resistance to Mao, the Soviets could claim that they were merely responding to "healthy forces" who had requested Soviet help. More ominously, the Chinese army was technologically inferior and over half its strength was committed internally. The Soviets clearly had the ability to carry off such an invasion. Indeed, prior to the Czech invasion Moscow ordered the largest test mobilization in history. It was well publicized and far too extensive to be aimed only at Czechoslovakia. The Soviets actually called up reservists and mobilized industrial equipment. Most Soviet cities near China were declared off limits for diplomats.[35]

The Soviets succeeded in conveying the threat perhaps too well. The serious nature of this threat created an unintended sense of unity in the Chinese leadership, and Mao immediately decided to terminate the army's involvement in the Cultural Revolution and deploy it against the Soviet Union.[36] Without the army, he could not continue the Cultural Revolution. Mao managed to convene a plenary session of the Central Committee in October that criticized Liu Shaoqi by name and expelled the "renegade, traitor and scab Liu Shaoqi" from the party.[37] However, members of the Liu-Deng group, including Deng Xiaoping, survived. They would be heard from again. In this sense, Soviet strategy was successful; Soviet military pressure ensured the survival of anti-Mao forces.

However, Soviet pressure generated an unexpected national unity. The Chinese quickly declared the Cultural Revolution a success, claiming that revolutionary committees had been established simultaneously in all provinces of China.[38] The regular Army units were withdrawn and replaced

[34]The Soviets understood this. See V. Pasenchuk and V. Viktorov, "Antinarodnii kurs pekinkikh praviteli," (Antipopular Course of Peking's Rulers), *Pravda,* June 22, 1968, pp. 4–5. This article points out that the forces opposing Mao were "extremely heterogeneous." They included "real Marxists and genuine internationalists" (in other words, pro-Soviet), and "those who share great power, hegemonic concepts, but disagree with present methods" (anti-Mao, not pro-Soviet).

[35]Paul Wohl, "Soviet show of power weighed," *Christian Science Monitor,* August 15, 1968, p. 1.

[36]Thornton, *China,* pp. 333–335.

[37]"Communique of the Enlarged 12th Plenary Session of the Eighth Central Committee of the Communist Party of China," *Peking Review,* October 31, 1968, supplement pp. v-viii; "Thoroughly Settle Accounts With the Renegade, Traitor and Scab Liu Shao-chi for his Towering Crimes," ibid., November 22, 1968, pp. 5–7.

[38]"Long Live the All-Round Victory in the Great Proletarian Cultural Revolution," ibid., September 13, 1968, pp. 3–5.

by regional militia.[39] Mao told the Red Guards they had done well and had them deported to the countryside. While many of the young Red Guards did not placidly accept the abrupt end of the Cultural Revolution, a tenuous balance was established between military authorities, the Red Guards, and the old cadres in the revolutionary committees. "We must strengthen unity between the Army and the people," ran the order of the day, "step up preparedness against war, strengthen our border defenses and our coastal and air defenses.... Should the enemy dare to touch China's sacred territory and launch an armed invasion, we will wipe him out."[40] The enemy was both the Soviet Union and the United States. The main threat, however, was the Soviet Union, as the Chinese press emphasized the importance of provinces on the Sino-Soviet and Sino-Mongolian borders.[41] The Cultural Revolution had to end because unity in China was needed: "We must smash disruptive activities by enemies at home and abroad...consolidate our border defense and turn our northwest and southwest border areas into an impregnable great wall of steel."[42]

Once the implications of Johnson's March 31 speech were clear, North Vietnam assumed a less important role in the Kremlin's China policy. What would be the adjusted role for Vietnam in Soviet strategy? A final decision would depend on the expected course of US policy, and that, in turn, would depend on the results of the 1968 presidential election.

Nixon Takes the Helm

On November 1, 1968, President Johnson decreed a complete halt to the bombing of North Vietnam, bequeathing that situation to his successor.[43] Although the election was close, Richard M. Nixon was elected on November 4, 1968.[44] Nixon's statements supplied the Soviets with two critical conclusions about the direction the new administration would take. First, Nixon would seek to reduce US combat involvement in Vietnam. Campaign statements and a major article in *Foreign Affairs* by candidate Nixon

[39]Thornton, *China*, pp. 333–334.

[40]"Long Live the All-Round Victory in the Great Proletarian Cultural Revolution," *Peking Review,* September 13, 1968, pp. 3–5.

[41]"Revolutionary Committees of Tibet and Sinkiang Simultaneously Established," ibid., pp. 9–10.

[42]Ibid.

[43]"Attacks end on the north," *Christian Science Monitor,* November 2, 1968, p. 1.

[44]Saville R. Davis, "Nixon two-part foreign policy," ibid., November 7, 1968, p. 5.

indicated that he felt US forces should be phased out of battle. The new American president was committed to finding a way out of Vietnam honorably.[45] Second, Nixon intended to press ahead with the attempted rapprochement with China. During the campaign, Nixon proposed negotiations with China and he was said to have adopted a "liberal" stance toward the communist regime.[46]

Time was running out for the Soviets if they wished to prevent a Sino-US rapprochement. As a result, the Soviets reacted to the US election with two near-term strategic decisions. First, they stepped up military pressure on China by sending more men and materiel to the Far East. The danger, of course, was that China would seek the United States as an ally to balance the pressure. This led to the second decision. In order to delay Chinese and American progress toward rapprochement, it would be necessary to prevent Nixon from rapidly reducing the US military presence in Vietnam, a move that could facilitate improved relations with China. Moscow therefore decided to further increase logistic support for North Vietnam and make the process of unilateral US withdrawal extremely dangerous and difficult.

This is important. One school of thought argues that the United States was the aggressor at every stage of the conflict and that the North Vietnamese and their supporters were responding to US escalations. If this were true, when the United States chose to deescalate, there should have been a like response from the other side. The November 1968 increase in Soviet support for North Vietnam came in response to overwhelming evidence that the United States wanted out of the war. In other words, the Soviet response to the bombing halt and Nixon's stated goal of withdrawing US forces was to escalate the conflict. This was all the more ominous because, given the bombing halt, the effect of the logistic surge would be greater. All of the increase would reach the battlefield because there would be no attrition due to bombing. The improved North Vietnamese military capability would limit Nixon's ability to conduct a phased withdrawal of US forces. Stated differently, the objective of Soviet actions was to prevent the withdrawal of US forces from Vietnam.

Richard Nixon's campaign stance had been carefully designed. He had to address the issue of Vietnam without undercutting the forces in combat. He had to criticize the Democratic administration without appearing to

---

[45]Ibid.; "Nixon Vietnam stance touches pulse of US," ibid., August , 1968, p. 4.

[46]Saville R. Davis, "Nixon adopts 'liberal' stance," ibid., August 8, 1968, p. 12.

criticize the country. He did this very well and in August the press indicated that he seemed to "touch the pulse of the nation."[47] He discussed a phase-out of troops and talked of the long-term requirement for peace in Asia.[48] Nixon surprised no one by saying that a president must negotiate with the Soviet Union, but he surprised many when he said the president also had to assume that there would be US negotiations with Communist China.[49] Nixon the candidate carried these positions over to Nixon the president-elect. His acceptance speech stated, "We extend the hand of friendship to all people...to the Russian people...to the Chinese people...to all people in the world."[50]

Nixon's approach to communism had changed. His approach in 1960, as with most in government and academia, had been based on a view of a monolithic communist world. But in 1968, according to Nixon, the communist world was split with great diversity. Nixon spoke of "national communism." There must be negotiations with the Soviets and "eventually with the leaders of the next superpower, Communist China."[51] Further, Nixon talked of a more effective prosecution of the war in Vietnam, although he put it in a context of a phase-out of US forces and long-term peace in Asia.[52] An external manifestation of Nixon's intentions in Asia came when Walter J. Stoessel, US ambassador to Poland, received instructions immediately from the new president that the United States wanted to press for contact with the Chinese charge d'affaires in Warsaw as soon as possible.[53] US efforts were publicized on November 18, 1968, and the United States received a public favorable response on November 26. Discussion of a proposed date for the 135th ambassadorial talks had heretofore met with negative results. Now, according to the Chinese:

> The United States is trying to postpone the 135th meeting of the Sino-US ambassadorial talks till February next year while shifting the responsibility for the postponement onto the Chinese side.... Actually, why should the US side have taken the trouble of doing all this? Since you find it necessary to

[47]"Nixon stance touches pulse of US," ibid., August, 5, 1968, p. 4.
[48]Ibid.
[49]Saville R. Davis, "Nixon adopts 'liberal' stance," ibid., August 8, 1968, p. 12.
[50]Saville R. Davis, "Nixon's two-part foreign policy," ibid., November 7, 1968, p. 5.
[51]Ibid.
[52]Ibid.
[53]Personal interview by the author with Ambassador Stoessel, June 12, 1977.

postpone the meeting, say it outright! The Chinese side can give consideration to it. Chen Tung, Charge d'affaires of the Embassy of the People's Republic of China in Poland, already wrote to the US Ambassador to Poland, Mr. Walter J. Stoessel, Jr., on November 25, making a concrete suggestion that the two sides might as well meet on February 20 next year. By that time, the new US President will have been in office for a month and the US side will probably be able to make up its mind.[54]

Against this backdrop, the Soviet Union on November 25, 1968, signed a new aid agreement with North Vietnam.[55] Unlike the July 1968 pact, which mentioned only continuing support and no details, this agreement stated that there would be "further expansion of economic and military assistance." During 1969, the Soviets would supply "food, oil products, vehicles, sets of equipment, ferrous and non-ferrous metals, chemical fertilizers, armaments, ammunition and other items and materials to strengthen the DRV's defense capability and promote its economic developments."[56] There would be non-repayable economic and military assistance, long-term credits, and trade. As the arms agreement was made public, the preparatory session for the expected "excommunication of China" conference announced in Budapest that the world conference of communist parties would be held in May 1969.[57] Meanwhile, tensions on the Sino-Soviet border increased.

The road ahead included open armed conflict between China and the Soviet Union in March 1969 and a "careful diplomatic minuet" leading to Sino-US rapprochement.[58] President Nixon achieved the phased withdrawal of US forces from Vietnam and the United States seized, temporarily, the initiative in world affairs. The role of Vietnam in Soviet strategy would change. Until 1969, Soviet actions resulted in escalated con-

---

[54] "Statement by Spokesman of Information Department of Chinese Foreign Ministry," *Peking Review*, November 29, 1968, pp. 30–31.

[55] Kotov and Yegerov, *Militant Solidarity*, pp. 186–187; "Krepnet bratskoe sotrudnichestvo mezhdu SSSR i DRV," (The Fraternal Cooperation Between the USSR and the DRV is Growing Stronger), *Pravda*, November 27, 1968, p. 1.

[56] Ibid.

[57] "Kommunike," (Communique), ibid., November 22, 1968, p. 1.

[58] "Zayavlenie sovetskogo pravitel'stva," (Statement of the Soviet Government), *Pravda*, March 16, 1969, p. 1; Richard M. Nixon, *US Foreign Policy for the 1970s, A Report to the Congress*, (Washington: May 3, 1973), pp. 16–25.

flict and were not designed to bring North Vietnam victory. After the US troop withdrawals began and the United States and China began clear, concrete movement toward improved relations, the Soviets would decide in 1970 to change the nature of Soviet assistance. The Soviets would conclude that a strong, unified, pro-Soviet Vietnam would play a key role in its containment of China strategy and, as a result, would supply North Vietnam with the military capability to conquer South Vietnam. The external expression of this decision would be a change in the type of armaments sent to North Vietnam to include tanks, heavy artillery, and other equipment needed for large conventional battles. After a long and tortuous journey, this decision, coupled with the drastic curtailment of military aid by the US Congress for South Vietnam, resulted in Soviet-made tanks rolling into Saigon in 1975.[59]

[59]See articles by the author, "The Third World in Soviet Strategy, 1945–1980," *Asian Affairs, An American Review,* July/August 1980, pp. 341–369 and "Vietnam and Soviet Asian Strategy," ibid., November/December 1976, pp. 94–116. Military appropriations for Vietnam totaled $2.168 billion for 1972–1973. This was reduced to $964 million the following year and $700 million the next. Although much has been publicized about the huge arsenal the United States left in Vietnam, much less has been written about this huge decline in appropriations that dried up the fuel, ammunition, and spare parts that made the arsenal run. The North Vietnamese fielded a better supplied and equipped armored and motorized force that conquered a South Vietnamese force that ran out of bullets and gas. People's War had nothing to do with it, nor was there anything inevitable about it. So many South Vietnamese soldiers and units distinguished themselves with incredible bravery and tenaciousness, that the claim of North Vietnamese moral superiority is false.

Afterword

When you write a couple of hundred pages on any topic, you hope there are a few pithy "universal truths" about which you can pontificate when all is done. There are many lessons here on the conduct of foreign policy by big powers in a global context. The main one, of course, is that nations, even the United States, formulate strategies to gain advantage or prevent loss. When a nation is found to be committing resources outside its borders, we may conclude that the leadership of that country believes that it has a reason for doing so—for example, the Soviet Union in Central America. Beyond this I choose not to go, because I don't want to lose focus on the central "lesson of Vietnam" that matters most to me.

It is clear that the political leadership of the United States—the Johnson administration—caused its armed forces to fight in an Asian jungle for two years without a meaningful goal. As I said in the preface, I felt something was wrong when I was twenty-three. So did the army as an institution. So did the nation. We just couldn't put our finger on what it was.

Now we can.

A great nation, one that is conceived in liberty with a government of the people, by the people, and for the people, does not have the right to abuse the trust, courage, endurance, and sacrifice of its soldiers—who are its own sons and daughters—this way.

It is true that soldiers don't really fight for King and Country. They fight, first of all, to survive, and second of all, not to let their comrades down. Sometimes those priorities are reversed. But somewhere in the back of the American soldier's mind is a childlike faith that somehow this horror really is worth it to the nation. To betray that faith, like the Johnson administration did in Vietnam, is contemptible. And that betrayal has probably killed that childlike faith of the nation's soldiers forever.

Appendix

Some Thoughts on the Cultural Revolution

There are many explanations for the Cultural Revolution. My argument does not dispute that there may have been a number of complex factors which contributed to the upheaval. But I maintain that the central issue of China's path to modernization caused domestic and foreign problems to be inextricably intertwined. The issue of Sino-Soviet relations was as much a domestic issue as it was a foreign policy problem. The fundamental question was, should China accept Soviet aid—and influence—and follow the Stalinist economic model of emphasis on heavy industry? How a Chinese politician related to the question of the nature of the threat posed by the American presence in Vietnam had larger implications. One view of the American threat would lead to a conclusion that it was necessary to unite with the Soviet Union, while the other view would lead to the opposite conclusion. How a Chinese politician felt about economic development probably influenced his view of the severity of the American threat in Vietnam—along with his sense of the impact of advocating those views would have on his own personal and political fortunes. The complexity arises because the leadership of the two fundamental sides in the debate had to compete for the allegiance of those who were uncommitted, or those who could be convinced to switch sides. Making analysis even more difficult, Zhou Enlai headed an organized but uncommitted group, though by the end of 1965 he had clearly shifted to a pro-Mao orientation.[1] However complicated all this may be, the press debate reflected the two interpretations of the threat to China posed by the Vietnam war, and the Cultural Revolution began precisely at a time when it was no longer possible for Mao to argue realistically that American strength in Asia was insignificant. If the conflict in Vietnam forced China to adopt a policy of unity with the Soviet

---

[1]For a fascinating discussion of the relationship between the crushing defeat of the pro-Chinese Indonesian Communist Party in September–October 1965 and Zhou's shift toward outright alliance with Mao, see Wedeman, pp. 183–208.

Union, Mao would lose also on the fundamental issue of China's path to development. Unity with the Soviet Union would simply have been inconsistent with a policy of breaking with the Soviet Union.

The victory of Mao's opponents on so fundamental an issue would have been a political defeat Mao could not have afforded. It might have permanently removed him from power. This is not to say "Vietnam caused the Cultural Revolution." Rather, the impact of developments in the Vietnam war were exploited by Mao's opponents and the Soviet Union in order to cause Mao a political defeat on a fundamental question. Faced with this threat, Mao took steps to counter his opponents by trying to remove them physically from their positions of power. The pro-Soviet group's own political power gave it the ability to resist and the resultant violence that very nearly reached civil war proportions is known as the Great Proletarian Cultural Revolution.

Since both sides in the debate were led by powerful figures who collectively represented China's national leadership, there needed to be some agreement on the public terms of debate. Beginning with the year 1966, the common line that developed was a two-edged sword that both sides could use, but twist to their own purposes by adding qualifications. Articles in the Chinese press from both sides acknowledged the US transfer of power to Asia, but attributed different meanings to the buildup. Mao's forces would use the lack of US mobilization to argue that the United States was stretched too thin even to handle the conflict in Vietnam, much less threaten China. Moreover, according to Mao, they had only achieved such a large ground presence in Vietnam by drawdowns in other areas, something they had managed to do because the Soviets had not pressured them in other regions. This made the Soviet Union a false friend of North Vietnam, seeking to exploit united action over Vietnam in order to establish control of China. Liu Shaoqi and Deng Xiaoping, on the other hand, would argue that regardless of how the United States had managed to transfer so much power to Asia, the transfer had been accomplished and was now a threat to China. Mao's supporters would add criticism of Chinese who acted in concert with the Soviet Union. The Liu-Deng group would criticize those who adhered to Mao's dogmatism in the face of the threat.

Mao's position was enunciated clearly in late December 1965 by Foreign Minister Chen Yi. Chen stated in an interview, "The Soviet Union is the largest European socialist country. If it really wanted to help Vietnam, it could have taken all kinds of measures in many fields to immobilize the forces of the United States...[but the Soviets] have in fact been giving the United States every facility so that it can concentrate its forces against Vietnam.... [They] want to make use of their so called aid to control the Vietnamese situation and bring the Vietnam question into the orbit of US-Soviet collaboration."[2]

The Liu-Deng group, on the other hand, focused on the fact that the American buildup had been accomplished. For example, in January an article discussed US plans to expand its bombing campaign to Laos and Cambodia and to blockade North Vietnam. If all this failed, war was "likely to spread to the whole of Indo-China and even to China.... The *Christian Science Monitor* reports US troops will be boosted to 350,000–400,000 this year."[3] Liu Shaoqi stepped forward in February with a message of support for Ho Chi Minh in the face of American troop deployments. Because of a mutual threat, Liu pledged support of the Chinese people in a joint struggle,[4] continuing with the idea that the threat was more significant than Chinese-Soviet ideological differences. A pro Liu-Deng article alleged that the United States was "the most brutal aggressor.... Afro-Asian countries should unite.... Thanks to their geographical proximity, the Asian countries share a higher degree of weal and woe, and there is all the more reason for them to unite to face the enemy."[5] In one of his final acts before being purged, Peng Zhen articulated the Liu-Deng position that Mao's uncompromising stance against unity with the Soviet Union was dogmatism. At a welcoming ceremony for delegates of the Japanese Communist party, Peng gave a speech that criticized revisionism but noted "at the same time we also oppose modern dogmatism."[6]

Both sides acknowledged and discussed the American buildup. For Mao's group, the buildup was evidence of Soviet unreliability as an ally. For Liu and Deng, the buildup was a threat to China that needed to be addressed and Mao's unrelenting opposition to cooperation with the Soviet Union over Vietnam was "modern dogmatism." The real issue was China's relationship with the Soviet Union. And China's relationship with the Soviets, or lack thereof, would determine China's path to modernization. The currency of debate was the meaning of the American military presence in Vietnam.

[2] "A New and Great Anti-US Revolutionary Storm Is Approaching," *Peking Review,* January 7, 1966, pp. 5–9.

[3] "How US Plots to Set All Indo-China Ablaze," Ibid., January 7, 1966, pp. 16–17.

[4] "China resolutely Supports DRV's Just Stand," Ibid., February 4, 1966, p. 4.

[5] "Unite to Combat Imperialism and Defend Peace," Ibid., April 1, 1966, pp. 6–7.

[6] "Rousing Welcome for Japanese Communist Party Delegation," Ibid.

Bibliography

Books

Barnett, A. Doak. *China After Mao*. New York: Columbia University Press, 1967.

Berman, Larry. *Planning a Tragedy: The Americanization of the War in Vietnam*. New York: W.W. Norton and Company, 1982.

Borisov, Oleg. *Soviet-Chinese Friendly Ties, A Historical Review*. Moscow: Novosti, 1974.

Brewin, Bob and Shaw, Sydney. *Vietnam on Trial, Westmoreland vs. CBS*. New York: Atheneum, 1987.

Brezhnev, L.I. *Otchet Tsentral' nogo Komiteta KPSS i ocherednye zadachi partii v oblasti vnutrennie i vneshnie politiki (Report of the Central Committee of the CPSU and the Main Tasks of the Party in the Areas of Internal and Foreign Policies)*. Moscow: Political Literature Press, 1976.

Brzezinski, Zbigniew. *The Soviet Bloc*. Fourth Printing, Cambridge: Harvard University Press, 1971.

Crawford, Robert W. *Call Retreat. The Johnson Administration's Vietnam Policy, March 1967-March 1968*. Washington: The Washington Institute for Values in Public Policy, Inc., 1987.

Dunn, Carroll H. *Base Development in South Vietnam, 1965–1970*. Washington: Department of the Army, 1972.

Ellison, Herbert J., ed. *The Sino-Soviet Conflict, A Global Perspective*. Seattle: University of Washington Press, 1982.

Fairbank, John K. *The United States and China*. Cambridge: Harvard University Press, 1979.

Fitzgerald, Frances. *Fire in the Lake*. Boston: Little, Brown and Company, 1972.

Gataullina, L.M., et. al. *V' etnam (Vietnam)*. Moscow: Science Press, 1969.

Gelb, Leslie H. and Betts, Richard K. *The Irony of Vietnam: The System Worked*. Washington: The Brookings Institute, 1979.

Giap, Vo Nguyen. *Big Victory, Great Task*. New York: Frederick A. Praeger, 1968.

Girginova, G., ed. *Reaktsionnaya sushchnost' ideologii i politiki maoizma (Reactionary Essence of the Ideology and Policy of Maoism)*. Moscow: Thought Press, 1974.

Glazunov, E.P. and Ognetov, I.A., eds. *Le Zuan (Le Duan)*. Moscow: Political Literature Press, 1971.

Glombinn'skii, Stanislov. *Kitai i SShA (China and the USA)*. Moscow: Progress Publishers, 1975.

Gorshkova, A.I. and Fokina, G.K., eds. *Opasnii kurs (Dangerous Course)*. Moscow: Political Literature Press, 1971.

Halberstam, David. *The Best and the Brightest*. Greenwich: Fawcett Crest, 1973.

Heiser, Joseph M. *Logistic Support*. Washington: Department of the Army, 1971.

Herring, George C. *America's Longest War: The United States and Vietnam, 1950–1975*. New York: John Wiley and Sons, 1979. (Revised edition 1986)

Isaev, M.P. and Chernyshev, A.S. *Istoriia sovetsko-v' etnamshikh otnoshenii (History of Soviet-Vietnamese Relations)*. Moscow: International Relations, 1986.

Isanov, O. *Soviet-Chinese Relations Surveyed*. Moscow: Novosti Press Agency Publishing House, 1986.

Johnson, Lyndon Baines. *The Vantage Point. Perspectives of the Presidency, 1963–1969*. New York: Holt, Rinehart and Winston, 1971.

Kahin, George McT. *Intervention. How America Became Involved*. New York: Alfred A. Knopf, 1986.

Karnow, Stanley. *Vietnam, A History*. New York: Pantheon Books, 1986.

Kim, Ilpyong J., ed., *The Strategic Triangle: China, The United States and The Soviet Union*. New York: Paragon House Publishers, 1987.

Kolko, Gabriel. *Anatomy of a War*. New York: Pantheon Books, 1986.

Komer, Robert W. *Bureaucracy At War. U.S. Performance in the Vietnam Conflict*. Boulder: Westview Press, 1986.

Kotov, L. and Yergerov, R., eds. *Militant Solidarity, Fraternal Assistance*. Moscow: Progress Publishers, 1970.

Lavalle, A.J.C., ed. *The Vietnamese Air Force 1954–1975. An Analysis of its Role in Combat, and Fourteen Hours at Koh Tang*. Washington: USAF Southeast Asia Monograph Series, 1975.

McChristian, Joseph A. *The Role of Military Intelligence, 1965–1967*. Washington: Department of the Army, 1974.

Mkhitarian, S.A. and Mkhitarian, T.T. *V'etnamskaya revoliutsiya: voprosy terii i praktiki (Vietnamese Revolution: Questions of Theory and Practice)*. Moscow: Science, 1986.

Nalty, Bernard C. *Air Power and the Fight for Khe Sahn*. Washington: Office of Air Force History, 1973.

Nixon, Richard M. *Foreign Policy for the 70s*. A Report to the Congress. Washington: Government Printing Office, 1973.

———. *No More Vietnams*. New York: Arbor House, 1985.

Oberdorfer, Don. *Tet!* Garden City: Doubleday, 1971.

Ognetov, I.A., et. al. *Demokratikcheskaya Respublika V'etnama (Democratic Republic of Vietnam)*. Moscow: Science Press, 1975.

Ott, David Ewing. *Field Artillery, 1954–1973*. Washington: Department of the Army, 1975.

Parker, F. Charles. *Soviet Strategy and Vietnam, June 1963–April 1965*. Unpublished M.A. thesis, Georgetown University, 1975.

———. *Strategic History of the Vietnam War, 1965–1968*. Unpublished Ph.D. dissertation, Georgetown University, 1987.

Pearson, Willard. *The War in the Northern Provinces, 1966–1968*. Washington: Department of the Army, 1975.

Porter, Gareth. *A Peace Denied*. Bloomington: Indiana University Press, 1975.

Palmer, Bruce. *The 25-Year War*. New York: Simon and Schuster, 1985.

Palmer Dave Richard. *Summons of the Trumpet*. New York: Ballantine Books, 1984.

Popov, G. and Serov, A. *The Soviet Union and the Democratic Republic of Vietnam*. Moscow: Novosti Press Agency Publishing House, 1975.

Pospelov, D.M. and Stepanov, E.D. *Pekin protiv V' etnama (Peking Against Vietnam)*. Moscow: Thought, 1983.

Rastorguev, V.S., ed. *SSSR-DRV (USSR-DRV)*. Moscow: Science Publishers, 1975.

Reutov, G.N. *Kollektivnauya bezopastnost' v ugo-vostochnoi azii i strategiya SShA (Collective Security in Southeast Asia and the Strategy of the USA)*. Leningrad: Knowledge Publishers of the RSFSR, 1975.

Salisbury, Harrison E. *A Time of Change*. A Reporter's Tale of Our Time. New York: Harper and Row Publishers, 1988.

Sharp, U.S. Grant. *Strategy for Defeat. Vietnam in Retrospect*. San Rafael: Presidio Press, 1978.

Sharp, U.S. Grant and Westmoreland, William C. *Report on the War in Vietnam*. Washington: Government Printing Office, 1968.

Sladkovskii, M.I., Akimov, V.I. and Morozov, A.P. *Problemy i protivorechiya industrial' nogo razvitya KNR (Problems and Contradictions of the Industrial Development of the CPR)*. Moscow: Thought Press: 1974.

Sladkovskii, M.I. *Velikoderzhavnaya politika maoistov v natsional' nykh raionakah KNR (Great Power Policies of the Maoists in the National Regions of the CPR)*. Moscow: Thought Press, 1972.

Summers, Harry G. *On Strategy*. Novata: Presidio Press. Third Printing, 1983.

Schlesinger, Arthur M. *Crisis of Confidence: Ideas, Power and Violence in America*. Boston: Houghton Mifflin, 1969.

Schandler, Herbert Y. *The Unmaking of a President*. Princeton: Princeton University Press, 1977.

Theis, Wallace. *When Governments Collide*. Berkeley: University of California Press, 1980.

Thompson, James Clay. *Rolling Thunder. Understanding Policy and Program Failure.* Chapel Hill: The University of North Carolina Press, 1980.

Thompson, Robert Graigner Ker. *Revolutionary War in World Strategy, 1945–1969.* New York: Taplinger Publishing Company, 1970.

Thornton, Richard C. *China: A Political History, 1917–1980.* Boulder: Westview Press, 1982.

Turley, William S. *The Second IndoChina War.* Boulder: Westview Press, 1986.

Turner, Kathleen J. *Lyndon Johnson's Dual War. Vietnam and the Press.* Chicago: The University of Chicago Press, 1985.

Ulam, Adam. *Expansion and Coexistence.* New York: Praeger Publishers, Inc., 1973.

————. *The Rivals.* New York: The Viking Press, 1971.

Vladimirov, O. and Ryazantsev, V. *Mao Tse-tung, A Political Portrait.* Moscow: Progress Publishers, 1976.

Westmoreland, William C. *A Soldier Reports.* Garden City: Doubleday, 1976.

Yurkov, S.G. and Petrov, G.P. *Vneshepoliticheskie kontseptsii maoizma (Foreign Policy Concepts of Maoism).* Moscow: International Relations Press, 1975.

Wolfe, Thomas W. *Soviet Power and Europe, 1945–1970.* Baltimore: The Johns Hopkins Press, 1970.

Zagoria, Donald, ed. *Soviet Policy in East Asia.* New Haven: Yale University Press, 1982.

————. *Vietnam Triangle.* New York: Pegasus, 1962.

Zhelokhovtsev, A. *The Cultural Revolution, A Close-up.* Moscow: Progress Publishers, 1975.

Pentagon Papers

Sheehan, Neil; Smith, Hedrick; Kenworth, E.W.; and Butterfield, Fox. *The Pentagon Papers. The Secret History of the Vietnam War as Published by the New York Times.* New York: Bantam Books, Inc. 1971.

The Senator Gravel Edition. *The Pentagon Papers. The Defense Department History of United States Decision Making on Vietnam.* 4 Volumes. Boston: Beacon Press, 1972.

U.S. Department of Defense. *United States Vietnam Relations, 1945–1971,* Books 1–12. Washington: Government Printing Office, 1971.

Documents

Vietnam: A Documentary Collection—Westmoreland vs. CBS. New York: Clearwater Publishing Company, 1987.

Vietnam Documents and Research Notes. Saigon: Joint United States Public Affairs Office, 1969.

Articles and Periodicals

Christian Science Monitor, London Edition. 1965–1969.

Current Digest of the Soviet Press. 1963–1969.

Izvestia. 1965–1969.

Kahin, George McT. "The Pentagon Papers: A Critical Evaluation," *American Political Science Review.* (June 1975) 675–686.

Lisannm Maury. "Moscow and the Chinese Power Struggle," *Problems of Communism.* (November-December, 1969) 32–41.

New York Times. 1963–1969.

Peking Review. 1963–1969. The *Peking Review* is an English-language weekly review published by the People's Republic of China. It carries translations of articles appearing in the major Chinese media. Thus, a quote or reference to an article in *People's Daily,* for example, may be followed by a citation from the *Peking Review.* The article appeared in English in the *Peking Review* with a notation that the article appeared earlier in *People's Daily.*

Pravda. 1965–1969.

Thornton, Richard C. "Soviet Strategy and the Vietnam War," *Asian Affairs,* No. 4 (March/April 1974) 205–225.

I used some 5,000 articles from the Chinese, US, and Soviet press. These are too numerous to list separately. Below I listed those authors whose by-lines appeared most frequently. Of course, many articles had no by-line.

Christian Science Monitor
Ashworth, George
Bourne, Eric
Brunn, Robert R.
Davis, Saville R.
Deepe, Beverly
Foell, Earl W.
Hughes, John
Oka, Takashi
Stanford, Neal
Strout, Richard L.
Willis, David K.
Wohl, Paul

New York Times
Baldwin, Hanson
Belair, Felix
Dale, Edwin I. Jr.
Frankel, Max
Langguth, Jack
Middleton, Drew
Raymond, Jack
Smith, Hedrick
Tanner, Henry
Topping, Seymour

Peking Review
Chen Yi
Chin Yu-kun
Lin Piao
Li So-feng
Liu Shao-chi
Mao Tse-tung
Peng Chen
Teng Hsiao-ping

Tseng-yun
Yang Pei-hsin
Commentator
Observer

Pravda/Izvestia
Aleksandrov, I.
Delyusin, L.
Demidov, P.
Dmitriev, G.
Fedosayev, G.P.
Gavilov, I.
Ivanov,I.
Kalkin, Oleg
Matveyev, V.
Mayevskyi, V.
Pasenchuk, V.
Shchedrov, I.
Simonov, Konstantin
Strel'nikov, Boris
Ter-Grigoryi,
Vasilev, G.A.
Viktorov, V.
Zanegin, B.
Zhurovski, V.

Interviews

Lieutenant General Charles A. Corcoran, USA, Ret. January 20, 1974. LTG
Corcoran was the operations officer (J–3) and later chief of staff for
MACV, I Corps Commander, Vietnam and finally, chief of staff for the
commander-in-chief of US forces in the Pacific.

Ambassador Walter Stoessel, June 12, 1977. Ambassador Stoessel was US
ambassador to Poland in 1969 when President Nixon's first overtures
to China were transmitted by Ambassador Stoessel to the Chinese
charge.

About the Author

Lieutenant Colonel F. Charles Parker IV graduated from the United States Military Academy at West Point in 1968. He commanded field artillery batteries in Germany and Vietnam, his Vietnam tour coming in 1970–1971. He spent two years with the 2nd Infantry Division in Korea and commanded a battalion at Ft. Bragg, North Carolina, from 1984 to 1986. Assignments in Washington include speechwriting for the army vice-chief of staff and serving as action officer in the secretary of the army's office for congressional liaison. In addition to his bachelor of science degree from West Point, he has an M.A. in Russian area studies and a Ph.D. in history from Georgetown University. He completed work on this book during a year as a visiting scholar at the Hoover Institution at Stanford University. He is married with two children, a boy and a girl.

He has recently been selected for promotion to colonel.

Index